Playing the Past

Playing the Past

History and Nostalgia in Video Games

*Edited by Zach Whalen
and Laurie N. Taylor*

Vanderbilt University Press • Nashville

© 2008 by Vanderbilt University Press
Nashville, Tennessee 37235

12 11 10 09 08   1 2 3 4 5

This book is printed on acid-free paper made
from 30% post-consumer recycled paper.
Manufactured in the United States of America

Library of Congress Cataloging-in-Publication Data

Playing the past : history and nostalgia in video games /
edited by Zach Whalen and Laurie N. Taylor.
p. cm.
Includes bibliographical references and index.
ISBN 978-0-8265-1600-8 (cloth : alk. paper)
ISBN 978-0-8265-1601-5 (pbk. : alk. paper)
1. Video games. 2. Video games—Psychological aspects.
3. Video games—Study and teaching. I. Whalen, Zach,
1979– II. Taylor, Laurie N., 1978–
GV1469.3.P483 2008
794.8—dc22
2007051878

Contents

Preface and Acknowledgments

It is now seven years since Espen Aarseth declared 2001 to be "year one" of computer game studies, and while this nascent, interdisciplinary field has seen its share of vigorous debate, studying games remains an increasingly rich and important intellectual endeavor. Whether one considers the so-called ludology v. narratology debates to be over, or ever to have taken place to begin with, this collection seeks to offer something different by discussing a specific set of ideas emerging from a central question: what do video games have to do with history, memory, and nostalgia? Rather than discussing how best to study video games or invoking video games as a generic metaphor, the authors in this collection put a variety of approaches into practice, reflecting the strengths of their respective disciplines, in order to unpack the complex negotiations of temporality and historical representation in games and gaming culture.

The present volume is the product of a conversation that began at the first game studies conference at the University of Florida in 2005. At this relatively small gathering, a diverse group of scholars met to discuss video games and nostalgia, and found surprising and deep interplay among our respective ideas and approaches. The result, this collection, encapsulates a broad and expanded conversation into a cogent statement that video games help us think about history and nostalgia in profound and important ways.

A note on terminology: throughout this collection, authors use the terms *video game*, *videogame*, *computer game*, and *digital game* to refer generally to the same kinds of objects. There are significant shades of meaning among these terms, and it may well be the case that selecting one term over the others may (consciously or not) predispose a given argument to certain assumptions. The prefix *video* is, perhaps, technically less accurate or inclusive than it may once have been, and even *digital* may not be a universal descriptor if one traces the prehistory of modern video games to include their analog and mechanical predecessors. It might be argued that *computer* satisfies the universality requirement, since some form of computation is nearly always involved in the phenomenon we're discussing, but since that term is often used (in the United States) to distinguish games made for personal computers from console-based games, *computer games* may not always correctly denote the same objects for different readers. While *video games* is arguably the most widely recognized of the terms in question, the decision of whether to separate the two or use the neologism *videogame* brings up another set of questions and possible assumptions. For example, in a comment thread on *gameology.org*, Ian Bogost defends his use of *videogame* in his book *Unit Operations* by arguing that he does so for rhetorical reasons: "Separating the words, in my opinion, suggests that videogames are merely games with some video screen or computer attached." Jesper Juul, on the other hand, compares Google results to argue that he uses *video game* in *Half-Real* because *video game* is used far more frequently and is thus already the accepted standard ("Videogames"). For the purposes of this collection, we have left the terminology up to each individual author, and although the term each author uses may betray regional, disciplinary, or rhetorical preferences, the reader should generally assume that *video game, videogame, computer game*, and *digital game* are interchangeable.

A book like this does not come into existence without the help and encouragement of many different people. The editors would like to thank, first of all, our contributors whose dedication and hard work in refining their chapters made this possible. Also, we'd like to thank Terry Harpold for reviewing drafts of our chapter, and Donald Ault for his advice and encouragement through the whole process. Finally, Betsy Phillips at Vanderbilt University Press deserves all of our thanks and appreciation for her enthusiasm for the project and her unending patience with two first-time editors.

— Zach Whalen and Laurie N. Taylor, *Editors*

Works Cited

Aarseth, Espen. "Computer Game Studies, Year One." *Game Studies: The International Journal of Computer Game Research* (*www.gamestudies.org*). 1.1 (2001). Accessed 27 June 2007.

"Videogames or Video games—What Are We Talking About?" Comment thread at *gameology.org* (2 December 2006). Accessed 27 June 2007.

Playing the Past

1

Playing the Past

An Introduction

Laurie N. Taylor and Zach Whalen

Outbreaks of nostalgia often follow revolutions.
—Svetlana Boym (2001)

In late 2006, Sony's PlayStation 3 console and Nintendo's Wii (codenamed "The Revolution") promised to usher in a new era of gaming with powerful graphics and innovative approaches to play. Joining the Xbox 360, these game systems complete the seventh console generation, and already (as of 2007) speculation is growing over the eighth. At the same time that gamers were lining up to pay over $700 for the PlayStation 3's high-definition capabilities, many other game enthusiasts were drawn to the moderately priced Wii—not for its graphics or even its motion-based input, but rather for the ease with which it allows players to reexperience classic games like *Super Mario Brothers* (1985) and *Donkey Kong* (1985) through its Virtual Console. Nintendo's branding has always emphasized its franchise characters like Mario and Yoshi; with the Wii, that nostalgic branding is fully realized in the form of a commodity—downloadable emulations of the actual games many of us grew up playing.

In the lead-up to the 2004 presidential election, game publisher Kuma Reality Games released a free downloadable game mission that allowed players to reenact the then-controversial Swift Boat patrol on which candidate John Kerry earned his Silver Star. (Completing the mission is not that easy, it turns out, and one may conclude that Kerry's actions were deserving of the medal he received.) At the same time that media outlets were running hotly-contested stories about the Swift Boat patrol, *Call of Duty* was one of the best-selling PC games of 2003, and it was recognized both with a Game Developers Choice Award and as the Academy of Interactive Arts and Sciences' Game of the Year.

Call of Duty is an intense first-person shooter (FPS) set during World War II. Its impressive visuals are frequently celebrated for their "cinematic" quality. As one reviewer observed, the game "shamelessly [recreates] scenes from such recent films as *Band of Brothers* and *Enemy at the Gates* … I've never played a game that captures the feel of Hollywood's version [of] World War II like *Call of Duty*. It really is like being in a war movie" (*GamesFirst*). This displacement of the documentary function of games—those ostensibly based on "actual" events—toward a Hollywood or pop-media measure of their realism suggests that something more is going on than the straightforward reenactment of history. In all of these examples (Nintendo's Virtual Console, *John Kerry's Silver Star*, and *Call of Duty*), video games operate with a clear—and a clearly *mediated*—relationship to the past.

As video games have become more complex and expressive, real world history has found an interesting place on the video game shelf among the fantasy, science fiction, and sports settings many games offer. As *Call of Duty* and the Swift Boat game demonstrate, games can use history for the purposes of politics, education, historical revision, or entertainment, but in all of these instances, a sense of nostalgia establishes the relationship between the real present and a virtual past. Similarly, the Nintendo Wii counts on its players' nostalgia for their experiences of old Nintendo games; its Virtual Console, like any emulator, reproduces a more or less faithful repetition of an actual, personally historical experience with gaming.

Games are finding their way into more and more aspects of our lives—in homes, cars, workplaces, and museums, and can even be found on city streets and crossing areas by way of mobile platforms like PDAs, mobile phones, GPS systems, handheld dedicated game systems, and more. As such, video games are playing an increasing role in communicating complex ideas—real world history, media ecologies, and gaming histories. In all of these instances, a playful intimacy grounded in nostalgia becomes an important element in how games express these ideas. The essays in this collection join a growing field of video game scholarship to explore the role of nostalgia as it configures playing in, of, and with the past.

As editors, we have found surprising and interesting connections among the approaches to history gathered within this volume. Moreover, a personal dimension of nostalgia has allowed us to recall our own histories with games. We have been lucky enough to see a cultural gaming literacy develop along with the creation and evolution of game studies as a nascent discipline. While we both began our academic careers in digital media during the rise of game studies, our interest in games and gaming long predates our scholarly engagements with them. As first players and now scholars, we have seen more generations of consoles than we have decades in our lives. Our first gaming experiences included the Atari, the Commodore 64, and the first Nintendo, but we began as *gamers* with the first Nintendo Entertainment System (NES); we are both members of the "Nintendo Generation."[1] Our early gaming memories are colored by the Nintendo Power Pad, *Nintendo Power* magazine, and Nintendo's famous game characters—Mario, Luigi, Princess Peach, Link, Zelda, Samus Aran, and many others. We have played games on every console since the mid-1980s. Now we can play all of those classic games again through emulation on our computers, the Virtual Console on the Wii, and retro versions and compilations for other systems, including iPods and mobile phones.

Wii's Virtual Console, notably, seems to make the old new again—bringing it back in a shiny package—while also preserving most of its "classic" qualities. This reconfiguration of the old within the new follows the logic of nostalgia that combines the past and the present in a way that can cause the past to become a fetish. Nostalgia is best understood as a process of looking back to an unattainable past and trying to bring that past into the present. This nostalgic turn can be seen as something negative in its desire to dwell in the past rather than to exist in the present.[2] However, nostalgia can also be understood in constructive terms, as the process by which knowledge of the past is brought to bear on the present and the future. As players, we look to the past for familiar games and to the future with memories of having played those games. As game studies scholars, we look to the past to study gaming history, game development, and the cultural significance of games both in their original forms and their influence on later works.

Game studies scholarship follows a logic of nostalgia in that it establishes a critical history for games and ties that history to a larger media ecology. As an academic field, game studies as such began by seeking to define its object of study. In her 1997 book *Hamlet on the Holodeck*, Janet Murray defines games as a new narrative medium, and by doing so brings to bear the long history of narratology on the new, interactive possibilities promised by video games. But this proposition has proven controversial. Other game scholars such as Espen Aarseth have broken ties to prior forms and chosen to analyze games in terms of their inherent and unique properties. For Aarseth, this means eschewing narrative-oriented theory in favor of an approach that begins by thinking of games in terms of their computational bases. Similarly, Gonzalo Frasca uses the term *ludology* (based on the Latin *ludus*, meaning "play") to define the study of video games as "ludic" or as forms that emerge from a history of play and games. "Ludological" and "narratological" approaches define video games as products of a particular history. Each of these general approaches can then seek to reinterpret prior works given new insights learned from game studies. For instance, game studies scholars have examined games in terms of particular concepts like quests and interactivity, and then identified those concepts in prior forms to see how insights derived from game analysis can inform and reshape prior critical thinking. One notable example is *Lady in the Lake* (1947), a film directed by Robert Montgomery and shot exclusively from the main character's first-person perspective. The film failed critically and commercially, but it represents an interesting and often-cited cinematic experiment. Alexander Galloway has noted that this use of a subjective shot in cinema is alienating or disturbing (first-person perspective is a cliché of horror films where the audience appears to see *through* the eyes of the killer) because it hints at the kind of player agency we take for granted in video games. In first-person shooters, for example, the unification of a perspective with the ability to act in the world seems natural because the form serves its function. In *Lady in the Lake*, the subjective form is ill-suited to the purposes of narration, so its effect is off-putting. The emphasis on form *and* function is often hinted at or explored in other media, but games bring the union of form and function to bear on the media experience itself.

Game studies, however, is not only wedded to theories of the past or of prior media; game studies is also carried out by game players who each bring to bear their personal histories with games and gaming. Jason Rutter and Jo Bryce have suggested that the recent surge in academic work on games is due not to a shifting emphasis in academia, but it rather "reflects the entry of researchers who grew up in the *PONG*, Atari, NES and BBC Micro years into academia" (2). Like us, many game studies scholars have played video games from early childhood. Others know video games from adult play or from their children's play. Each of our experiences with games as players and scholars shapes our understanding of video games and our approaches to their analysis. This shaping of the present and the future through prior experience implies, as we have suggested, that a nostalgic turn is fundamental to game studies as a field.

Therefore, in order to investigate games' past, present, and future, we look to nostalgia as a critical structure. By examining specific moments and representations of history in games, each of the chapters in this collection explores an aspect of gaming in terms of time and memory. We have grouped the chapters according to their—often complex and inconsistent—relationship to the past: "Playing *in* the Past: Nostalgia and Classic Gaming," "Playing *and* the Past: Media History and Video Games," and "Playing *with* the Past: Real and Revisionist History in Video Games." Together, the chapters and divisions demonstrate multiple nostalgic movements.

Situating Nostalgia

Nostalgia begins with memory, but it is more than simply the displaced memory of a past event; nostalgia (both personal and cultural) operates within a complex negotiation of temporality. Video games operate on similar organizations of time and space. For many games, even an expert player will often find herself having to replay some sections; in a narrow sense, game play itself frequently requires memorization or at the very least applying the lessons of past failures. Many racing games, for example, include a feature where players can compete against a ghost car that acts out that player's previous run through the course.

As texts that are increasingly set in versions of reality, video games also offer experiences of remembering that may be either personal or cultural. As the latter, video games act as public records of events and objects and can even be mnemonic and memorial devices. Public arcade games memorialize past games by displaying high scores, and games can also act as memorials of the past testifying in the present, as with ghost actors in museums' interactive history exhibits who play as now-dead characters in order to educate the present. For example, in his chapter in this collection, "Performing the (Virtual) Past: Online Character Interpretation as Living History at Old Sturbridge Village," Scott Magelssen explores how ghost actors perform the past as a system of play within the present. Significantly, what unites games to these interactive history performances is the users' experience of presence. Whether acted out in person or mediated through a machine interface, games communicate history most effectively by situating the player within the time and space of the memorial event. These features of temporality and situated presence distinguish video games and electronic literature from other media; their ability to record aspects of the reader/player's interaction and alter their content and expression accordingly gives them unique potential for mnemonic function. In another sense, video games may record artifacts of their use (cookies and memory caches track webpage access, many games perform automatic saves, and others allow players to create photo albums of in-game events), and they also rely on physical media, including hard drives and memory cards that store a player's progress through the texts. However, like other mnemonic devices, these devices are subject to failure, so memory is always incomplete, failing to record certain aspects of the experience. Memory cards can fail, losing data and erasing records of the reader/player's history, so experiencing one of these texts, therefore, invokes a certain amount of anxiety about the potential inability to return to the present moment of play.[3] Despite the presupposition of atemporality, game players in this way develop a kind of nostalgia for the present within that anxiety.

While nostalgia may be a longing for a past that can be projected onto a present or future time and place, memory necessarily implies sequence. This may or may not conform to chronological sequence, but it does operate within the constraints in which memories are formed and are then remembered. These sequences, however, do relate to the way nostalgia is created; "what triggers nostalgia in the first place, making it into a distinct aspect of memory, is precisely a critical discrepancy between the present and the past" (Ritivoi 30). This discrepancy creates a gap or fissure in the sequence of memory, and when memories cross that gap, they conjure other memories or potential memories.

Playing *in* the Past:
Nostalgia and Classic Gaming

In the 1970s and 1980s, video games emerged as a popular form of entertainment, and a rapidly growing industry quickly brought those arcade games into homes with familiar titles like *PONG, Pac-Man,* and their numerous imitators. After the industry's crash in the early 1980s, Nintendo revived and forever altered the market with the release of its Famicom or Nintendo Entertainment System, associating game playing more explicitly with younger children through their "cartoony" characters and family-oriented themes. As the so-called "Nintendo Generation" has matured, we have grown to associate video games with our early childhood and adolescence, and our memories of the iconic characters of those early games become a way of activating nostalgia for that period. In this way, video games themselves have become quotations of our shared past, referencing their role in a general experience of youth. As game technology has improved and as daily life becomes more saturated with media technology, these early video games have also become objects of nostalgia in that their low-resolution aesthetics have come to be perceived as a retrospective ideal. Despite the massive (by comparison) computing power and visual photorealism available to modern games, the so-called "Golden Age" of gaming occurred in the late 1970s and early 1980s, when many of the game genres that dominate today's market were in their in-cunabular stages. The nostalgic impulse that idealizes these games may embrace their relative crudeness as a figure for the good old days, but what does this phenomenon of retrogaming reveal about video games' investment in their past? What are the theoretical and critical implications of memory as it informs game play?

The first group of essays in this collection addresses these concerns and related ideas by turning to classic gaming, video game sequels, and the structures and limitations of early video game technology. Sean Fenty's "Why Old School Is 'Cool': A Brief Analysis of Classic Video Game Nostalgia" directly addresses games in relation to nostalgic impulses from gaming culture. Similarly, in "Homesick for Silent Hill: Modalities of Nostalgia in Fan Responses to *Silent Hill 4: The Room*," Natasha Whiteman studies a specific case where players respond to change in the *Silent Hill* series and analyzes their motivations as they create an idealized gaming history. In both cases, there is a sense in which older games are shown to exert a negative influence on games that follow; that is, much as Romantic poets wrote in the shadow of Milton, new games must negotiate the experiences their audiences have had with the early classics of the medium. This is a tenuous assumption, and the authors of these two chapters provide valuable insights into its applicability for the receptions of these texts.

While video games and game play may enable and evoke memories of other games, game creators and players fuel this often idealistic vision of classic games, which leads to retrogaming as an independent, even anachronistic phenomenon. The fact that gamers often express opinions like "games used to be better" means that there is a market for reselling and repackaging older games. These arguments are part of a larger cultural commodification of memory through consumable media forms. In reference to a similar phenomenon with regard to Hello Kitty, Brian McVeigh argues that "appeals to nostalgia encourage a reconnection with the past by buying certain products united by one leitmotif; *same* commodity, *same* individual, *different* ages/tastes/styles/desires" (227). Therefore, the memory and nostalgia for game play as it is commodified, repackaged, and sold to consumers illustrates the manner in which video game nostalgia operates. Matthew Payne's "Playing the Déjà-New: 'Plug it in and Play TV Games' and the Cultural Politics of Classic Gaming" discusses the marketing logic and intellectual property issues surrounding the popular dedicated controller devices. Comparing the games licensed for these plug-and-play units with the open source MAME (Multiple Arcade Machine Emulator), Payne argues that these commercially licensed properties create a revisionary, almost mythological narrative of gaming history that downplays the gritty reality that MAME and the homebrew community celebrate. In a similar vein, Ruffin Bailey's "Hacks, Mods, Easter Eggs, and Fossils: Intentionality and Digitalism in the Video Game" analyzes the digital basis of that grittiness and posits a theory of digitalism for game studies. Bailey argues that by properly understanding the ideologies and aesthetics embedded in games by the technology they are composed of, game scholars can explore more deeply how games create meaning and express ideas. The final chapter in this section, Terry Harpold's "Screw the Grue: Mediality, Metalepsis, Recapture," takes on a particular kind of expression produced by the unique constraints imposed by game software. For games that create a story world, that world is bounded not only by the scope of the narrative but also by the features and limitations of the platform itself. Classic text adventures, for example, are restricted in their agency by the phrases the text parser is prepared to respond to. Harpold discusses what happens when those boundaries collide and the restrictions of one layer of the game world erupt into another.

Because the very forms of video games belie attempts at constancy, nostalgia grows for a return to the original text through repetition—even through the commodified representation of the original. Replay value is a quality of any good game, but replay value that survives through multiple platform changes illustrates the impact of these texts on the players and the nature of video game textuality itself. Since each time one plays a game level is likely to be at least slightly different in some way (or wildly different, depending on the game), the memory of previous attempts only goes so far. Similarly, nearly all video games are complex enough that replaying a game from beginning to end will be different each time—the player may choose to take quests in a different order, or she may simply require fewer attempts to clear a certain room. In both cases, therefore, the structure of nostalgia works within the critical discrepancy between a player's current game and her prior experiences of play.

As many of us have grown up with video games, this aspect of the structure of digital text is part of a complex media ecology in which games play a crucial and influential role. Florian Brody speculates on the future of digital media replacing books as memory technology and suggests that as media changes from "a conveyor of memory rather than messages," it will impact "our memory technologies" and thus "the very way we metaphorize our lives" (143). Games and electronic literature—forms often represented as played in childhood or as representing childhood—thus come to stand for a nostalgic desire to return, a desire reinforced by the very structure of games. Games like *Ratchet and Clank* (2002) that return the player to an initial start point at the conclusion of the game's narrative or that, like *Silent Hill 4* (2004), maintain a central "home" node to which the player returns after each level demonstrate the emotional function of nostalgia tied in with the memorial structure of playing in our pasts.

Playing *and* the Past:
Media History and Video Games

As a medium that relies on players' memory and a technology that is itself built using computing memory, video games operate within a rich new media ecology and inform how we think about memory, history, and nostalgia through other types of media. Jay David Bolter and Richard Grusin advance the idea of *remediation* in their book of the same name. In exploring how different forms of media relate to one another, Bolter and Grusin argue that new forms of media can be said to "remediate" older media, particularly in terms of how they construct a user interface. Early cinema, for example, began by mimicking theater to the extent that many early films consisted of a single shot of a fixed stage. Video games also mimic formal elements of other media, but games are also themselves subject to remediation. In its basic construction, remediation is a one-sided projection of something old onto something new, but as games have matured and changed rapidly, films like *Run Lola Run* (1999) and *eXistenZ* (1999) explicitly adopt formal elements originating from gaming.[4] This exchange is not always productive, however. Though the term "cinematic" is often applied to games as an indicator of their photorealistic visual accomplishments, reversing the terms to label a film "video gamey" generally signifies a negative assessment. In many ways, the formal structures of video games and related media like film, television, and (increasingly) mobile phone content look forward and backward to borrow properties from other platforms and media. Is this temporal relationship afflicted with a kind of medial nostalgia? What happens when the complex temporalities and spatialities of play transform the text? Does nostalgic remediation in games comment on the ideologies embedded in the older form, or does it suggest a sense of loss? The chapters in this second section investigate these and other issues in terms of classic cinema, television, and mobile phones.

When a game migrates to a new platform, it invites a nostalgic turn as players recall the attributes of prior versions. In addition, new versions of texts force players or readers to operate within an anachronistic framework that rewrites the memory of the original. An environment populated by these texts, such as Nintendo Wii's Virtual Console, is self-reflective in that it presents classic games in a new package and console. Though players will be familiar with many of the games, they must relearn them using affordances of the Wii's (new) Classic Controller. As an analogy for temporal relationships across media, video games resonate with themes of memory and nostalgia in other forms like film, TV, and comics. Each of these forms, furthermore, responds and adapts to developing technologies, including the increasingly popular all-in-one handheld mobile communication devices. The fact that these devices can be conduits for multiple media that nevertheless retain their unique identities indicates the connection each holds to its rich tradition. The first chapter in this section, Sheila Murphy's "Unlimited Minutes: Playing Games in the Palm of Your Hand," examines changes in gaming as it moves into the mobile arena.

All media call attention to formal constraints of memory and representation; in this way, they indicate with varying degrees of directness the importance of nostalgia as a cultural concept. Film in particular has much in common with games, and even though some theorists are critical of applying film studies' analysis to video games, some formal parallels and thematic concerns cannot be ignored, especially when games explicitly reference cinema aesthetics. Studying video games within a larger media ecology that includes films allows those who study games to draw upon and reflect directly on recent movements in film studies, some of which highlight memory and nostalgia. Pam Cook notes the growing preoccupation in film studies with memory and nostalgia and continues with the observation that this interest comes within larger questions of history and identity. These trends are also "partly a response to the emergence of the nostalgic memory in film itself, which reconstructs an idealized past as a site of pleasurable contemplation and yearning" (4). Video games reconstruct memory in similar ways to film (the use of narrative flashbacks in cut scenes, for example) and even reconstruct memories of older cinematic moments or styles. *Max Payne* (2001), for example, clearly and cleverly invokes the mood of *film noir*, reconstructing its generic qualities in the formal constraints of game play and the graphic novels that serve as interstitials. Andrew Jankowich examines another such reconstructions in "Visions and Revisions of the Hollywood Golden Age and America in the Thirties and Forties," arguing that the aesthetics and even physics of *Crimson Skies* (2000) and *Prince of Persia: The Sands of Time* (2003) invoke specific qualities of Golden Age cinema. Tom Gersic finds a productive contrast in comparing the uses of music in *Resident Evil Zero* (2002) and Hitchcock's *The Birds* (1963). Gersic's chapter, "Toward a New Sound for Games," concludes that, although game music and film music are related, successful sound composition for games depends on understanding the fundamentally new context that games create. In other words, games are more than mere hybrid forms that mix elements from other media. Instead, video games depend on a unique textuality that, while related, opens possibilities for expression unavailable to film or television.

As both representational and experiential forms, video games can recall other texts in playful ways and make unique contributions to a story spread across multiple media forms. Anna Reading and Colin Harvey explore this by introducing the concept of *nostalgic-play* in their chapter, "Remembrance of Things Fast: Conceptualizing *Nostalgic-Play* in the *Battlestar Galactica* Video Game." Like Natasha Whiteman in her chapter on *Silent Hill 4*, Reading and Harvey discuss the ways in which a specific game text modifies an established narrative. Because *Battlestar Galactica* is a long-running franchise with multiple instantiations as a television and film series, its adaptations in video games invite reading relationships among different media in terms of *nostalgic-play*. Reading and Harvey conclude that nostalgia is a critical conceptual tool in understanding the complex intertextuality of game play. Therefore, as an area of inquiry, gaming invites richer understandings of mediated temporality and memory, and as forms of representation, video games exploit that complexity toward communicating ideas, information, and attitudes about the real world.

Playing *with* the Past: Real and Revisionist History in Video Games

Video games frequently operate within fantasy or science fiction frameworks; that is, in imagined worlds and eras with their own histories and timelines. But strikingly, more and more games that seek to be realistic (in terms of visual fidelity) use World War II as a setting.[5] As video game technology has increased its power and offered better-quality photorealism, it is logical that game developers have also harnessed games' powers of simulation to convey narratives about the past. In this way, games would seem to be best at offering nostalgists an opportunity to "relive" the past, but what is crucially at stake here is the assumption that games *play* with the narrative and settings. As Frasca and others have argued, video games provide unique opportunities for conveying ideas because the environment a game constructs allows the designer to build in a set of relationships (an ideology, for example) even before the player confronts a narrative based in that environment. The effects of these changes on historical representation operate similarly to nostalgia's desired return to a particular moment or to a mythical state of innocence. In this context, play becomes a way of relating to the past and a means of addressing our loss of innocence by temporarily allowing us access to that innocent condition. Critical genres and artistic disciplines often look to World War II as the center of this century's nostalgic conscious (after which innocence is always tainted by the knowledge of evil) so World War II games are an important example of nostalgia expressed with video games.

James Campbell's essay, "Just Less Than Total War: Simulating World War II as Ludic Nostalgia," approaches the question of ludic representation regarding the specific era of World War II. This period is crucial for understanding the extent to which video games are successful at retelling the past, not only because WWII is a turning point in human history, but because in packaging this period as "playable," game design decisions favor particular narratives of the war at the expense of others. Similarly, in "Performing the (Virtual) Past: Online Character Interpretation as Living History at Old Sturbridge Village," Scott Magelssen shows how museums offer nostalgic representations of real world histories through online actors who perform characters from a specific historical period. Like the game design decisions that affect the narration of history, the mediated presence of an online interaction also influences interpretation, even when the goal is explicitly educational. Taking this notion of intention and interpretation even further, Tracy Fullerton's chapter, "Documentary Games: Putting the Player in the Path of History," examines games that have attempted the opposite: using game design explicitly to interpret a historical event. The John Kerry game mentioned earlier is one such interpretation, and others like the more recent *Super Columbine Massacre RPG* (2005) have proven even more controversial. What is interesting about such games, and what Fullerton discusses, is the sense in which these games can be subjective simulations, placing the player in a specific place to allow her to experience an event from a particular point of view.

These chapters all share a concern with how players relate to history through gaming, and how players relate to these games. Taking a closer look at subjectivity, Robert Fletcher's "Of Puppets, Automatons, and Avatars: Automating the Reader-Player in Electronic Literature and Computer Games" uses the examples of the adventure game *Syberia* (2002) and the electronic literature piece "3 Proposals for Bottle Imps" (Poundstone) to examine the manner in which the player operates in a metaphorically symbiotic relationship with the game interface and apparatus.

Fletcher argues that game players and games function akin to symbolic relationships between puppet masters and puppets. Fletcher's discussion not only explains many gaming operations, but also explains games within a practical and metaphorical history of media reception, use, and control. As such, this chapter provides a logical bridge connecting all of the sections of this collection.

Ultimately, each of these chapters approaches games and their relationship to real world histories in different ways. However, in doing so, each shows the many and complicated connections among games, history, and nostalgia.

Conclusion

The chapters in *Playing the Past* deal generally with the role of nostalgia in video games, but each also points to its role in culture at large. Our culture of nostalgia demands critical attention in order to understand better how the history of past media bears upon the present. Video games present a unique context within which to study nostalgia because they carry with them associations with childhood, technology and technological change, as well the influence of prior forms of media. Video games also rely on remediating structures of earlier forms, and they explicitly address the past through their representations of history. While nostalgia enacts a return or a longing to return, the first gesture of nostalgia is based in memory, and as the record of past events and hoped-for futures, memory allows the longing that is nostalgia. Different media forms use metaphors of memory and history within the logic of information retrieval that employ representations of nostalgia through their interfaces. As forms of new media, video games have often been treated as wholly new phenomena, distinct from older media and their analysis by virtue of their unique logical structures. Because digital texts function on logical structures that do not only depend on the technology, digital media works are situated within a much longer and much older narrative of media history. Jesper Juul, for example, approaches video games as continuous with the history of all games, including those that predate digital technology and the other forms of interaction which some video games clearly rely on. This places digital media works both temporally and spatially within a complex intertextual and intermedial structure of influence. As many have argued, recognizing this history takes into account histories of gaming as well as histories of media technology (cf. Aarseth). Nostalgia similarly foregrounds the connections between time and space in memory and in the act of remembering. When new media texts are separated from their past by virtue of their newness, they abandon their historical and conceptual roots. This means that new media scholarship often focuses on broad potentialities or technical minutiae rather than contextual or ecological operations. Nostalgia thus becomes a way for new media study to reclaim an appropriate temporal perspective. The essays in this volume seek to do this with two principal vectors in mind—video games as both objects for and subjects of nostalgia.

Notes

1. See Sheff for a full discussion of the "Nintendo Generation."
2. The term *nostalgia* (coined as a neologism in 1688 by Johannes Hofer) originally designated a pathological condition of longing for one's home country. Anna Reading and Colin Harvey, in their chapter in this collection, discuss how this etymology informs nostalgia as a cultural concept.
3. *Eternal Darkness: Sanity's Requiem* (2002) for the GameCube exploits this aspect of play in one of its well-known "Sanity Effects." When a player's Sanity Meter is low, she may see the game switch itself to the menu screen and move of its own accord to erase all saved game data. This is revealed as a trick, but the moment of panic it induces in the player exploits the memory structure of the game. *Eternal Darkness* is also noteworthy in terms of memory and history because one must play through the entire game three times to achieve the final, "real" ending to the game. Each time through the game amounts to a different version of the same sequence of events, but the overarching narrative of the game requires that all three (mutually exclusive) story arcs come to resolution.
4. *Run Lola Run* features a character who must deliver a sum of money to her boyfriend in less than twenty minutes. After each unsuccessful attempt, Lola starts over and tries again, effectively hitting the "reset" button. *eXistenZ* is far more overt regarding its relationship to gaming as it presents a frame story with characters immersed in a pervasive virtual reality. At a broader level, however, *eXistenZ* calls into question the audience's expectations of the fictionality of film.
5. At the time of this writing, a Wikipedia index page lists about eighty such titles. This list only scratches the surface, however, since it mainly includes major releases. (See "List of World War II video games.")

Works Cited

Aarseth, Espen. *Cybertext: Perspectives on Ergodic Literature.* Baltimore: Johns Hopkins University Press, 1997.

Brody, Florian. "The Medium is the Memory." In *The Digital Dialectic: New Essays on New Media.* Ed. Peter Lunenfeld. Cambridge: MIT Press. 130–50.

Bolter, Jay David, and Richard Grusin. *Remediation: Understanding New Media.* Cambridge: MIT Press, 2000.

Cook, Pam. *Screening the Past: Memory and Nostalgia in Cinema.* New York:

Routledge, 2005.

Dika, Vera. *Recycled Culture in Contemporary Art and Film: The Uses of Nostalgia.* Cambridge, UK: Cambridge University Press, 2003.

Frasca, Gonzalo. "Videogames of the Oppressed: Critical Thinking, Education, Tolerance, and Other Trivial Issues." In *First Person: New Media as Story, Performance, and Game.* Ed. Noah Wardrip-Fruin and Pat Harrigan. Cambridge: MIT Press, 2004.

Galloway, Alexander R. *Gaming: Essays on Algorithmic Culture.* Minneapolis: University of Minnesota Press, 2006.

GamesFirst. "Review of *Call of Duty.*" *www.gamesfirst.com* (1995). Accessed 1 June 2005.

Juul, Jesper. *Half Real: Video Games between Rules and Fiction.* Cambridge: MIT Press, 2005.

"List of World War II video games." *wikipedia.org.* Accessed 8 June 2007.

McVeigh, Brian J. "How Hello Kitty Commodifies the Cute, Cool and Camp: 'Consumutopia' versus 'Control' in Japan." *Journal of Material Culture* 5.2 (2000). 225–45.

Murray, Janet. *Hamlet on the Holodeck.* Cambridge: MIT Press, 1998.

Poundstone, William. "3 Proposals for Bottle Imps." *The Iowa Review Web* (*www.uiowa.edu/~iareview*) 5 (1 February 2003).

Ritivoi, Andreea Deciu. *Yesterday's Self: Nostalgia and the Immigrant Identity.* Lanham, MD: Rowman and Littlefield, 2002.

Rutter, Jason, and Jo Bryce. *Understanding Digital Games.* Thousand Oaks: Sage, 2006.

Sheff, David. *Game Over: How Nintendo Zapped an American Industry, Captured Your Dollars, and Enslaved Your Children.* New York: Random House, 1993.

Games Cited

Call of Duty. Santa Monica, CA: Activision, 2003.

Crimson Skies: High Road to Revenge (Xbox). Redmond, WA: Microsoft, 2003.

Donkey Kong. Redmond, WA: Nintendo, 1985.

Eternal Darkness: Sanity's Requiem (GameCube). Redmond, WA: Nintendo, 2002.

John Kerry's Silver Star. Kuma Reality Games, 2003. Available at *www.kumawar.com/ Kerry/description.php.*

Max Payne. Finland: Remedy Entertainment, 2001.

Prince of Persia: Sands of Time (Xbox). Montreal: Ubisoft, 2003.

Ratchet and Clank. San Mateo, CA: SCEA, 2002.

Resident Evil Zero. Sunnyvale, CA: Capcom, 2002

Super Columbine Massacre RPG. Ledonne, 2005. Available at *www.columbinegame. com.*

Super Mario Brothers. Redmond, WA: Nintendo, 1985.

Syberia. Montreal: Microïds, 2002.

Part I

Playing *in* the Past
Negotiating Nostalgia and Classic Gaming

2

Why Old School Is "Cool"

A Brief Analysis of Classic Video Game Nostalgia

Sean Fenty

I first played a video game in 1981; I was four at the time. I remember going to my neighbor's house, where a boy a little older than me asked if I wanted to play *PONG*. I asked what *PONG* was, and he showed me a plastic box with wood paneling connected to the television. I am not sure which of the many *PONG* systems it was, but my best guess now is that it was a five-year-old Tele-Games Super *PONG* machine. The system did not have a slot for cartridges; it did not need one, because it only played one game—*PONG*. I was very excited about playing it, but when he booted it up, it seemed unimpressive—just a vertical line down the center of the screen, one shorter line on the far left, and another on the far right. My neighbor gave me one of two detachable controllers with a knob on it and explained that I could move the "paddle" on the right up and down by turning the knob on my controller to block the square "ball" that bounced across the screen. He then proceeded to defeat me in several games before I got bored with losing and left.

Video games have come a long way since *PONG*. Thanks largely to the accuracy of Gordon Moore's now famous prediction that computing capacity would double every eighteen months, video games have become an increasingly sophisticated, immensely popular entertainment medium. The advances in computer power—which in part have been driven by our desire to play more advanced video games—have pushed the medium from its simple, blocky, two-dimensional graphics and synthetic blips and beeps to richly rendered, photorealistic, interactive, three-dimensional environments. All media, of course, are affected by technological advances. The written word, for instance, was changed radically by the invention of the printing press. But new media, tied as they are to quickly developing technologies, change more rapidly. Film, for instance, in just over a hundred years, has developed from its silent, low frame-rate, black-

and-white roots to the vivid colors of computer-rendered animations and surround sound explosions that make our insides vibrate. Television has also changed tremendously in form and content in the past fifty years. In the last couple of decades in particular, both film and television have been enormously changed by the computer revolution that continues to push the boundaries of what is visually possible in new media to fantastical heights. Video games, however, were born in the circuitry of this everything machine that is the computer. It was born and bred in an acceleration engine where rapid change is a constant. Not only do games and technology change rapidly in the personal computer and arcade sectors, but in the video game industry's primary arena—home and portable gaming devices—the technology of production and consumption undergoes radical changes every half decade when new consoles and handhelds make old models obsolete. It is an industry fueled by the promise of a tomorrow of more—more visual detail, more immersion, and more interactive freedom.

One would think that in such a medium (when tomorrow is always better than today, and certainly better than yesterday) that the past would be left behind—"played out," so to speak—but many gamers' lists of their top ten favorite games include classic games right at or near the top. In particular, many older gamers view games they played in their youth as some of the best games of all time—"classic" games played in noisy arcades in intervals measured in quarters and skill. In many cases, players have not played these games in years, having long since lost access to the original systems or arcade machines on which the games were played. Or players have played them emulated on their PCs or redistributed in "Classic" bundles on current consoles, but for some reason, after getting over the glee of familiarity, the players could not help but be slightly disappointed. Some say that these games are not the same, somehow, as the ones they played years ago. Something not quite distinguishable is inauthentic—the sounds, the colors, the feel of the controller, and the smells, even—if they, like me, spent hours playing *Galaga* (1981), *Donkey Kong* (1981), and *Ms. Pac-Man* (1982) in a laundromat close to home, filled with the smell of dirty clothes and strong detergent. These games occupy an important space of memory for many gamers, and are remembered fondly and even nostalgically. Indeed, for some, classic video games have become powerful nostalgic artifacts, not only as reminders of another time and place (a tether to a longed-for past) but as yearned-for states of being, desired spaces in and of themselves—digital homes to which gamers yearn to return. This fact is seemingly at odds with the technology-driven, future-orientated medium of video games, but it is not surprising when we consider the nature of nostalgia, the revolutionary nature of video games, and the specific characteristics of classic video games.

Nostalgia is the emotional by-product of change. People feel nostalgia—the yearning to return to some past period or irrecoverable condition—because the current condition is somehow different. It is no surprise, then, that in its most extreme pathological cases, nostalgia afflicts those who have suffered the radical and painful changes wrought by war (Boym xvi). It is easy to understand how someone affected by an actual military war would yearn for a return to a time or state prior to the conflict. Like military wars, cultural wars can also cause nostalgia. Marshall McLuhan, in *War and Peace in the Global Village*, states that "every technology necessitates a new war" (98). He says that new technology causes pain and misery (39). This pain is caused by the tremendous changes brought about by technology, and afflicts two main groups—those totally of the old technology and those stuck in the middle between the old technology and the new. Those completely of the old technology long for a return to a past where the new technology does not exist. They reject the new technology and their pain comes from a longing for a return that can never be. Those stuck in the middle experience a different pain—a pain of transition; they struggle with the pain of being caught between two worlds. Those born totally within the new technology do not suffer through these pains, because for them, this technology is not new—it is the state of things.

McLuhan was speaking of the radical changes wrought by new media in the transition from a print to an electronic culture. Most of those playing and studying games were born totally within this age, so much of the cultural change McLuhan describes in his early works does not affect us in this way. Of course, we have our own new technologies to deal with, as the process McLuhan puts forth continues and in fact accelerates in our own digital times. At the center of this technological upheaval is one of the most provocative and pervasive terms accompanying the computer revolution—*interactivity*. It has come to characterize so much of what has seduced us about computer technology, in all its ever-more ubiquitous forms, and peppers the rhetoric of advertisers and academics alike. The majority of the growing number of discussions—ranging from the apocalyptic to the rapturous, about what the computer revolution has done, is doing, and will do to how we write and read, teach and learn, create and play—are at some level grappling with the issues of computer-enabled interactivity. It is this participation within virtual spaces that make video games such a revolutionary medium and video games such powerful sites of nostalgia.

Nostalgia is the yearning to return to a place—to a state of being; and video games are places—they are states of being; and because they are stored, unchanging data, they tease with the hope for a possibility of return, if only we can regain access to them. William Blake's claim that we can "see a world in a grain of sand" seems prophetic in light of the silicon-rendered reality we now can play in with ever-increasing ease (150). Though created in a medium that is constantly changing, and as paradoxical as it may seem within an experience that insists upon movement and change, we cannot help but think of these virtual playgrounds as perfect and immutable constants that we can return to for comfort as our world changes around us. Of course, the nostalgia felt for them are multilayered. Certainly, video games represent times and places in gamers' lives to which they may want to return, but that is merely one superficial aspect of video game nostalgia.

Video games may be, for some, artifacts of a past they want to return to, but video games also offer the seduction of a perfect past that can be replayed, a past within which players can participate, and a past in which players can move and explore. As Lev Manovich says of all new media spaces in *The Language of New Media*, within video games all time is spatialized and all spaces are spaces of navigation (252). Though requiring us to move within them and change within them, they themselves, as a whole, never change; video games are always there, like Keats's Grecian Urn, only set in motion and ready for us to enter in the activities, waiting for us to return to their patterns and repetitions, which we learned like the rhythms of a dance we practiced time and again. Once we learn the rhythms, we are home—player and game, dancer and dance, one and the same. And if, years later, we can only remember the steps and relearn the patterns, we can return to that place and time and dance the dance, or so the seduction goes. However, since nostalgia is a yearning for a return to an irrecoverable condition, it would not be nostalgia if a return were possible. Though we may desire to go back, we never really can. Not because the games are different, but because we as players are different. We have changed, and the games themselves have helped us to change.

Marc Prensky, in his book *Digital Games-Based Learning*, suggests that we are now a part of what he calls the "games generation," which he identifies as beginning with those born in the last forty years or so—a period that not coincidentally coincides with the emergence of what are now called classic video games. While many radical technological innovations have emerged and changed us over the last few decades, altering our formative experiences and our interests, Prensky identifies video games as being particularly influential, creating cognitive shifts in the ways players learn and experience the world. He is not alone in this research; others (like James Paul Gee in *What Video Games Have to Teach Us About Learning and Literacy*) also discuss how video games have changed players as learners and how video games can be used as learning tools. Like our experiences with all media, our experiences with video games change us, as a culture and as individuals. These changes greatly affect players—especially those at the beginning of the "games generation," in the transitional state McLuhan describes—and create a particularly rich breeding ground for nostalgia.

The nostalgia felt for classic video games by those who first ventured into arcades and played the first home console and computer games in the late 1970s and early 1980s is at one level a nostalgia unique to that generation, as one that experienced a profound cultural shift into computer-mediated play and representation. However, the emergence of video games is more than just an historical moment of transition. Video games are a continual source of transition and so, at another level, all of those who have played video games may feel nostalgic about them. In this sense, the nostalgia felt for video games is not nostalgia for a past state before the trauma of the games disrupted us, but a desire to recapture that mind-altering experience of being in a game for the first time. It is a yearning for liminality itself—for the moment of transition. Not the liminality of being caught between the two worlds of pre-video games and video games, but the liminality of being between the two worlds of the real and the game world—of being on the threshold. It is here to which we want to return—to the sheer joy of beginning to know another world and the contrast between that world and the one in which we normally reside.

We may ask ourselves if this process really is revolutionary. After all, in many ways, the worlds of the video games that we immerse ourselves in by learning the rhythm of the games are similar to the worlds created by other entertainment media such as books, television, and film—in which, to varying degrees and with huge variations within each medium, we must also learn the rhythm of things. Certainly, video games share many characteristics with each of these media. Surprisingly, in fact, video games are in some ways closer to novels than much of television and film. All of these media are highly focused on world creation, but in novels, as in video games, significant effort is required to enter this imaginary space. As Umberto Eco tells us in his "Postscript" to *The Name of the Rose*, a novel is first and foremost a world, and entering this world requires effort. Much to the chagrin of his editors, Eco purposely made the first hundred pages of his novel difficult and demanding, because he insisted that if a reader wants to enter the world of his novel, the reader will have to accept its pace. The novel thus teaches the reader the ideal rhythm of reading it requires. Eco compares entering a novel to climbing a mountain, saying that readers must "learn the rhythm of respiration, acquire the pace; otherwise you stop right away" (520). In short, there is a learning curve involved, and if readers do not get past it, they will never gain entry into the novel. Similarly, if players do not learn the patterns of a video game, they will never fall into the flow of the game; they will never be fully in its world. One can play *Ms. Pac-Man*, for instance, without realizing that each of the ghosts has its own personality—its own pattern of movement of pursuit and retreat—but playing it well requires such a realization. If a player does not learn these patterns, the player will not be able to continue on into the game. Entering these worlds requires effort; the experiences are active ones.

With a book, the reader must interpret the words on the page and imagine the world they describe. They must read on for its events to unfold, and read thoughtfully to understand these events. In fact, if the text is well-written, the reader really *must* continue. Without effort, everything stops, and if the text is compelling, the reader cannot let it stop. The reader wants to keep moving through the text. So it is with video games: players must play on, if the game is a good one, and to play on, players must learn how to play better, learning the patterns of the game in order to continue in it. This process alters players, making return impossible. Film and television, of course, are not entirely passive; they too require effort for entry, though not often to the extent of novels and video games, which often take many hours to get through, and often require rereading and replaying. At the very least, however, viewers of films and television, as well as readers of books and players of video games, must suspend disbelief to become immersed. Sometimes this is not enough, but even when it is, it is a remarkably active feat of self-deception.

All worlds on screen or in print, no matter how strenuously authors and directors and game designers try to cover this fact up, are incomplete and limited. Readers, viewers, and players connect the dots and ignore the gaps to immerse themselves in the texts. Creators of entertainment help us to do this by relying on conventions of the media and the genres that they are working in that draw attention to that which we are supposed to see and what we should expect to see, and away from that which cannot be seen and what is not shown. But video game designers have a tougher time with this, since video games are interactive in ways that other media are not. While video games share much with other media, and much of what they share contribute to the nostalgia we feel for them, it is the ways in which video games are different that make them particularly suited as objects of nostalgia.

As an interactive medium, video games give over a great deal of control to players that other media retain in the presentation of their content. In part, it is this control and the illusion of freedom that makes play possible and video games enjoyable and memorable. Players enjoy the relative freedom that they have in a game world versus other fictional worlds represented in books, television, and movies; they enjoy the control that they have over video game avatars and the struggle of learning how to succeed in the game world. It is the effort involved—the struggle to learn and overcome—that makes the games memorable, and these memories feed into the process where earlier games are idealized and game-play operates nostalgically for players.

Though freedom and control are key elements of video games, to keep players engaged, video games must also have boundaries and naturalized limitations. A game must have rules and goals, as Katie Salen and Eric Zimmerman have already delineated (*Rules of Play*). The rules of the game limit the freedom of players, but they also give the game meaning. A game must get players to play it and want to keep playing it. One of the best ways to do this is to make the play meaningful and provide desirable goal states for the players. At the most basic level, to do this, video games must first work. The game world cannot be buggy and crash accidentally. The games need to run on a stable system able to support consistently the space designed within it. Beyond that, the cosmology of the game world must have discernable physical rules: a player must be able to determine that their actions have consistent consequences within the game. Once this is established, game designers can build spaces in which the player can play, but designers still need to get the player interested in continuing through the game. Designers must motivate players to put forth the effort involved in playing. They need to set goals and give rewards; they need to set up a situation that will make players want to succeed at the game and want to learn the rhythm of things, or the player, like Eco's reader, will never make it up the mountain. Players do not feel nostalgic about such games; they forget them. Games players feel nostalgic about are games they put effort into to learn the game patterns and rhythms. People feel nostalgic about games they enjoyed being a part of—games that changed them. The games must offer players the allure of interactivity—the freedom to be in the world of the game—but they must make actions within that world compelling. They must create a place where players not only want to *be*, but a place in which players also want to *do*.

Two of the ways video games do this is through the use of schemas and affordances. The idea of schemas comes from cognitive psychology and is based on our reliance on past experience in determining our actions in a given place or situation. In one respect, schemas can be thought of as deeply ingrained social conventions. For instance, when we go into a restaurant, those of us who have been to restaurants and learned the restaurant schema know that certain behavior is acceptable or required and certain behavior is not. We wait to be seated, or we place our order at the counter. Variations, of course, exist, and with each new restaurant experience our schema expands and becomes more complex. Game designers can use schemas to reasonably limit or anticipate players' behavior. Classic video games by and large do this quite well. There is not much else to do in *Ms. Pac-Man*, for instance, other than to chomp pellets and to run from and chase ghosts. Newer games sometimes have a more difficult time with this, since they put players in worlds more similar to our own and thus have to contend with far greater expectations of freedom. In *Donkey Kong*, players can only climb, jump, or smash barrels. In many newer games, however, with naturalistic-looking environments, players confuse gaming and real-life schemas, expecting to be able to do things that games may not allow them to do. Players may, for instance, expect that a vase will break when shot or that a door lock will open when shot, but the game world may not be designed this way. In fact, there is likely nothing behind the doors we cannot open. This is a limitation of the game world and it must be naturalized to keep players immersed in the game. Game designers use schemas to dictate what a player can expect to be able to do within the game world. If the video game is a football simulation, for instance, players usually do not attempt to run off the field and into the stands in the middle of the game. The game world does not allow this freedom, but neither do players expect it. The illusion of freedom is maintained and the player stays in rhythm with the game. Remaining within the flow of the game allows the play to be idealized, and to remain in the nostalgic memory of the player.

Another method employed by designers to naturalize gaming limitations, thus adding to the illusion of freedom within the game-space, is building in affordances into the various levels of interface. *Affordance* is a term Donald Norman uses in his book *The Design of Everyday Things*. He defines affordance as "the perceived and actual properties of the thing, primarily those fundamental properties that determine just how the thing could possibly be used" (9). For example, in a game such as *Donkey Kong*, players learn quickly that they can be killed by barrels thrown down at them by a large ape, so players take into the game world the affordance that being hit by large wooden objects is a bad thing and respond by jumping over them. In other words, players are given signs about what affordances they can take from the real world and apply to the game world. In doing so, these affordances tie a simplified version of the real world to the representational space of the game world. This aligns the game worlds with a real world that has never existed. As long as these affordances are reasonably consistent and numerous, players allow themselves to overlook the many things that cannot be done in the game-space. All of this, if done well, creates the illusion of freedom of interaction within the game-space, helping players to ignore the gaps and missing pieces in the game world—issues that filmmakers and television show creators do not have to worry about since they always control the audience's movement through time and space.

Thus video games, as a whole, because they are interactive, offer different sets of challenges for both makers and players, and different rewards as well. They put players on the threshold of another world and make players work to enter that world. In the case of classic video games, unlike most new games, it is an experience of being on the threshold of something entirely different—not a real space or a virtual space trying to be real, trying to fool us with illusions of graphic detail, but a distinct, abstract, computer space—a game world of symbolism, graphic minimalism, and ideal forms. New games continue to evolve increasingly complex and sophisticated graphics, incorporate increasingly complex storylines, and in general offer an interactive space for cinema-like representation. As such, they can evoke nostalgia for earlier days in much the same way as cinema, but with the added allure of interactivity. Video games can represent the past as it was, or as it never was, but they can also represent how players wish to remember it, revisiting or revising the past to make players yearn for it, and they can offer players the possibility of not only *being* there but of *doing* things there—of *playing the past*. Because of advances in computer technology, new games can do all of this in ways classic video games could not. They can portray emotions or emotionally consequential events far more effectively than their predecessors. In short, they can evoke the nostalgia that players feel for other objects, people, and places with increasing effectiveness that rivals—and in some ways surpasses—other media. But as transformational play experiences and nostalgic artifacts in and of themselves, newer video games are, in some ways, less powerful than classic games in that the transition between the real world and the game world is less profound.

One could argue, as Marie-Laure Ryan does in *Narrative as Virtual*

Reality: Immersion and Interactivity in Electronic Media, that new games "through increasing attention devoted to sensorial representation of the game world" have become more immersive experiences than classic video games (309). This depends, of course, on our concept of immersion. Under such a premise, new video games are more immersive because they represent the game world more realistically and thus require less effort on the part of players to fill in the blanks, allowing them to immerse themselves more easily in the game world. An alternative view—more appropriate to our understanding of classic video games as objects of nostalgia—is proposed by D. B. Weiss in his novel *Lucky Wander Boy*, a work that is in large part about classic video game nostalgia in its most pathological sense. It is a view based on Marshall McLuhan's concept of hot and cold media as put forth in *Understanding Media*, the idea being that video games are heating up—becoming more like films and less like books. Though, as mentioned earlier, all video games require effort on the part of the player, classic video games require more effort in many ways. They are "cool," in McLuhan's sense of the word. Further, because they require more effort and participation than new games, they bring players deeper into their worlds than do new games. "In cool games," says Adam Pennyman, the protagonist of *Lucky Wander Boy*:

> graphic minimalism goes hand-in-hand with the absorptive, World Unto Itself quality that makes these games special . . . When we play these games, the sketchy visual detail forces us to fill in the blanks, and in so doing we bind ourselves to the game world. Even more, we participate in its creation, we are a linchpin, a co-creator, crucial to the existence of the game world as it is meant to be experienced. (66)

Pennyman is an obsessed classic video game fan—pathologically nostalgic—so perhaps he is overstating his case, but his position has some merit.

Classic video games offer players another world to play in, but one that requires effort—even more effort than that required by newer games. It is a space of ideal forms—of abstracted geometry and characters. As points of comparison to other media, painting in the western tradition shows a similar progression of form. As Marie-Laure Ryan points out:

> In pre-Renaissance times painting was more symbolic representation of the spiritual essence of things than an attempt to convey the illusion of presence. Its semiotic mode was signification rather than

simulation . . . All this changed when the discovery of the laws of perspective allowed the projection of three-dimensional space onto a two-dimensional surface. (2)

If the discovery of perspective was a watershed event in painting, so too was the increased processing power of the computer that has allowed for the technologically deterministic advancement of graphical and spatial sophistication in video games. This progression in what can be done in the medium of video games has changed the way players experience them, for the most part. Certainly, while developers can make games more visually sophisticated and realistic, they do not have to, just as paintings do not have to use perspective, and comics can adopt a realistic style or a more abstract cartoonish one. However, by and large, computer, console, arcade, and even handheld games are evolving toward more graphic detail and spatial complexity.

One of the by-products of this advancement has been a gradually growing scarcity of classic video games as original hardware becomes obsolete and more difficult to find. This increased unavailability has in fact added to the nostalgia felt for these games, as objects of an irrecoverable past. Yet as the technology has advanced and continues to advance, we have also seen the development of emulators such as MAME that allow players to play classic games once again on their PCs. More recently, there has been even more widespread availability of these games with the re-release of many classic video games bundled in anthologies for contemporary consoles, as well as video game download services such as the Nintendo Wii's Virtual Console and Microsoft's Xbox 360 Live Arcade. There are also plug-and-play devices that contain several classic console games from Intellivision, Activision, and Atari, and even reconfigured classic gaming consoles such as the Atari Flashback, which takes another step in trying to recapture the original game-play experience with controllers approximating the original.

If the development of video game technology has been a progression, certainly the success of these releases is in part due to the nostalgia felt for them. Of course, part of it can also be attributed to the fact that such anthologies are often good values in terms of game-play per dollar spent, and fundamentally, from a strategic standpoint, the best of classic games are just as fun and engaging and often more so than their more modern counterparts. In addition to the sincere nostalgia felt for these games, the culture of "cool" that values all things retro-chic is certainly being played to by corporate entities ever willing to turn the past into a commodity. But what does this renewed availability mean for those sincerely nostalgic for recapturing the magic of their foundational video game-play experiences?

Playing these games again can be a pleasurable experience at a certain level. As play-experiences, the games can still be fun. Add to that the pleasure associated with the feeling of remembering the original experiences one has had with these games, and overall, replaying them can be a rewarding experience. However, as indicated earlier, for many, the experience is not the same. It can never be a true return, and that, of course, is what makes classic games true objects of nostalgia. We may try to recapture the joy of playing these games years ago, but something is not quite the same. Some might suggest that an emulated version of *Dig-Dug* (1982) or a plug-and-play version of *Asteroids* (1979) is not the same, because the controller is different, the display is different, or the emulation is not quite accurate—the sound is off, or the color—but even if these things are true, more importantly, we ourselves are different. In *Lucky Wander Boy*, Pennyman denied this truth and strove for more accurate experiences, moving from emulators such as MAME to the original consoles and arcade games, but he still found them to be lacking. They were missing their aura. He became obsessed with the one game that he could not find emulated, the one game that was in no archive or anthology— *Lucky Wander Boy*. His quest to find this game, to play it once again, and to get to its unattainable third level becomes all-consuming precisely because it is his last hope for return. Whereas all the other games eventually fell short in allowing him the recovery of his former state, the one yet to be rediscovered still held hope. But such a return is not possible. While the feeling of nostalgia can be evoked by these games—while they may remind us of our past—they cannot truly return us there because we have changed. The games themselves have helped change us. This is the essence of classic video game nostalgia and indeed all nostalgia. The past object or event holds us as a desire delayed—an anticipation of what might yet be. In the novel, Pennyman replays possible endings to his story—possible ways in which his dream can be fulfilled. He dreams of going to the game's creator and finding an untouched *Lucky Wander Boy* machine, just waiting for him to play it. He says, in one of Weiss's endings—in the last ending, in fact:

> . . . the *Lucky Wander Boy* machine, enshrined in its very own dark corner, a corner so dark it refused to spit out a single shard of light. I could not think of a single better thing to do, a single better place to

be, than right in front of that machine. I wanted to want something else, I tried to want something else, but it was impossible . . . This was what I had come to find. (271)

Finally, he did find it and he reached into his pocket full of an infinite number of quarters, and the story ends as he puts his first one in, just as he is about to fall into the game, stop time, recapture the moment, and live in it forever. This is the dream of classic video game nostalgia taken to its pathological extreme—a dream, whether small and restrained as it is in most cases of nostalgia, or large and all-encompassing as it was for Pennyman, that is, ultimately and perpetually, deferred.

Works Cited

Boym, Svetlana. *The Future of Nostalgia.* New York: Basic Books, 2001.

Eco, Umberto. *The Name of the Rose.* Trans. William Weaver. New York: Harcourt Brace, 1983.

Gee, James Paul. *What Video Games Have to Teach Us About Learning and Literacy.* New York: Palgrave Macmillan, 2004.

Manovich, Lev. *The Language of New Media.* Cambridge: MIT Press, 2001.

McLuhan, Marshall. *Understanding Media.* New York: New American Library, 1964.

___. *War and Peace in the Global Village.* New York: Bantam Books, 1968.

Norman, Donald. *The Design of Everyday Things.* New York: Doubleday, 1988.

Prensky, Marc. *Digital Games-Based Learning.* New York: McGraw-Hill, 2004.

Ryan, Marie-Laure. *Narrative as Virtual Reality: Immersion and Interactivity in Electronic Media.* Baltimore: Johns Hopkins University Press, 2000.

Salen, Katie, and Eric Zimmerman. *Rules of Play: Game Design Fundamentals.* Cambridge: MIT Press, 2003.

Weiss, D. B. *Lucky Wander Boy.* New York: Plume, 2003.

Games Cited

Dig-Dug (arcade). Tokyo: Namco, 1982.

Donkey Kong (arcade). Kyoto: Nintendo, 1981.

Galaga (arcade). Tokyo: Namco, 1981.

Ms. Pac-Man (arcade). Tokyo: Namco, 1981.

PONG (Tele-Games Super *PONG*). New York: Atari, 1976.

Asteroids (arcade). New York: Atari, 1979.

3

Homesick for Silent Hill

Modalities of Nostalgia in Fan Responses to *Silent Hill 4: The Room*

Natasha Whiteman

Serial forms of entertainment rely upon and must contain varying degrees of textual change and transformation. Change, in terms of the "successive differences in form or configuration"[1] between titles or episodes, is necessary if a series is to evolve. Yet, in the face of audience expectations, innovation must be balanced against the provision of established title or genre characteristics/elements. New episodes of television programs, and the release of film and video game sequels and prequels, have the potential to both unsettle and build upon that which is already established—that which has already been experienced.

Nowhere is the expectation of audiences more heated than in the fan cultures on the Internet, and nowhere is audience dissatisfaction with series developments as visible. This chapter examines the responses of one such fan "community" to the release of *Silent Hill 4: The Room* (2004), the fourth in Konami's series of survival horror video games. In examining fan talk about *Silent Hill 4*, I want to suggest a move beyond conceptions of nostalgia in terms of interest in classic or retrogaming—the way in which it has typically featured in writing on video games—towards thinking of nostalgia relationally. This involves a consideration of the ways that gamers deal with the multiplicity of textual consumption by essentializing and constructing frames of reference relating to their favored "loved objects," and thinking about nostalgia in relation to fan affiliation to and longing for these games is expressed online and challenged in the face of new games/developments. This broadening move resonates with a number of the chapters in this volume, including Sean Fenty's examination of nostalgia as "the emotional by-product of change."

The term "fan" suggests a degree of allegiance to a text, persona, or practice that goes beyond that of a casual consumer. The relationship between fan and text (or indeed fan and producer) is, however, by no means straightforward or necessarily harmonious. In the context of video game fandom, allegiance may keep a gamer returning to a specific video game title, series, or games site (which may privilege one title or series over and above others).[2] It may also result in excitement, optimism, and anticipation surrounding the release of new titles. However, this allegiance can be threatened when the texts that inspire fan devotion are taken in new directions. Enthusiasm and excitement surrounding new releases is frequently tempered by the voicing of loss, criticism, and disappointment, and in extreme circumstances, anger, which feed into the creation of websites, petitions, campaigns, and tirades left on bulletin board forums and discussion groups.

These sources of publicly displayed disapproval and conflict provide us with an opportunity to examine the voicing of expectations about media texts and the negotiation of textual "authenticity" by fans in ways that, I argue, privilege nostalgia (in terms of a desire or longing for a return to an idealized state). This is not to suggest a unified or established reference point. Nostalgia in such contexts can instead be seen as an emergent, strategic, and only temporarily stable phenomenon of the oppositions and alliances that pattern the activity in which people are enabled to recognize themselves as participants of fandom. My interest here is in considering how these positions are expressed in moves that both idealize and essentialize the nature of *Silent Hill* via the identification of key elements of what *Silent Hill* "is" or "should be."

In thinking about nostalgia in this way, I am drawing from theoretical approaches to the fixing of meaning in language, specifically the concept of *points de capiton* or "quilting points" in Lacanian psychoanalytic theory (Lacan; Laclau and Mouffe; Žižek). This is based on an understanding of language as involving a constant slippage of meaning; in this conceptualization of language, quilting points provide temporary points of stability. The major element to be taken from this work in relation to my interest here is that the fixing of meaning is always at the expense of alternate fixings—it is always a political act. This idea has particularly interesting implications in sites such as *Silent Hill Heaven*, where struggles over the fixing (and unfixing) of what *Silent Hill* is are tied into the formation of dynamic encampments and divisions as fans respond to the new by making reference to the old.

Video Game Fans, Cultures, and Change

There is increasing academic interest in the cultural practices surrounding gaming. Acknowledgment of the social contexts within which games are situated has begun to challenge the stereotype of the isolated, socially incompetent gamer (Gee; Jenkins "Reality Bytes"). The emergence of fan cultures on the Internet—the fan sites and forums, homepages, shrines, and universities[3] devoted to video games—have represented numerous sites for examination for those interested in the nature of media texts and fans' relationships with them. Such interest clearly ties into earlier work on media fandoms. However, as the celebration, analysis, and subversion of video games by fans has become increasingly visible and accessible, work has begun to focus on the practices and cultures of video game fans online (Flanagan; Consalvo; Rehak; Simons and Newman; Newman). As well as representing part of a broader move from "real" to "virtual" sites of investigation, these studies have also been part of a shift of attention from TV and print forms of fan-favored texts to digital, "interactive" texts that appear to raise new questions about fan identification, consumption, and authorship. Much of the work on video game fans to date focuses on the expansion and recontextualizing of games through fans' creative and analytical practices (such as the creation of walkthroughs, fan art, mods, histories of video game characters, etc.). In contrast, my focus here is on nostalgia in the context of evaluative statements voiced by video game fans online.

The expression of fan critiques and disapproval in response to media products and transitions in series has been described elsewhere in both academic work and in the popular gaming press. Though new releases can provide explicit pressure points and sources of conflict and disagreement, discussions about texts are part of the "everyday" activities of fans—practices that have been examined in media and cultural studies of both off and online fan cultures. In Henry Jenkins's *Textual Poachers*, one of the key early texts on media fans, Jenkins notes the importance of disagreements in maintaining the debate central to fan practices while also arguing that heated disagreements are rare and that "a high degree of consensus shapes fan reception" (95). Jenkins argues that certain episodes of television shows, in this case *Star Trek*, are particularly disliked because of fans' responses to the formal elements of the text, suggesting that "many fans justify these judgments according to general criteria applicable to any classical narrative" (97).[4] He goes on to add:

More often, however, individual episodes are evaluated against an idealized conception of the series, according to their conformity with the hopes and expectations the reader has for the series' potential development. This program "tradition" is abstracted from the sum total of available material and yet provides consistent criteria for evaluating each new addition. (97)

This abstraction may be regarded as providing stability from the multiple experiences of the text. Although Jenkins presents descriptions of the workings of fan cultures and fans' engagements with media texts,[5] his focus is not sociological. Issues relating to oppositions and hierarchies within fandoms,[6] for example, are played down in favor of an emphasis on documenting the productivity of alliances within fan cultures from an insider's perspective. His discussion of that which serves to create the ideal *Star Trek*—the "meta-text against which a film or episode is evaluated" (98)—is however clearly significant in relation to my interest in nostalgia in this chapter.

Fan evaluations and dissent in the face of an "ideal" meta-text are seen elsewhere in work on media fans. Will Brooker's study of the reformulation of the comic-book character Batman through various media and mediums (including comics, TV series, and films), for example, contains a description of fan protests against Tim Burton's 1989 film *Batman*. These protests, including criticisms of the casting of Michael Keaton in the lead role, contrasted the new film to the earlier comic books of the series, with this heritage presented as the defining reference point for many fans. Brooker references Camille Bacon-Smith and Tyrone Yarbrough's suggestion that "the movie *Batman* failed to enter into fan 'continuity' as an 'authentic' representation of the character" (288). Further, Brooker himself notes that, "To many fans, they got it wrong. They blew it. And, worse, they didn't care" (288). He then recounts how responses on discussion boards to the even more derided, Joel Schumacher-directed *Batman & Robin* (1997) involved the expression of (more conventionally understood) nostalgia for Burton's earlier Batman films in the face of Schumacher's "camp" spectacle.[7]

In literature relating to video games we find similar criticisms by fans of the formal elements of new titles. James Newman, for example, quotes postings from the *Zelda Guide* website to demonstrate the "mix of anger, denial and reverence" in responses of fans to early shots demonstrating the introduction of a new cell-shaded aesthetic in *The Legend of Zelda: The Wind Waker* (2003). He notes:

> For some, the comic book visual style with its wide-eyed, boldly coloured characters and environments that harked back to the Laserdisc visuals of *Dragon's Lair*, for example, was wholly at odds with the series that, in previous incarnations, had conformed largely to a *Dungeons and Dragons*-style "fantasy" aesthetic presently in vogue as a result of the film adaptations of the *Lord of the Rings* trilogy and interestingly referred to as "realistic" by Zelda fans. (153–54)

Journalistic coverage of new games contain similar references to fan responses to change. In an article about the title *Legend of Zelda: Twilight Princess* (2006), *Edge Magazine* notes "the rift in the fanbase that *The Wind Waker* caused," describing that game as "the most contentious game in the Zelda series. It doesn't take long for any discussion among Zelda fans to turn to raking over its coals: the controversial visual treatment, the slender conclusion, the long stretches of sailing" (73). Such notions of "rifts" (seen elsewhere in the academic recording of crises—or what Bacon-Smith refers to as "schisms"—within specific fandoms) may suggest an overemphasis of the stability and the unity of the fan culture. Media texts clearly inspire multiple sites and spaces of fan interest and devotion, and the response to changes can be localized and are context-dependent. In this chapter, I am not attempting to make claims about a *Silent Hill* "fanbase." My focus instead is on how evaluation, and with it nostalgia, is expressed within one specific site, *Silent Hill Heaven*.

Studying Nostalgia @ *SilentHillHeaven.com*

Silent Hill Heaven is one of the most high-profile unofficial fan sites for the *Silent Hill* series. Along with information about the four games and related media (official publications, guides, etc.), and links to affiliated *Silent Hill* fansites, *Silent Hill Heaven* houses lively and active forums in which each of the *Silent Hill* games, the 2006 *Silent Hill* film,[8] and more general topics are discussed. As is typical in many bulletin boards, activity is maintained and regulated by a number of moderators and administrators who police the site, reining in flaming and maintaining order in each of the forums. The posting activity discussed in this chapter took place on the site's public forums where posts were accessible without necessary membership or registration at the time I wrote this chapter. I was a frequent visitor to *Silent Hill Heaven* from June 2004 to February 2006 during the production of my doctoral thesis, which explored informal pedagogies in online fan cultures (Whiteman). When I started visiting the site, *Silent Hill 4* had not yet been released, and I began to follow discussion relating to the new game as the release date (in the UK, 17 September 2004) drew closer. The longitudinal nature of my study meant that I was able to follow the move from exchange of information and rumors to pre-release excitement and anxiety, and then to early reviews and then queries relating to the new game, post-release.

The analysis presented here is based predominantly on observation of forum activity from September and October 2004. It draws from fan talk across threads in the *Silent Hill 4* forum, as well as my experience of the site and its bulletin board as a whole. My specific empirical focus however, is on one thread titled "Im disappointed and my head hurts" (a thread that, at the time of archiving, contained 139 posts). "Im disappointed and my head hurts" is one of a number of threads that were deleted from the forums during a spring clean of the site in 2005 (or in the parlance of the setting, a "forum flush") and is therefore no longer available online. This "flush" served to demonstrate the contradictory nature of audience/fan research on the Internet—an environment in which data appears often overwhelmingly plentiful, but is also transitory and ephemeral. Ethical guidelines for carrying out research in such environments remain contested. Although this was a public thread, extracts from the postings to it are here presented in anonymous form[9] (and cannot be retrieved via the use of search engines).

The analysis presented in this essay is strongly influenced by the sociological approach of social activity theory (Dowling *Sociology,* "Social," and "Timely"; and Dudley-Smith)—which is distinct from Engeström's similarly-titled *activity theory.* Social activity theory is concerned with the institutionalization of practices and patterns of relationships within sites of social activity, defining the social in terms of the formation, maintenance, and destabilization of alliances and oppositions. My focus in this essay is on *Silent Hill Heaven's* forum as a social setting and the modality of practice within it—in particular, the positions and relations marked out in relation to the game object. The analysis does not go beyond this data (in terms of making assumptions about the "real" gamers/fans, for example).

Fan Responses to *Silent Hill 4: The Room*

The *Silent Hill* series of survival horror games are characterized by an atmospheric occult horror aesthetic and linear exploration style of gameplay, with games 1–3 involving (to differing degrees[10]) the exploration of the threatening and mysterious town of Silent Hill.[11] When *Silent Hill 4:*

The Room was released in Japan in June 2004, word quickly spread online and in the gaming press that many Japanese gamers were disappointed with the game experience it offered (see GamesRadar). The game's production history had been complex. It had gone into production just before *Silent Hill 3*, initially as a separate title, which was pulled into the franchise during the production process (a fact that was not missed by *Silent Hill* fans). *Silent Hill 4* maintains elements of the series formula in terms of atmosphere, aesthetic (and, it could be argued, gameplay), and references and extends the *Silent Hill* mythology. It also, however, represents a number of changes to the *Silent Hill* "formula" (not least the fact that the game is not set in the fictional town of Silent Hill but instead its neighboring town, South Ashfield). These changes include the introduction of a first-person perspective (the previous games were played fully in the third person), new characters and storyline, a new menu system, and the removal of two key *Silent Hill* items: the flashlight and radio.

Most significantly perhaps, *Silent Hill 4* marked a move away from the linear exploration models of games 1–3, to a new scenario.[12] *Silent Hill 4* begins with a new protagonist, Henry Townshend, trapped in his apartment, Room 302 of South Ashfield Heights—the room of the title. Henry is able to escape—through an opening portal in his bathroom—but only in order to visit a range of levels/worlds, including subway, forest,[13] and apartment building levels. Having successfully negotiated and survived these hostile environments (the horror genre characteristics of the game ensuring that these worlds are inhabited by monstrous enemies), Henry awakens from "sleep" to find himself once again trapped within the apartment. The repeated—and inescapable—returns to the room and to the worlds that surround it instill both frustration and anxiety, the feeling of claustrophobia increased by the fact that the "safe" haven of the apartment does not remain safe for long.

The changes outlined briefly above were to inspire heated debate in *Silent Hill Heaven*'s forums, with the *Silent Hill 4* forum soon displaying members' responses to the game in public pronouncements of both praise and criticism. Some initial responses were particularly hostile:

> I feel betrayed, the ones we love betray us in the end and team
> Silent is no exception, they took our money and ran. And that's the
> difference between Dracula and Underworld and SH2 and SH4. Look
> kinda the same don't they only two numbers apart, not even close my
> friends. SH4 can dress up in its big brothers clothes but it still trips
> over the pant leg . . . Well you get the idea, SH4 sucks the root!

Soon after the game's release, critical voices in a number of threads suggested that *Silent Hill 4* was not a "proper" *Silent Hill* game but a "spin off," a "side story," or (drawing from its early status as a stand-alone title) that it should rightfully just be titled *The Room*. As one member noted:

> I didn't like it as a Silent Hill game, but I liked it as a survival horror game [. . .] I understand some people don't like this game, because it's not Silent Hill. But why don't you at least TRY to like it as something else?

Many of those who criticized the game supported their opinions by highlighting formal elements that displeased them (in a similar way to the *Star Trek* fans cited by Jenkins), including frustration with the repetitive scenario, with technical elements, and with the characters and quality of the voice acting. These criticisms of formal elements of the game tied into the public reminiscence of personal experiences of gameplay:

> it starts of ok . . . and by ok i mean on the bad half of ok (Ghosts???
> i thought i traded in fatal frame . . .) then, you get to go to a subway.
> with a pipe. and it looks like it is day time in that motherfucker . . .
> then you meet a really hot chick . . . but she dies . . . (m . . . m-maria?
> huh? no, she has black hair . . .) then you go back to the house . . .
> apartment . . . thing . . . so know im like, ok, so maybe it is just slow
> at the beggining, it will get better . . . i mean, come on, its silent hill
> it has to get better! but NO! you go to a forest. and it looks like it is
> daytime in that motherfucker . . . then . . . the bat-bird-bee-hornet-
> things come . . . and i remember another bad game . . . called tomb
> raider. but no, im playing silent hill, the game that used to give me
> nightmares, it can't be resorting to tomb raider shity ass cheap thrills
> . . . but it does . . . and i wept for Konami . . . i wept . . .

> The game cheated it's gamers [. . .] After you beat the first half of this game, the levels are recylced and it makes the entire experience feel CHEAP!!! Plus Wlater . . . oh my fucking god. ARGH!!!!!!!

Made along textual lines, comparisons in terms of quality positioned the game not just in relation to existing games but also to other media texts (as can be seen in the references to *Tomb Raider* and *Fatal Frame* in the first of the two extracts of posts above). A number of posts made reference to the survival horror series *Resident Evil*, with one poster commenting that "its exactly like what you said—a bad RE game. And Most RE games are bad. The portals? The worlds? Are we playing Silent Hill, or Spyro the Dragon?" Such comments situated the new game within broader genre-based debates and prejudices.

In contrast to these negative posts, a number of posters focused on the unique qualities of the game, praising what they regarded as an original storyline and reconfiguring the frustration of the repeat returns to the room in positive terms as inducing a pleasingly claustrophobic horror: "Why do I like this game so much? The complexes. Mothers, wombs, sacrifices, serial killing, detachment, isolation—I think this was a pretty goddamn good mixture of things." As those who praised the game focused upon elements of the games that deserved celebration, many used intertextual references to attribute quality in a way that reflected moves on the site to demonstrate the artistic value of *Silent Hill*. Comparisons to culturally valid (in the context of this site) auteurs such as David Lynch and Clive Barker, and the "revelation" of references to Japanese folklore within *Silent Hill 4*, for example, appeared to attribute "depth" to the new game.

In some ways the responses and debate surrounding *Silent Hill 4* fit quite snugly into the surrounding discourse within *Silent Hill Heaven*'s forums—particularly that relating to the other games in the series. Familiar forum activity included the discussion of typical themes (to do with place, character, motivation, the opinions of the producers, etc.), inter- and intra-textual negotiation, and consideration of the *Silent Hill* mythology. The discussion surrounding the fourth game did, however, appear to be both particularly heated and specifically fixated on the game in terms of its difference and similarity to the *Silent Hill* canon. One poster suggested that the new game "is ultimately turning out to be the most 'Love it or Hate It' out of the series."

Before moving on to consider a number of posts in more detail, it is worth noting that the polarization of criticisms and praise towards *Silent Hill 4* that I briefly suggested above was founded on key elements that individual posters argued the new game either did or did not demonstrate. In both supportive and critical responses to *Silent Hill 4*, the identification of these elements was used to support individual readings of whether the game was or was not an authentic representative of the series. These elements represent a range of moves to define individual versions of an ideal *Silent Hill*—personal responses to the new game voiced in a public space.

Modalities of Nostalgia:
"Im disappointed and my head hurts"

The voicing and negotiation of the essential elements of *Silent Hill* and resulting conflict between posters can be seen in the thread "Im disappointed and my head hurts." The thread opens with one member posting a negative review of *Silent Hill 4*, a review which presents a number of criticisms of the new game and its position in relation to the perceived cohesiveness of the preceding texts:

> All of the first three had a universal feeling. They had something to do with each other, or a similar story process, or something. Like they were continuing chapters in the same story. Each character going to Silent Hill, encountering new worlds and monsters. This game it feels like a spin off, a bad spin off.

The post ends with an appeal for opinions relating to the game,[14] an invitation that privileges evaluative statements. For much of the thread, the postings remain "on-topic" (although as an argument between two of the posters descends into flaming, discussion begins to focus on the nature of online behavior and then attempts at getting the discussion back on track). The responses to the game posted in this thread can be examined in terms of the nostalgic stances that posters are voicing in relation to the referent object, the game (with alternative stances serving to create encampments of members in the pro- and anti- *Silent Hill 4* groups and stoking the flames of argument).

For example, one post included the following criticism of *Silent Hill 4*:

> I'm sorry, but SH is SUPPOSED to be in SH. Not Subway world, not forrest world, not water prison world, not let's all gather around a hospital and masterbate world. All of these things have had their place in silent hill and that's what made them so creepy. To the classic brookhaven hospital, to the school of the damned (where any SH fan forgives the blocky graphics of game one and gets involved again) to Blue Creek apartments, and to my new personal favorite, the Chapel of god (ala SH3) . . .

This definition of what *Silent Hill* is "SUPPOSED" to be is here used to provide a critical perspective for evaluating the new game. This definition is supported by another member who suggests that this poster "had it right on, Silent Hill is suppost to be Silent Hill." The changes of *Silent Hill 4* are here set against a fixed, ideal-version *Silent Hill*—in this case one that is defined as being set within the town of Silent Hill, rather than the worlds or levels of *Silent Hill 4*. The "classic" features of the previous games are presented as exemplars of "proper" *Silent Hill* settings, which "should" be set within context of the town rather than as separate levels. The privileging of location is expressed in terms of reminiscence, the sharing of memories, and reflection upon previous game experience(s).

As well as this focus on location,[15] I would suggest that in terms of the establishment of the game world this post demonstrates a broader synchronizing move in which the gamer desires a return to an established, fixed game universe or chronotope (Bakhtin), considering this universe "as if it were frozen in time" (Chandler 12).

This synchronizing move can be seen elsewhere in the thread. Another post offers a similar fixing, one that privileges somewhat different elements in its critique despite repeating the criticism of the loss of the town feel and dissatisfaction with the new game's levels:

> I just started playing this yesterday (for about 2 hours) and didn't get hooked up at all. I must say the game plays in a VERY different manner to previous games. The controls and weapons are similar but the way you fight, the enemies, etc. has changed. Although SH3 was a bit disappointing to me it still played quite a bit like the previous ones, apart from lack of the town it kept the same feel.
>
> It's much more action oriented now and you have to walk through big areas without much to do. Also it's level based so you don't get the "town feel."
>
> The graphics are jaw-dropping, particularly in certain locations. Most times it's very photorealistic.
> I'll keep playing it hoping it gets better, but so far I'm not thrilled about it.

This post presents a more explicitly defined notion of that which grounds this poster's allegiance to *Silent Hill*—the desire to reexperience the "town feel," an atmosphere that is related to a specific style of gameplay. This is based on a more exploratory mode of action, rather than the emphasis on fighting that the post makes reference to in the comment, "It's much more action oriented now." This emphasis means that, although *Silent Hill 3* is presented as different from the games 1 and 2—lacking the emphasis on the town, it is still regarded by this poster as demonstrating an authentic *Silent Hill* feel. This appears to be, as suggested, due to the privileging of gameplay style rather than location.

In these posts, the changes or "innovation" of *Silent Hill 4* result in disappointment and a look both to the past (gamers' individual experiences of *Silent Hill*) and also to the voicing of varying—albeit related—conceptualizations of an idealized textual universe (what Silent Hill should be, and, in the case of *Silent Hill 4,* is not). In the first case, this is a universe which is founded in a mythical place (Silent Hill), and in the second, a universe that is experienced in a certain way (involving a specific form of gameplay) and provides a specific feel. In each, the previous *Silent Hill* games are referenced as being more authentic than the most recent title. Each harks back to a desired sameness about the games, against which *Silent Hill 4* is different and unsatisfactory, and also to the idea of a commonality which must hold the individual parts of a series together. In each, *Silent Hill 4* is read as failing to demonstrate sufficient elements of this universe. In contrast to an ideal version of *Silent Hill*, the changes are read as corrupting elements, destroying the "*Silent Hill* experience." In each post a longing to return is tangible.

Like these two posts, many of the responses in the thread demonstrate a critical stance in relation to *Silent Hill 4* that desires a fixed universe and privileges the preceding *Silent Hill* titles as demonstrating more satisfactorily an ideal version of *Silent Hill*, against which *Silent Hill 4* is read in negative terms. In contrast, however, a number of posts demonstrate more positive responses to the new game and exhibit enthusiasm for *Silent Hill 4*'s changes. As suggested earlier, these posts tend to consider the new game on its own terms, rather than viewing it through a longing for the previous games—the "past"—and praise the developments in gameplay and storytelling that it represents. More significantly, the focus in these posts is on the dynamic nature of the game series, which suggests the possibility of a diachronic mode of nostalgia, which is fixed through affiliation to this particular game but also open to change and development over time.

One poster's response to critics of the game exhibits just this sort of openness to change:

> I think some of you should really take the time to think about:
> What if the series never changed? We would get the same game with a few new ideas. I for one do not want that. I don't think I would like the whole process of new game, same place, over and over again, Do you guys really hate innovation? We must wean ourselves sometimes,

and I think some of us want to just have Silent Hill stay the same story and everything the same.

This poster rejects the desire to remain within the synchronic textual universe—to keep repeating the same elements *"over and over again"*—instead arguing that the game must develop in order to maintain interest. Innovation, change, and newness is privileged, with the reference to weaning suggesting that growth through change is necessary in terms of development of the fans—perhaps into "good" fans?—as well as the game series. Another poster agrees, sharing this privileging of the diachronic, calling for an evolving textual universe, and privileging openness rather than closure:

> It isnt nessacary to get into a huge philisophical debate about why the games are diffrent. The point is was silent hill 4 a fun experience to play? I love the new controls. Its fun to charge up a swing with the rusty axe. The story was good and it gave some fresh new perspective. That should be the common ground instead of whining about. "It doesnt take place in silent hill" or something dumb like "henry runs bad". I have a goofy run but who cares. Thats placing emphasis on something that isnt that important to begin with.

These two posts privilege a dynamic text rather than a desire to return to previously offered experiences.

The voicing of this alternative position suggests division within the site members, as seen in the comment, "I think some of us want to just have Silent Hill stay the same story and everything the same." However, while these posts voice disagreement with the two more critical reviews of the game, they are similar in that they also represent a privileging of elements that are "important" in relation to *Silent Hill*. Extracts from two of the more positive posts relating to *Silent Hill 4*—posts that also make reference to the location shift mentioned earlier in the paper—demonstrate how criticisms of the game in terms of loss of town feel were resisted. Here, the significance of the location is trivialized, and the developments of *Silent Hill 4* justified and sanctioned in relation to the posters' ideas of what a *Silent Hill* game should involve:

> The game definately has the feel of a Silent Hill game, there's much much more to the series than just wandering aimlessly in a foggy town.

I think the point of this game is that the evil is spreading, and that you don't have to go to Silent Hill, it now comes to you.

I am going to refer to the opposition between the fixed and dynamic as a distinction between synchronic and diachronic modes of nostalgia. In doing so, I am not suggesting that these are essential or stable modes, but rather that they help mark out positions taken in specific utterances—the idea that "we might usefully differentiate between categories of text in pointing at the different strategies that they foreground (or, rather, that we might foreground in their analysis)" (Dowling "Timely"). As I have suggested, my analysis involves a distinction between stances that privilege transformation and/or modification of the game world, and stances that privilege an ideal version of *Silent Hill* that the fan/poster wishes to return to. In addition to this opposition, however, there is another distinction that can be made, between the modes of comportment or authorship within these posts. Among the quotes referenced earlier, for example, are references to both the agency of the producer (Konami) and to the game players (the fans as "agents" within the game-worlds). In each of the two positive posts, we also see respect for (and to some extent the celebration of) external authorship, which is in contrast to the criticism of artistic choices in the previous two negative posts. In terms of comportment or authorship, we can therefore consider an internal/external opposition in relation to the fan. Each of these oppositions—between the diachronic and synchronic, and between the internal and external authorship—can be summarized within the following analytical schema, which provides four modes of nostalgia:

		Comportment	
		Extrovert	Introvert
Chronotope	**Synchronic**	Repeat	Explore
	Diachronic	Spectate	Mod

The terms *explore, repeat, mod,* and *spectate* serve in a sense merely as placeholders for the varying modes I am suggesting here, but they do also resonate with the modalities I am introducing. The *explore* mode, for example, involves a form of synchronic nostalgia in which the fan desires a fixed universe, but one that can be investigated further through the fan's agency. In contrast, the *repeat* mode stands for a form of nostalgia in which there is the impossible desire to reexperience something lost. In contrast, the *mod* mode involves some transformation of the textual universe by the fan author, and the *spectate* mode, the transformation or development of the universe by an author other than the fan (the official producer, Konami, for example).

The posts that I have introduced here serve as examples of positions within the synchronic (the first two negative posts) and the diachronic (the two positive posts, which emphasize the *spectate* mode). It is somewhat ambiguous as to which of the two synchronic modes the two negative posts would represent, as each desires a return to a fixed notion of the *Silent Hill* universe apparently both to repeat and explore further. It is, of course, possible for a post to exhibit more than one mode.

Although there are other examples of these positions within the threads in the *Silent Hill 4* forum, and indeed in the thread to which I am primarily referring, examples of the *mod* mode that the schema presents are less frequent—although more numerous in different forums within the bulletin board, reflecting the site's organization by topic and content. It can be seen in terms of the mentioning of a fanfic relating to the game in which the authorship of the fan acts transformatively upon the textual universe:

> On a seprate note, to anyone who might give a damn. I am intent on finshing my SH fan fic this time. I will do it like previous games, have one or two references to the them but mainly be a new story. And yes I will end it well. But the word well can be subjective. Main character survives but has to live as a dark wizard for eternity.....you will find out what that means eventually.

The immediate response to this post, by a member of the site, suggests a rejection of fan authorship in favor of the official game producers—a response that is far removed from the supportive/creative nature of fan communities represented in some of the literature:

> You're right I don't give a damn. All of the Fanfics I've read suck Donkey Balls and are far less Imaginative than anything Konami would ever produce (Including my own) . . . So I doubt I will think yours is any better. Sorry for the rude comments I was just thinking outloud with my fingers.

This response involves rejection of the *mod* mode in favor of the *spectate* mode, voicing a preference for external authorship rather than the authorship of fans in terms of possible future *Silent Hill* texts.

It may seem odd to suggest that a desire for change and transformation, and a privileging of the diachronic, can be described in terms of a mode of nostalgic engagement with a video game. Nostalgia may conventionally be seen in terms of retrospection, rather than involving forward momentum or constituting a preference for development and transformation. I would argue that the diachronic can be regarded as nostalgic in the way that it, like the synchronic, is anchored by key elements that stem from past experience of the game. In order to establish an object of fandom, the dynamic has to be fixed in some in some way, or the allegiance would not be held. It might be argued, therefore, that the synchronic is necessary to fan practices, in that it produces quilting points in respect of diachronic nostalgia: the affiliation to a changing product or text must be fixed in order for the fan to remain allied to it. As suggested in the privileging of elements in both the pro- and anti- *Silent Hill 4* posts above, it is possible to examine these fixing points through the identification of the features that are prioritized by the gamer as the core attributes of a legitimate *Silent Hill* game, such as place—references to the absent "town feel" and location shift being two of the major reasons for posters' dislike of the game (this is perhaps unsurprising for a series which takes its title from a fictional town)—as well as atmosphere, gameplay, and story. Each has been privileged in "Im disappointed and my head hurts" and in other threads relating to *Silent Hill 4* by both those who like or dislike the game.

Conclusion

In this essay I have suggested that in settings such as online forums, monolithic or static definitions of nostalgia might be challenged in favor of examining how individual perspectives construct nostalgic stances in respect of the object of fan affiliation. The modalities of nostalgia I have introduced in this chapter provide a way of distinguishing between the positions voiced by fans (within one forum) in respect to *Silent Hill 4*, illuminating the sometimes problematic negotiation of fans' relationships with their favored media texts. In such contexts nostalgia can be regarded as strategic in that it involves the fan making appeals to potential (or existing) alliances within the site that celebrate the text in the same way. This, of course, also involves the marking out of oppositions within the setting. While my focus here has been on thinking about the points that secure, albeit temporarily, meaning and affiliation at the level of the game as a whole—what *Silent Hill* is and should be—it would also be possible to examine more micro-level symbolic fixings in forum discussion relating to formal elements of this game such as specific levels/worlds or characters. As well as marking out fans' responses to the new game, however, the nostalgic macro-level responses to change examined in this chapter provide a focus for considering issues relating to the dynamism of community formation and the ways in which members negotiate their roles (and status) within such settings. Such considerations are invaluable for those interested in the workings of online fan cultures.

Notes

1. *Series*: "A group of objects related by linearly varying successive differences in form or configuration" (*dictionary.reference.com*).
2. Gamers may favor specific genres of games rather than specific titles, but in terms of this paper, my focus is on allegiance to specific series within video game genres.
3. For example, the *Civilization III* Apolyton University (see Squire).
4. "Episodes are often disliked because they fail to resolve the questions they raise, because they develop too many plot lines to be presented with depth and coherence, or because performances or scripting are perceived as flat and one-dimensional" (Jenkins 97).
5. See also Bacon-Smith for a different ethnographic perspective on fan cultures published in the same year.
6. Issues that have since been examined in greater detail (for example, see Macdonald; Williams).
7. "In a curious but perhaps inevitable twist, Burton's *Batman* therefore became something of a 'good object' within the Internet debates of 1997. The campaign against Michael Keaton's casting and the discrepancies between 1989's screen Batman and the comic book Dark Knight it was meant to resemble were apparently forgotten— by these fans at least—in the face of Schumacher's reinterpretation. Fewer than eight years had passed since *Batman*'s release, but already a nostalgic revisionism had settled around the movie and by association, the summer of 1989" (Brooker 299).
8. For discussion of fans' responses to the *Silent Hill* film, see Whiteman.
9. All typos in the extracts presented are intentional.
10. Only part of *Silent Hill 3* is set in the town.
11. The series has received interest from games researchers (see Carr; Lankoski).
12. "Since it's the fourth title, we wanted to have a major difference to past games. We wanted to introduce a new play style. If it's just like a linear map, it's a one-way route and the story proceeds one way. But if we put a central part in the middle, the storyline is more three-dimensional." (GamesRadar)

13. Discussion on the boards has confirmed that the "forest world" is located near to Silent Hill.
14. The post ends with: "So this is a dark day for me and the whole of the SH sub-culture. Mabey a nice soy based snack will calm me down. So I hope to have my feelings changed in the remaining game. So I will end my heresy now and will ask what you all think of the game."
15. Which ties into concern on the site about the geography of the Silent Hill universe as the mythology of the series had developed—seen in moves to create meta-maps of Silent Hill across the different games (and to deal with inconsistencies between the individual game maps).

Works Cited

Bacon-Smith, Camille. *Science Fiction Cultures.* Philadelphia: University of Pennsylvania Press, 2000.

Bakhtin, Mikhail. *Speech Genres and Other Late Essays.* Austin: University of Texas Press, 1986.

Brooker, Will. *Batman Unmasked: Analysing a Cultural Icon.* London: Continuum, 2000.

Carr, Diane. "Play Dead: Genre and Affect in *Silent Hill* and *Planescape Torment.*" *Game Studies: The International Journal of Computer Game Research* (*www.gamestudies.org*) 3.1 (May 2003). Accessed 25 July 2005.

Consalvo, Mia. "Zelda 64 and Video Game Fans: A Walkthrough of Games, Intertextuality and Narrative." *Television & New Media* 4.3 (August 2003).

Dowling, Paul. *The Sociology of Mathematics Education: Mathematical Texts/Pedagogic Texts.* London: Falmer Press, 1998.

___. "Social Activity Theory." *www.ioe.ac.uk/ccs/dowling/sat2001.htm.* Accessed 22 August 2005.

___. "A Timely Utterance." *homepage.mac.com/paulcdowling/ioe.* Accessed 16 August 2005

Dudley-Smith, Russell. "A Social Activity Analysis of the Institute of Fiscal Studies "Virtual Economy" Internet Site." MA dissertation, University of London, 2000.

Flanagan, Mary. "Mobile Identities, Digital Stars, and Post-Cinematic Selves." *Wide Angle* 21.1 (January 1999). 76–93.

GamesRadar. "Official: Silent Hill 4 a 'Pain in the Ass.'" *gamesradar.com.* Accessed 19 August 2004.

Gee, James Paul. *Situated Language and Learning: A Critique of Traditional Schooling.* London: Routledge, 2004.

Jenkins, Henry. *Textual Poachers: Television Fans and Participatory Culture.* London: Routledge, 1992.

Jenkins, Henry. "Reality Bytes: Eight Myths About Video Games Debunked." *www.pbs.org* (2005). Accessed 10 August 2005.

Lacan, Jacques. "The Quilting Point." In *The Seminar of Jacques Lacan: The Psychoses, Book III, 1955-1956.* London: Routledge, 1993. 258–70.

Laclau, Ernesto, and Chantal Mouffe. *Hegemony and Socialist Strategy: Towards a Radical Democratic Politics*, London: Verso, 1985

Lankoski, Petri. "Building and Reconstructing Character. A Case Study of Silent Hill 3." *www.gamesconference.org/digra2005*. Accessed 27 July 2005.

Macdonald, Andrea. "Uncertain Utopia: Science Fiction Media Fandom and Computer Mediated Communication." *Theorizing Fandom: Fans, Subculture and Identity*. Eds. Cheryl Harris and Alison Alexander. Cresshill, NJ: Hampton Press, 1998. 131–52.

Neale, Steve. "Questions of Genre." *Film and Theory: An Anthology*. Eds. Robert Stam and Toby Miller. Oxford: Blackwell, 2000.

Newman, James. *Videogames*. London: Routledge, 2004.

Rehak, Bob. "Mapping the Bit Girl: Lara Croft and New Media Fandom." *Information Communication and Society* 6.4 (2003). 477–96.

Simons, Iain, and James Newman. "All Your Base Are Belong to Us: Videogame Culture and Textual Production Online." *www.gamesconference.org/digra2003*. Accessed 27 July 2005.

Squire, Kurt. *The Higher Education of Gaming: Or How Game Consumers Became Game Producers*. Presented at the *CAL'05 Virtual Learning?* conference. University of Bristol, 11 April 2005.

Whiteman, Natasha. "The Establishment, Maintenance and Destabilisation of Fandom: A Study of Two Online Communities and an Exploration of Issues Pertaining to Internet Research." PhD thesis, University of London, 2007. Available at *homepage.mac.com/paulcdowling/ioe/studentswork/whiteman(2007). pdf*

Williams, Rebecca. "'It's About Power': Spoilers and Fan Hierarchy in On-Line Buffy Fandom." *Slayage* (*slayageonline.com*) 11–12 (2004). Accessed 29 June 2005.

Žižek, Slavoj. *The Sublime Object of Ideology*. London: Verso, 1989.

Games Cited

Legend of Zelda: Twilight Princess. Kyoto: Nintendo, 2006.

Legend of Zelda: The Wind Waker. Kyoto: Nintendo, 2003.

Silent Hill. Redwood City, CA: Konami, 1999.

Silent Hill 2. Redwood City, CA: Konami, 2001.

Silent Hill 3. Redwood City, CA: Konami, 2003.

Silent Hill 4: The Room. Redwood City, CA: Konami, 2004.

4

Playing the Déjà-New
"Plug it in and Play TV Games" and the Cultural Politics of Classic Gaming

Matthew Thomas Payne

In D. B. Weiss's novel *Lucky Wander Boy*, the protagonist Adam Penny-man reflects on the cultural and material fate of the world's first commercial video games:

> The games themselves would live on thanks to MAME [Multiple Arcade Machine Emulator] and other such emulation programs, but due to their diversionary status and their laudable but deceptive simplicity, they would likely be taken at their face value—and to live on in fleeting moments of others' wistful nostalgia is not to live at all. It was important that someone begin to peel back the layers of meaning beneath their colorful surfaces, because they were a crucial strata in the bedrock on which a generation was built . . . in 1981, the videogame industry's $5 billion take was more than Hollywood and Vegas combined—and so much of it was taken one quarter at a time. (36–37)

There are three noteworthy points in Weiss's passage that underscore the need for the continued development of video game studies, or ludology (See Frasca). First, video games, like other contemporary media artifacts (e.g., DVDs, novels, CDs), are brimming with meaning and must be excavated for their social, cultural, and historical significance. Second, video games demand scrutiny because of their broad economic impacts. In fact, the US gaming industry reached a new high in 2006, grossing over $12.5 billion (eclipsing its previous 2005 record of $10.5 billion) (Brightman). Finally, Weiss's novel reminds us that antiquated video games live on in gaming memory well after they have vanished from arcade floors, retail shelves, and computer hard drives.

The Golden Age of video games, which lasted from the early 1970s until the industry crash in 1984, engendered play experiences that constitute a cornerstone of many gamers' identities (Wolf 53). After all, arcades were the social and historical sites of the world's first popular reception of video games, and hence were witness to the emergence of the world's first generation of video gamers. It is of little surprise then, that when these classic titles were re-released in the form of "Plug it in and Play TV Games'" (PNPs),[1] they quickly became the number one selling game device in the United States from April to June 2004 (Keighley 2). These self-contained, miniaturized consoles typically come in one of two varieties: either as a vehicle for an already successful entertainment property (e.g., SpongeBob SquarePants, Spider-Man), or as a retro-chic product that contains one or more classic game properties (e.g., *PONG* [1972], *Frogger* [1981], *Pitfall!* [1982]). This chapter is concerned only with the latter of the two types of PNPs. To appreciate this toy's implications for classic game communities, retro style PNPs will be analyzed as cultural products that engender particular gaming practices. I begin this chapter by framing classic gaming practices as evidence of collective gaming memory, and I then compare the highly stylized, commercial PNP device to its freely distributed online counterpart. Finally, I contend that the PNP's cultural condition is understood best as postmodern pastiche, and that by collapsing the retrogaming experience into a simple, easy-to-use device, PNPs threaten to efface or supplant other gaming histories that include marginal games and alternative play experiences.

Collective Memory

Memory has been widely and varyingly conceptualized by scholars as a solitary experience, as a psychological exercise that operates with discrete informational units, or as images stored in one's head. In fact, a number of dominant metaphors have been used in Western thought to try to elucidate this complex phenomenon (see Draaisma). For example, Plato saw memory as a wax table with orality as its vehicle; Aristotle believed it to be an inherently physical experience grounded in one's senses and in nature; Freud called memory a "mystic writing tab"; and the French phenomenologist Maurice Merleau-Ponty argued that memory's subjectivity was woven into the fabric of one's own lived body. But while philosophers differ on how memory ought best to be understood, they have generally defined it as a solipsistic experience. In contrast, scholars interested in "collective memory," a term coined by French sociologist Maurice Halbwachs, study a group's shared experiences and their representations of their past. Generally speaking, collective memory is not interested in researching "objective" histories, but rather *how* a group re-presents its past and how it propagates and disseminates this narrative. This is not to suggest that the study of collective memory is in any way less concerned with factual accuracy or scholastic rigor, however. Recent academic interest in collective memory has resulted in a flood of articles on the topic, and a proliferation of differing definitions, conceptualizations, and even basic labels (e.g., *collective memory, history of memory, collected memory, social memory,* and *cultural memory*).[2] The term *collective memory* is adopted for this chapter's purposes.

Gaming communities are largely defined by their choice of core games and the social practices that contribute to their "imagined community" (Anderson). When studying the collective memory of gaming communities, it is essential to identify the games they play (their texts), and how and where they play them (their practices and social spaces). For example, computer gamers playing *Counter-Strike* (1999) at a LAN party is a fundamentally different techno-social configuration than a gamer playing *Grand Theft Auto IV* (2008) alone on an Xbox 360, which is likewise different from playing *World of Warcraft* (2004) with hundreds online. With this need for specificity, this chapter adopts James Wertsch's concept of collective memory to explore how a specific classic gaming group identifies itself as such.

Wertsch's concept of collective memory argues that a community's sense of a common past is founded on its shared "textual resources." These resources mediate the commonly held experiences of its members, lending credence to a group's claims of collective identity. Borrowing from the Russian literary theorist Mikhail Bakhtin, Wertsch argues that a community's textual resources are composed of two primary elements: first, the structure of the artifact itself, and second, the use of that text by a "concrete speaker in a concrete setting" (15). Therefore, the classic game form and the video gamer are the twofold components of Wertsch's textual resources.

By today's standards, the classic game form is characterized (and sometimes stigmatized) by its low-resolution graphics, limited sound effects and music tracks, and its elementary physical interface (i.e., few buttons and limited controls). Yet, according to Mark J. P. Wolf, the video game industry owes its current success to classic games' lack of technical sophistication and simulated abstraction. Wolf reminds us that "it is easy to forget that the video game interface, with its hand-eye coordination

linked to onscreen action, was not always as intuitive as it now seems"
(49). Unlike its predecessor *Spacewar!* (1962), *PONG*'s simplified control
and now iconic presentation proved that the video game could become
a commercially viable entertainment product. Beyond facilitating a kind
of bare-bones video game literacy—that operating the controller results
in onscreen effects—abstraction in classic video games invites one to participate in the mental construction of the game world, filling in for the
games' technical shortcomings (Wolf 64). Wolf's aesthetic of abstraction
resonates with what collective memory scholars have said about the stay-
ing power of certain images over time. James Fentress and Chris Wickham argue that images, like words, are part of social memory:

> Images can be transmitted socially only if they are conventionalized
> and simplified: conventionalized, because the image has to be
> meaningful for an entire group; simplified, because in order to be
> generally meaningful and capable of transmission, the complexity of
> the image must be reduced as far as possible. (47–48)

It is hardly surprising, then, that the simplistically designed titular heroes
of *Pac-Man* (1979), *Q-Bert* (1982), and *Mappy* (1983) are also the first
digital avatars-cum-celebrities. Yet, the second component of Wertsch's
textual schema suggests another, more convincing reason why many classic game elements (e.g., characters, levels, weapons, soundtracks) enjoy
iconic status.

For Wertsch, the *process* of remembering is far more central to collective memory than memories proper. The latter connotes a static collection
of discrete moments, whereas the former suggests that collective memory is always in flux and is constantly being redefined and reevaluated;
memories are something we have, but remembering is something we do
(17). The game and the gamer (or the text and the speaker, in Wertsch's
nomenclature) are the historically contingent dialectic that are the foundational elements of classic gaming culture. Just as the storyteller cannot
be excluded from an adequate conceptualization of shared memory in
oral cultures, neither can the player be removed from gaming memory in
an interactive epoch.

The interactive and reiterative nature of video game play reinforces
the likelihood of forming (what might later become) shared memories.
Susanne Küchler and Walter Melion's "Introduction" to *Images of Memory*
describes image production as a practice that reinforces memory through
the interplay of the hand and the mind.

Memory may enable image production, but it is neither prior
to nor discrete from the artificing functions of the hand. By the
same token, the hand, when it inscribes an image on a material
surface, is precipitating memory, shaping and consolidating it. The
image documents this complex interplay between recollection and
handiwork. (7)

It is only a small step from drafting with a pen on parchment to interacting in a virtual world with a joystick. Because video games are by their
very nature interactive, players form lasting memories through the mental and physical act of repeated game play. Mediated game play is a psy-
chosomatic event that bolsters the likelihood that gamers will remember
a game's characters, levels, and rules of play well after it disappears from
popular circulation. Hence, the simple and repetitive operations at the
core of the classics *Frogger*, *Missile Command* (1980), and *Galaga* (1981)
are major reasons for their cultural longevity. Küchler and Melion reit-
erate that the value of collective memory is that it can account for the
material nature of image production, and, by extension, interactive game
play (7).

The foregoing discussion about collective memory has two major
implications for gaming communities. First, gamers must speak to each
other about the games and through the games (by way of game play) in
order to maintain their community's collective memory. For example, a
broad research question might ask, how do local LAN communities remember their play differently than MMO communities (Massively, Multiplayer Online games), and how might these groups differ from communities of offline arcade patrons? The second point is that the collective
identity and authority of a group on a subject is socially and historically
contingent and is never a foregone conclusion. Classic gamers, who (as
their name suggests) would appear to be the authority on classic gaming
are nevertheless vulnerable to outside forces. As the following sections
explain, gaming communities are not immune from ideological contestation over how we remember our gamings past.

MAMEs (Multiple Arcade Machine Emulators)

It is important not to lump gaming practices and practitioners into broad,
ambiguous social groupings. For this chapter's purposes, classic game en-
thusiasts are understood as a substratum of video gamers, a group that
could clearly be subdivided into more precise groupings, such as by plat-

form (e.g., Intellivision, Atari 2600), by years of interest (e.g., 1970–1984), or by gaming franchise or publisher (e.g., *Sonic the Hedgehog*, Namco). MAME groups are the classic gaming communities of interest here because their collective mission and community organization offer an excellent counter-position to the logic inherent in the commercial PNP format.

Classic gamers know that collecting and playing retro games is neither a novel commercial innovation nor a new social practice. In domestic spaces, classic game compilations have been available for game platforms and the PC for nearly a decade (e.g., PS2's *Activision Anthology* [2002], Xbox's *Atari Anthology* [2004], and the PC's *Atari 2600 Action Pack* [1995]). In public arenas, arcades continue to offer coin-op cabinets loaded with single and multiple retro titles. Compared to participatory MAME culture, retro game compellations are static, ahistorical, and offer little more than simulated and uninspired "reruns." This situation changed, however, on 5 February 1997 when Nicola Salmoria, inspired by the open source philosophy,[3] released the first video game emulator.[4] The software's professed *raison d'être* was "to document the hardware (and software) of the arcade games. There are already many dead arcade boards, whose function has been brought to life in MAME. Being able to play the games is just a nice side-effect" ("MAME"). Online and offline MAME communities quickly converged around Salmoria's project, providing gamers with a counter-position to classic gaming through commercial offerings. The differences between a game culture engendered by MAMEs and game play produced through commercial compilations are highlighted when these opportunities are placed side-by-side. Most significantly, MAMEs destabilize the corporate firm's authoritative hold on authoring, distributing, and mediating the classic game experience. Additionally, online MAME communities encourage its constituency to discuss the act of classic gaming—placing a premium on digital dialogues—whether it is articulated in chat forums or through peer-to-peer file sharing.

The primary objects of interest that unite classic gaming cultures are the games themselves. For MAME groups in particular, these texts are played, shared, and stored. MAME software politicizes video game play, shifting the focus of activity from playing alone with classic properties to becoming amateur archivists. With MAME technologies, gamers preserve and curate their own collections and need not depend on profit-driven firms to decide what constitutes an authentic and sanctioned canon of classic games and, by implication, the classic gaming experience. Thus, MAMEs free gamers to author their own narratives of gaming memory and catalyze the potential proliferation of multiple gaming histories and textual canons. The monolithic corporate game history is no longer the only "game" in town. Indeed, players' idiosyncratic classic gaming libraries, which are the constitutive building blocks (the union of player and played) of a community's shared expression of a common past, challenge the singular history offered by the for-profit game collection. MAMEs lead to a kind of Classic Ludological Reformation, giving previously atomistic consumers the technological means to become community participants in developing their own emergent historical narrative and collective identity.

How gamers come into possession of classic titles is the second substantial difference introduced by MAME software. This online, open-source project circumvents the technological barriers inherent in offline console gaming that limited player access to a single game space at a particular time (e.g., at a coin-op in an arcade, or a console in a living room). Conversely, MAME communities have flourished online where free and open game-swapping practices allow their preservation efforts to succeed. The hierarchical top-down producer-to-retailer-to-consumer distribution model that corporations rely on to generate capital now competes with a free, egalitarian, and comparatively flat peer-to-peer distribution network.

Another major difference between PNP-producing companies and MAMEs is that while the former is interested in turning a profit, the latter seeks to cultivate a dynamic and emergent public record. These divergent imperatives are manifest in the current legal contention over MAME activity. MAMEs require two components to operate: the emulator, which allows software to run on hardware different than what it was created for, and the ROMs,[5] which contain a game's code and associated files. Until now, MAME groups have garnered little press and legal attention, but given the popularity of PNPs and their money-generating potential, this may not be the case for long. It is reasonable to expect that copyright owners may begin prosecuting game collectors with vigor, à la the Recording Industry Association of America (RIAA)'s campaign against music file sharing. According to Wikipedia's MAME entry, "It is rumored that the operators from the *mame.dk* website have shut down their site because they were concerned about personal liability, and not because of the expense of running the website." The following section reviews JAKKS Pacific's financial success with their PNP lineup and argues that, though MAME networks may undermine the full profit potential of entertainment companies, our highly litigious intellectual property regime (supported by big business) more substantially threatens the long-term sustainability of a noncommercial game community.

Profiting from Pastiche

JAKKS Pacific, Inc., the United States' fourth-largest toymaker, bought the toy company Toymax in 2002 and with it "a battery-operated control pad that housed a low-tech videogame that plugged into a TV" (Keighley 1). JAKKS's recent acquisition generates a staggering $66 million (or fifteen percent of the company's revenue) and is a major reason why JAKKS was named 2005 Toy Vendor of the Year by Wal-Mart (JAKKS Pacific). Why the success? According to Anson Sowby, a spokesman for JAKKS Pacific, "The plug and play games are very popular because they're simple to use. You don't need an Xbox for it. They're also fairly inexpensive" (Bhatnagar 2).[6] *Forbes* columnist Kenneth Fischer adds, "Parents love the ease of use. That's why, in a weak toy market, JAKKS should be able to increase its sales 13% [in 2005] to perhaps $540 million" (1). Other business columnists give a more nuanced breakdown of the product's successful formula. According to Geoff Keighley, the PNP is profitable due to four factors: cheap content (relatively inexpensive licensing agreements); inexpensive hardware (Taiwanese electronics and Chinese hardware); retro packaging (or, retro styled, custom designed by artists); and mass appeal ("low retail price and retro cachet helped JAKKS break into mainstream stores" [e.g., Best Buy, Urban Outfitters, and Bed Bath & Beyond]) (Keighley 1-2).

Not surprisingly, JAKKS is rapidly expanding its PNP line-up[7] and is in development with long-time industry favorite Capcom. Nelo Lucich, the vice president of JAKKS Interactive, notes that Capcom's celebrated *Street Fighter* PNP will "feature original arcade game play" and that "fans will experience the same thrill as they did when they first played the game in 1992" (JAKKS Pacific).[8] Lucich's comment is illustrative of how these retro style entertainment devices have been framed and marketed by the TV Game companies.[9] The advertised fidelity of the product is such that playing it will produce a rich and faithful nostalgic experience. But how exactly is nostalgia built into the PNP format, and what might its programming suggest about its cultural condition?

John Dewey has been quoted as saying, "Every well constructed object and machine has form, but there is aesthetic form only when the object having this external form fits into a larger experience" (Becker 103). The question before us is, how does the PNP fit into our world, aesthetically and politically? The literary and cultural genre of pastiche is a productive heuristic for investigating the PNP's dual functions as a disposable consumer good *and* as a vessel for venerated games.

The genre of pastiche is generally defined as a "'stylistic medley' or blend of diverse ingredients"; it is both the "imitation of a masterwork and the '*pâté*' of components" (Hoesterey 9). Once held in caustic disdain by cultural elites, the progressive art movements of the 1960s and 1970s reframed the genre's cut-and-paste aesthetic and its playful appropriation of cultural masterworks. The works of Andy Warhol, Roy Lichtenstein, and Jasper Johns argued for a renewed evaluation of pastiche's artistic and social potential, as did earlier projects by Marcel Duchamp. "Pastiche, the least classical of genres, can now be posited as a challenge to the canonization of the classical, whose material presence it problematizes as ideological" (Hoesterey 24). Pop Art, in particular, reconceptualizes artistic practice as generating social reality, not simply reflecting it. With this aesthetic shift came the prerogative for artists to frame and deconstruct previous art movements as products of language, ideology, and power. Given the genre's political potentiality, do PNPs offer resistant play opportunities to gamers, are they just cheap plastic economically-driven transmogrifications of once-great great games, or is it a complicated conflation of the two? Unpacking two retro style PNPs offered by JAKKS Pacific—*Ms. Pac-Man* and the *Atari Paddle*—will help us arrive at a satisfactory answer.

Playing the Déjà-New

At the intersection of PNPs and pastiche are two philosophical dilemmas. The first is a question of authorship and agency. With the PNP, who or what shapes the gaming memory engendered through game play, the corporation or the user? The second issue raised by PNPs is one of history versus memory. Fredric Jameson's oft-cited critique of the postmodern condition includes a discussion of the "crisis of history," and his insights offer a springboard for theorizing the contestation between the PNP's corporate *history* and the MAME's community *memory*.

Several of JAKKS's retro style controllers are replicas of classic joysticks. For example, JAKKS's *Atari Paddle* (Figure 4.1) is a faithful, but not identical, copy of the paddle that was released for Atari's home console. The PNP device is longer and taller than the original and it has an additional power switch and menu button. The PNP housing is larger because it is powered by batteries, and since there is no AC power cord, the device's only wire is the AV cable that connects to the television. The device's installation process is therefore far simpler and quicker than most game systems, which has been hyped by the PNP marketers. As for those PNPs that lack console system referents (e.g., *Classic Arcade Pinball*, *Ms. Pac-Man*), JAKKS's artists have fashioned controllers that are inspired by their respective games. For example, the *Ms. Pac-Man* unit has roughly

Figure 4.1. JAKKS's *Atari Paddle* PNP unit.
Photograph © 2007 Matthew Payne.

Figure 4.2. JAKKS's *Ms. Pac-Man* PNP unit.
Photograph © 2007 Matthew Payne.

the same size joystick as its arcade cabinets, but the control is mounted on a small boxy plastic housing and covered with decals of the Namco titles programmed into the unit (Figure 4.2). The PNPs' start-up menus list the prepackaged titles and allow the gamer to select and play its various games. Pressing the "menu" button returns the gamer to the main navigation screen without any significant loading time.

With respect to its content, all of JAKKS's retro style PNPs contain at least two titles and no more than thirteen (the lone exception being the *Mortal Kombat* unit). These game licenses are generally optioned from other companies and then compiled into a thematically congruous and financially reliable product. JAKKS Pacific organizes its lineup's content[10] according to game brands (e.g., Namco), game type (e.g., pinball), genre (e.g., sports), and target market (e.g., children's titles).

The toy's most noteworthy characteristic is not the constellation of titles that it re-presents or those that it omits, however, but that these games are hard-wired into the device itself. New titles cannot be added to the PNP, and the pre-packaged games cannot be removed. The rehistoricized gaming that JAKKS and its competitors sell is not too different from traditional game compellations that facilitate a limited, immutable retro experience. So unlike the open-source ethos that undergirds MAME communities, this commercial format bars gamers from curating their own collection of retro titles, preventing gamers from authoring their own personally meaningful collections. The deeper significance of this technological restriction is that it proscribes the variety of Wertsch's textual resources (the synthesis of game and game play) available to a community's collective memory processes. The history performed by PNPs is monolithic and corporate—a stark contrast to the organically evolving game memory that grows out of MAME communities. The PNP's revisionist history replays only economic successes, ignores marginal texts, and frames classic gaming as a cheap and kitschy, easy-to-use novelty.

Furthermore, MAME groups do not jeopardize the viability of PNP firms nearly to the extent that PNP producers threaten MAME communities. Indeed, it is hard to imagine why any committed MAME user would choose to become an avid PNP user. Instead, these devices' cultural impacts are far more significant to casual classic gamers. Without access to a counter-dialog, PNPs dominate the gaming memory of non-MAME groups with their sanitized, commercially viable but ultimately incomplete historical record. But purchasing and enjoying retro style PNPs does not automatically reflect negatively on a gamer's understanding of or appreciation for classic gaming culture. It is easy to see the appeal of retro PNPs to the consumer; after all, the controller, deck, and games are collapsed into a single device—all of the advertised nostalgia with none of the obsolescent mess. Gone are the dusty controllers, half-working cartridges,[11] the cumbersome console and its outdated wiring. But along with jettisoning all the technical inconveniences of yesteryear, gone too are the physical markers of a console's age and the likelihood of placing it into a larger historical timeline. The stickers and retro-chic design tell you that it is to be read as "classic," but its cheap signifiers say more about the PNP's marketing strategies and mode of production than it does about classic games. Retro style PNPs forcefully foreground a style, not a history. Yet style is never just poetics and aesthetics; style is invariably political and bound up with material relations of power.

Fredric Jameson's acclaimed critique of the postmodern condition and its excesses summarizes the PNP's stylistic "attitude." According to Jameson and similarly minded neo-Marxists, postmodernism is the mighty cultural equalizer. Postmodernism collapses all histories, discourses, and narratives (both significant and marginal) into an undifferentiated whole. In its view, all "stories" (e.g., history, sciences, art) have equal validity and worth. Jameson objects to postmodernism on a number of fronts, but it is his ethical opposition that proves most compelling. Postmodernism's erasure of morality from popular discourse obliterates the moral underpinnings that bolster social causes and progressive projects. Without ethics, be they grounded in pious religion or secular humanism, there is no social progress. The history of slavery, for instance, is not on par with other historical accounts; it is not just one story among a throng of stories.

The crisis of history according to this neo-Marxist critique is the end result of capitalism's successful conquest of the cultural sphere. Nothing is immune from commoditization under postmodernism. All styles, from all eras, can be reappropriated as consumer goods. The cutting and pasting together of styles effectively collapses a materialist history, or destabilizes it at the very least. Temporality, then, is one of postmodernism's first victims. In his introduction to postmodernism, Medan Sarup cites Jameson's privileged example of the nostalgia film as style run amuck. Sarup writes:

> And so, in a world in which stylistic innovation is no longer possible all that is left, Jameson suggests, is pastiche. The practice of pastiche, the imitation of dead styles can be seen in the "nostalgia film." It seems that we are unable to focus on our present. We have lost our ability to locate ourselves historically. As a society we have become incapable of dealing with time. (146)

The clear analog to the nostalgia film in gaming is the PNP. Separated from its authentic past, PNPs situate the gamer in the "perpetual present" (Sarup 176). These games offer a warm, welcoming embrace of a faux-nostalgia, engendering a longing for a past that never was. Jameson would likely point to PNPs as additional evidence of our current cultural predicament, noting how (with very few exceptions) these devices eschew the popularly derided violence of today's best-selling games. With most PNPs, players are safe from *Doom III*'s BFGs (Big Fucking Guns), fragging in *Halo 2*, or carjackings in *Grand Theft Auto IV*.

The most pernicious aspect of the postmodern attitude, as far as cultural critics are concerned, is the narcotizing and depoliticizing effect that it has on object analysis. Postmodernism reaffirms the unquestioned naturalness that grafts itself to cultural artifacts. The "pastiche of the stereotypical past, endows present reality and the openness of present history with the spell and distance of a glossy mirage" (Jameson 21). Postmodernism's distaste for cultural hierarchies, morality, and ethics in tandem with its love of illusion and simulacrum elides inequitable power relationships. So unlike the pastiche of the 1960s and 1970s, which was mobilized as a tool of resistance, retro style PNPs are imbued with a safe, "plastic-y" pastiche. The classic games genre has been appropriated and declawed by JAKKS and its competitors so as to make game history easy to package, and even easier to consume; classic games have been decontextualized for their economic replay value.

For Jameson, the postmodern condition is a sign of our collective inability to express our current cultural and economic situation. Postmodernism is "an elaborated symptom of the waning of our historicity" (21). But despite much of Jameson's pessimism, tacit in his argument is the assumption that people will, if given the opportunity, organize themselves into communal, egalitarian groups. What makes MAME culture such an excellent research object is that their collective historicity is not waning. In fact, because their peer-to-peer network actively constructs their shared memory, MAME communities place the onus for producing and policing their shared memory on themselves, refusing to rely on an extraneous commercial entity to package and sell them a common past. And while theirs is a history that will never be complete, as it is a never-ending, ever-emergent process, it is one that remains free and open to all.

Back to the Future of PNPs

PNP gaming continues to grow in popularity. JAKKS Pacific acquired the popular Yu-Gi-Oh™ property, based on the card game and animated series of the same name, and JAKKS also hopes to capitalize from the boon of interest in poker with their *World Poker Tour* PNP. The company has not, however, neglected its retro line of PNPs. In addition to expanding their classic offerings, including a Tecmo Games PNP, the company is redefining the format's basic hardware capabilities. For example, in a press release, JAKKS announced their plans to develop a wireless *Ms. Pac-Man* PNP, further updating one of the world's most recognizable classic video games. And, as a seeming response to this chapter's observations, the company is also developing a "Gamekey Expansion Pack" for their Capcom PNP. This modification allows gamers to add other classic Capcom titles to their TV Games toy. It is too early to speculate as to whether the PNP is gravitating towards the traditional game system format that utilizes distinct game cartridges or if this hardware innovation is more exploratory in nature.

What the aforementioned modification has not changed, though, is JAKKS's framing of retro style game play. The streaming commercials embedded in the individual retro PNP webpages at *www.jakkstvgames.com* speak to the toy's cultural positioning and reaffirm many of this work's observations. On the *Ms. Pac-Man* page, the narrator booms that the PNP is "an entire arcade in one joystick!", suggesting that the toy's contents are whole and its vision of classic gaming complete. Similarly, the narrator hypes the *Mortal Kombat* toy as containing the seed from which an entire genre was born. The voiceover proclaims, "The legend is reborn with a vengeance" and "Just plug it and play it to experience the game that started it all." Lastly, the game play on the EA Sports PNP is hocked as being "just like the good old days—only better!", seeming to confirm many of Jameson's likely suspicions. The continued success of PNPs is a testament to the lasting power of classic gaming texts, the nostalgic hold of past game play, and the deft ability of entertainment firms to delimit and reconfigure that complex history into small, plastic goods. Despite their size and disposable plastic shells, PNPs speak volumes about our contested relationship to our larger gaming histories, including the titles we choose to deify, those we forget, and how free gamers are to remember, play, *and* replay the past.

Notes

1. I am using *PNP* as shorthand for all "Plug it in and Play TV Games" devices.
2. Connerton, Halbwachs, and Zerubavel offer valuable observations on how social groups constitute, maintain, and modify their shared historical narratives.
3. For more information about the definition, philosophy, and articulations of the "open source" movement, see Wikipedia's entry ("Open source").
4. For more information on MAMEs, see *mamedev.org* and *www.retrogames.com*.
5. "A ROM image, or simply ROM, is a computer file which contains a copy of the data from a read-only memory chip, often from a video game cartridge, a computer's firmware, or from an arcade game's main board. The term is frequently used in the context of emulation, whereby older games or computer firmware are copied to ROM files on modern computers and can, using a piece of software known as an emulator, be run on the newer computer" (en.wikipedia.org/wiki/ROM_image).
6. Most PNPs retail for around $25.
7. JAKKS's complete TV Game lineup is available at www.jakkstvgames.com.
8. The company is also procuring the licenses to other classic Capcom titles, including *1942, Mega Man 3, Ghosts'N Goblins, Commando,* and *Gun Smoke.*

9. Again, the majority of PNPs do not play classic titles. JAKKS's retro style PNP competitors include Toymax, Majesco Sales, and Radica Games.
10. The PNPs investigated here are the *Ms. Pac-Man* and the *Atari Paddle*. The *Ms. Pac Man* PNP includes itself and four other Namco titles (*Galaga*, *Pole Position*, *Xevious*, and *Mappy*) while the *Atari Paddle* houses thirteen Atari titles (including *Breakout*, *Circus Atari*, and *PONG*).
11. PNPs eliminate the fine art of fixing ostensibly broken cartridges with a variety of DIY remedies (e.g., rubbing alcohol, blowing air into the deck, etc.).

Works Cited

Anderson, Benedict. *Imagined Communities: Reflections on the Origin and Spread of Nationalism*. London: Verso, 1991.

Becker, Carol. "The Education of Young Artists and the Issue of Audience." In *Between Borders: Pedagogy and the Politics of Cultural Studies*. Eds. Henry A. Giroux and Peter McLaren. New York: Routledge, 1993. 101–12.

Bhatnagar, Parija. "Hot in 2004: Movie Toys and Singing Barbie." *money.cnn.com* (10 February 2004). Accessed 15 January 2005.

Brightman, James. "Breaking: U.S. Video Game Industry Totals $12.5 Billion in 2006." *biz.gamedaily.com* (11 January 2007). Accessed 1 March 2007.

Bruno, Giuliana. "Ramble City: Postmodernism and *Bladerunner*." *October* 41 (1987). 61–74. Available at *www.stanford.edu/dept/hps/bruno/bladerunner.html*.

Connerton, Paul. *How Societies Remember*. New York: Cambridge University Press, 1989.

Draaisma, Douwe. *Metaphors of Memory: A History of Ideas About the Mind*. New York: Cambridge University Press, 2000.

Fentress, James and Wickham, Chris. *Social Memory*. Cambridge, MA: Blackwell, 1992.

Fischer, Kenneth L. "Portfolio Strategy: End Your Gloom." *forbes.com* (28 March 2005). Accessed 28 March 2005.

Frasca, Gonzalo. "Simulation versus Narrative: Introduction to Ludology." In Wolf and Perron. 221–36.

Gaggi, Silvio. *Modern/Postmodern: A Study in Twentieth-Century Arts and Ideas*. Philadelphia: University of Pennsylvania Press, 1989.

Halbwachs, Maurice. *On Collective Memory*. Chicago: University of Chicago Press, 1992.

Hebdige, Dick. *Subculture: the Meaning of Style*. New York: Routledge, 1979.

Hoesterey, Ingeborg. *Pastiche: Cultural Memory in Art, Film, Literature*. Bloomington: Indiana University Press, 2001.

JAKKS Pacific. "JAKKS Named Toy Vendor of the Year by Wal-Mart." *excite.ccbn.com* (20 April 2005). Accessed 20 July 2005.

___. "JAKKS Pacific Adds Yu-Gi-Yo! Property to Award-Winning TV Games Line." *biz.yahoo.com* (15 June 2005). Accessed 20 July 2005.

___. JAKKS Pacific Ms. Pac-Man Wireless TV Games." *prn.newscom.com* (16 February 2005). Accessed 20 July 2005.

___. "JAKKS Pacific Offers TV Games Game Key for Classic Capcom Games." *biz. yahoo.com* (8 March 2005). Accessed 13 March 2005.

Jameson, Fredric. *Postmodernism, or, The Cultural Logic of Late Capitalism.* Durham: Duke University Press, 1991.

Kariel, Henry S. *The Desperate Politics of Postmodernism.* Amherst: University of Massachusetts Press, 1983.

Keighley, Geoff. "New Life for Old Games." *Business 2.0 (www.business2.com)* (1 September 2004). Accessed 15 January 2005.

Küchler, Susanne, and Melion, Walter, eds. "Introduction." In *Images of Memory: On Remembering and Representation.* Washington, DC: Smithsonian Institution Press, 1991. 1–46.

"MAME." *Wikipedia.org.* Accessed 13 March 2005.

"Open source." *Wikipedia.org.* Accessed 13 March 2005.

"Pastiche." *Wikipedia.org.* Accessed 13 March 2005.

Sarup, Madan. *An Introductory Guide to Post-Structuralism and Postmodernism.* Athens: University of Georgia Press, 1993.

Weiss, D. B. *Lucky Wander Boy.* New York: Plume, 2003.

Wertsch, James V. *Voices of Collective Memory.* Cambridge: Cambridge University Press, 2002.

Wolf, Mark J. P. "Abstraction in the Video Game." In Wolf and Perron. 47–66.

Wolf, Mark J. P., and Bernard Perron, eds. *The Video Game Theory Reader.* New York: Routledge, 2003.

Zerubavel, Eviatar. *Time Maps: Collective Memory and the Social Shape of the Past.* Chicago: University of Chicago Press, 2003.

Games Cited

Activision Anthology (PS2). Santa Monica: Activision, 2002.

Atari Anthology (Xbox). Chicago: Atari Games Midway, 2004.

Atari 2600 Action Pack 2 (PC). Santa Monica: Activision, 1995.

Breakout (Atari 2600). Chicago: Atari Games Midway, 1978.

Circus Atari. (Atari 2600). Chicago: Atari Games Midway, 1978.

Classic Arcade Pinball (PNP). Malibu: JAKKS Pacific, 2004.

Commando (NES). Sunnyvale, CA: Capcom, 1986.

Doom III (PC). Santa Monica: Activision, 2004.

Frogger (arcade). San Francisco: Sega, 1981.

Galaga (PNP). Malibu: JAKKS Pacific, 2004.

Ghosts 'N Goblins (arcade). Sunnyvale, CA: Capcom, 1985.

Grand Theft Auto IV (PS2). New York: Rockstar Games, 2008.

Gun Smoke. (NES). Sunnyvale, CA: Capcom, 1988.

Half-Life: Counter-Strike (PC). Bellevue, WA: Sierra Entertainment, 1999.

Halo 2 (Xbox). Microsoft Game Studios, 2004.

Madden 1995 (PNP). Malibu: JAKKS Pacific, 2004.

Mappy (PNP). Malibu: JAKKS Pacific, 2004.

Mega Man 3 (NES). Sunnyvale, CA: Capcom, 1990.

Missile Command (arcade). Chicago: Atari Games Midway, 1980.

Mortal Kombat (PNP). Malibu: JAKKS Pacific, 2004.

Ms. Pac-Man (PNP). Malibu: JAKKS Pacific, 2004.

1942 (arcade). Sunnyvale, CA: Capcom, 1984.

Pac-Man (arcade). Chicago: Midway, 1980.

Pitfall! (arcade). Santa Monica: Activision, 1982.

Pole Position (PNP). Malibu: JAKKS Pacific, 2004.

PONG (Magnavox Odyssey). Chicago: Atari Games Midway, 1972.

Q-Bert (arcade). Providence: Hasbro Interactive, 1983.

Sonic the Hedgehog (Genesis). San Francisco: Sega, 1990.

Spacewar! (DEC PDP-1). Cambridge: MIT, 1962. Available at www3.sympatico.ca/
maury/games/space/spacewar.html.

World of Warcraft (PC and Mac). Irvine, CA: Blizzard Entertainment, 2004.

Xevious (PNP). Malibu: JAKKS Pacific, 2004.

5

Hacks, Mods, Easter Eggs, and Fossils

Intentionality and Digitalism in the Video Game

Wm. Ruffin Bailey

The term "interactive digital media" contains an often-overlooked adjective, *digital*. Espen Aarseth has given us a detailed study of the aesthetics of cybertext; Nick Montfort, the textuality of interactive fiction; and Mark J. P. Wolf, a strict review of the hardware requirements for a work to be labeled a video game. These authors provide useful, high-level work that introduces a young field, but only begin to provide an in-depth look at the digital underpinnings of gaming software and digitalism's undeniable influence on the creation of virtual realities.

The "digital" in digital media needs to be examined to gauge its characteristics' influence upon the creation of virtual spaces. Every web page lives on a digital host, forcing preschoolers to grandmothers to become familiar with the highly technical standards of Universal Resource Locators (URLs) and Hypertext Markup Language (HTML) that enable digital interpretation. Engines that drive video games are mediated by similar digital hosts. Games are limited in size by their ability to access their host's physical memory. They are limited in complexity by their authors' ability to construct decision-making algorithms that approximate the authors' visions of virtual realities. Theorists may be able to observe the results of these virtual realities, but in the absence of an interrogation of the fundamentals of computer science, they will not be able to effect a complete study of digital media and its creation.

This chapter seeks to establish a rhetorical method—of terminology and taxonomy—by which to explore what is unique to software-based digital media, starting with a nostalgic application of the method to the Atari 2600 (the first truly modular home gaming console) and watching how its workings continue to reflect and inform studies of games written nearly two decades later. Such a methodology currently requires a multidisciplinary cultural approach and is instrumental in grasping how interactive digital media, here video games in particular, operate.

This study begins by reviewing Montfort's study of interactive fiction, which provides an accessible introduction to video game studies by focusing on the games' use of narrative and riddle—two conventional approaches to text—before launching into code. I then review two foundations of a digitalistic approach that are currently housed in the field of computer science, the concepts of Boolean logic and memory addressing. These prove crucial for studying the operation of video game engines and creating a technical taxonomy for video game content. I end with a consideration of several video games to demonstrate how a nostalgically informed study of code can be employed in practice to shape game studies, using examples as varied as programmers innocuously hiding graffiti of their names in Atari 2600 games to more modern artifacts like Rockstar Games' "accidental" inclusion of a hidden sex game in *Grand Theft Auto: San Andreas* (2004). In sum, because digital media is heavily influenced by technical characteristics, game studies will not achieve its full potential until considerations of computer science are more fully integrated into its methods.

The Bias of Accessibility or Limited Approaches

Montfort's enlightening study of interactive fiction (IF), *Twisty Little Passages*, recommends approaching IF, a subset of video games, in three ways: as narrative, as riddles, and as computer programs (14–15). The first two have received a great deal of discussion, largely through scholars like Montfort constructively framing games as texts. Purely by virtue of being accessible, however, these two approaches risk garnering inordinate attention within cultural studies at the unfortunate detriment of the third.

In the field of cybertext, six years prior to Montfort, Aarseth expressed his "wish to challenge the recurrent practice of applying the theories of literary criticism to a new empirical field" (14). This "recurrent practice" is one possible symptom of over privileging customary approaches—including narratives and riddles. At the same time, scholars' familiarity with these approaches is one reason that Montfort's book on interactive fiction (a style of game with a high affinity for the common codex) is a proven and popular introduction to the field.

Aarseth admits that "[traditional literary] approaches are useful for establishing the legitimacy of the field [of hypertext literary theory]" (76). *Twisty Little Passages* does a fine job establishing such legitimacy by dissecting IF-as-narrative and riddle. Still, both authors ultimately privilege the experience of IF's and cybertext's content without giving the same level of sustained attention to how that content was shaped by its digital hosts, a topic crucial for the study of both IF and cybertext.

Guarding against unfairly strong remediations of old media approaches into the study of the new proves a major difficulty in many studies, exemplified in part by John Muckelbauer's critique of a recent collection of essays regarding the rhetoric of film. Muckelbauer warns against exploiting that which is unique to a medium to support conclusions that were reached exclusively via historically more familiar means of compiling evidence: "This [narrative bias] is particularly striking insofar as discussion of things like images and sound—things that would seem to be important elements of film's distinctiveness—are relatively invisible in this collection" (905). In the case of video games, this warning translates directly, and it is this tendency to ignore games' "distinctiveness" that ludology and other multidisciplinary approaches must avoid.

The importance of truly digital approaches is evident in a section of *Twisty Little Passages* where Montfort heuristically recommends initially treating an IF work's engine, called a parser, "as a black box that accepts input and generates output." He goes as far as to proscribe "making reference to a program's specific data structures, functions, objects, and so forth" (23). However, to complete his analysis, Montfort (himself an author/programmer of several impressive works of IF) ultimately does move to his third approach: looking at IF compositions as computer programs. When he compares *Adventure* (1976) to a successor, *Zork* (1982), he lists a number of ways that *Zork*'s parser is superior to *Adventure*'s. Montfort states that *Adventure* "only accepts commands of one or two words" and that *Zork*'s parser understands longer directives. *Adventure* requires explicitly mentioning the object a player wants to use in commands, but *Zork*'s parser can "disambiguate" the item a user implicitly requested to employ with certain actions (e.g., a player's avatar might dig with its hands if another object was not mentioned). *Zork*'s parser can also understand prepositions, unlike *Adventure* (108–9).

Montfort's conclusions about IF engines—that one parser is limited to one or two words, that it never understands prepositions, or that its content is limited to a certain size —cannot be stated with full confidence without an in-depth, open-box understanding of the works' parsers.[1] Perhaps *Adventure* anachronistically understands the sentence, "Climb over the northern mountains, read Sam Lantinga's blog, and then summarize any advantages of using OpenGL over DirectX." If one were to take *Twisty Little Passages*' initial proposal to treat game engines as black boxes until every possible sentence has been tried, a task of ridiculously irrational scope, its conclusions could not be stated in absolute terms and likewise could not be authoritatively woven into critical works. Determinations about maximum work lengths or the potential to display graphics could not be made. As Montfort's and Ian Bogost's forthcoming *Platform Studies* series' concentration on just these issues attests, it is crucial for scholars of digital artifacts to now move past accessible remediations and forward toward understanding the inner workings of these artifacts' platforms. To analyze these inner workings requires the explicit introduction of a number of concepts from computer science.

Digitalism

For digitalism, the first steps involve further pursuing Montfort's third approach to IF works: to treat them as computer programs. Commercial video games, thus far, are digital creations.[2] I argue that scholars studying works of digital media must, as an essential position for rhetorical and cultural studies of games, approach the content on an equal footing with those games' creator(s) or author(s).

Digital means a system of representation based on discrete digits rather than any sort of continuous spectrum. What this means in practice becomes especially evident in the way computer programs make decisions. The simplest flow chart that includes at least one decision step makes the point obvious.

In each decision step, there are one or more discrete choices for exit. Even in the most complicated piece of branching logic, entry into each potential branch is, at its core, mediated by a simple test of true/false (that is, Boolean) logic. Either the condition or conditions for taking the branch are all true statements and the branch is taken, or at least one condition is false and the branch is avoided. By convention, conditions that point towards taking a branch evaluate to a Boolean value of "true," usually represented by the digit "1." Conditions that would stop the branch's execution are given a value of "false," and are usually represented by the digit "0."[3]

In technical terms, Boolean data types that hold these values are often called *switches*, and these evaluations act like switches on a railroad track. If "on," the train of logic will travel down one track; if "off," the logic will proceed down another. For trains, taking a third choice is disastrous. In digital hardware, a third choice, much less an infinite spectrum of choices, is—by design—impossible. This is precisely why cybertext so

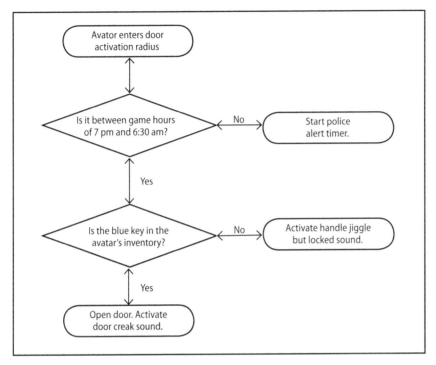

Figure 5.1. A simple flowchart

naturally gave rise to a system that, as Aarseth remarks, is "forcing the reader to pay attention to the strategic links" between portions of text (78). The reader is *being forced to act digitally*—to select one of a finite number of branches for their progression in a work. The operation of a cybertext interface can be reduced to nothing more than the most trivial of covers above the Boolean logic being evaluated beneath.

Exactly like they do in the thinly veiled interfaces of most hypertexts, Boolean evaluations or switches drive decision-making even in the most complicated representational systems created by video games. A player's avatar may approach a locked door that only operates during the night and if the avatar is carrying the appropriate key. Here there are at least two conditions to be evaluated. If the value of the night switch is "true" and a key inventory switch is also "true," the engine will allow the code to open the door to be executed. To the player, the checks in this example happen behind the scenes. Regardless, the digital switches are still there, evidenced by the consistent appearance of if-statements in the representation of Figure 5.1's logic shown in Figure 5.2's pseudo-code.

```
if (measurer.pointDist(p1,p2) < 20)        {
    if (   Game.currentTime() < Game.MORNING_TIME
           &&
           Game.currentTime() >= Game.EVENING_TIME
    ) {
            if (inventory.key(BLUE_KEY))  {
                    blueDoor.open();
            }      else    {
                    Game.sounds.
play(handleJiggle());
            }
    }      else    {
            police.soundAlarm();
    }
}
```

Figure 5.2. Pseudo-code for opening a door

This Boolean logic also introduces the method for creating "hacks." Hacks occur when an unsanctioned third-party or independent programmer changes a program's code to function in non-standard but not necessarily unintended ways. If a hacker could change the above example's logic to read, "If the night switch is 'true' and the key inventory flag is also 'true,'" or "1 = 1" (that is, simply adding a trivial expression that makes the evaluation of the whole always true), the hacker could easily short-circuit the game's door to open regardless of the time of day within the game or whether the avatar is carrying an appropriate key.[4] This is precisely what happens in certain "god mode" cheats in games that, for instance, allow players' avatars to walk through walls. By locating the Boolean evaluation where the collision detection occurs, a hacker can essentially insert a switch that makes the game's engine believe that collisions never occur. The new switch permanently sets the collision state to "false" for every check. The avatar can then move through any wall in the game. The game is now full of "not-collisions."

Certain games establish a documented standard where modifications can be added by placing the homespun content at certain memory addresses on the computer. *Memory addressing* is the second important digital concept computer science lends to ludology.[5] Every instruction in a computer has a memory address of one sort or another. Much as street addresses, hotel room numbers, or the line numbers in a BASIC program label potential locations for their users, digital computers use discrete numbers to reference specific hardware memory addresses that contain the code or data necessary to perform their tasks. Most, if not all, contemporary games have abstracted this process so that the machine's literal memory addresses do not have to be known. These games can situationally reference the correct address for, as an example, a folder as represented by a user's operating system rather than a specific spot on a stick of RAM or a hard disk.

Still, anyone who has experienced a "Blue Screen of Death" on a Windows computer has had every layer of abstraction ripped from her or his interface when the memory address describing the location of a deal-breaking error was displayed, usually as a particularly befuddling hexadecimal number similar to "71d633e5." Memory addressing is also why game console developers remain so intent on letting gamers know what was an 8-bit, 16-bit, 32-bit, or 64-bit system. Each increase indicates an exponential growth in the maximum number of addresses, meaning (at least indirectly) more resources with which the consoles could construct games.

Hacking Nostalgic

At this point, it is useful to revisit the term *game engine* to help establish how games are "hacked." Since the earliest days of home consoles, a game engine has been the part of a video game that interfaced with a game's content and evaluated Boolean logic. An engine, if run alone, is not able to provide a traditional gaming experience. In some ways, engines enforce the rules of their virtual worlds, but they are not worlds themselves. Engines are often created to be reusable, supporting more than one package of content, as with those displayed in Table 5.1.

It is sometimes difficult, especially in classic games, to know where an engine ends and content begins, as they may contain engines that were not designed for reuse and seem inextricably wedded to their content, like *Space Invaders* (1979) for the Atari 2600. Some contemporary "games," however, are hardly games at all; instead, they are little more than specialized engines with a minimum of content added before their release, begging third-party modification, like *Quake 3* (1999).

Atariage.com remarks that *Space Invaders* for the Atari 2600 home gaming console was the first arcade game licensed for home use ("Atari 2600—Space Invaders (Atari)"), and the ability to create the arcade experience in the home gave the 2600 its iconic stature. Yet *Space Invaders*, like

Table 5.1: Selected popular first-person shooter engines with implementations

Engine	Release	Implementations
Wolfenstein 3D	1992	*Wolfenstein 3D, Rise of the Triad, Spear of Destiny*
Doom	1993	*Doom, Doom 2, HeXen, Strife, HacX*
Quake 1	1996	*Quake, Half-Life,* * *HeXen 2, X-Men: Ravages of the Apocalypse*
Quake 2	1997	*Quake 2, Soldier of Fortune, Heretic 2, SiN, Kingpin, Daikatana*
Quake 3	1999	*Quake 3, Star Wars: Jedi Academy, American McGee's Alice*
Unreal 1	1998	*Unreal* (original), *Unreal Tournament, Deus Ex, Harry Potter and the Sorcerer's Stone, Star Trek: The Next Generation: Klingon Honor Guard*
Unreal 2	2002	*Unreal 2, America's Army, Thief: Deadly Shadows, UT2003, UT2004, Unreal Championship 2, Tom Clancy's Splinter Cell, Star Wars: Republic Commando, XIII*
Lithtech 1.0	1998	*Shogo, Blood II: The Chosen*
Lithtech 1.5	2000	*No One Lives Forever, Alien vs. Predator 2*
Lithtech 2.0	2002	*No One Lives Forever 2, Tron 2.0, The Matrix Online*
Halo	2001	*Halo, Stubbs the Zombie, Red vs. Blue* (machinema)

**Half-Life* contains a heavily modified *Quake 1* engine with some code from *Quake 2* as well.

a number of 2600 arcade ports,[6] was not nearly as true to the original as even the limited 2600 hardware would allow. In 1999, using new tools like modern emulators, Rob Kudla hacked *Space Invaders'* code in a doubly nostalgic attempt to re-create more faithfully the coin-operated arcade version of *Space Invaders* on the 2600 ("Atari 2600 Hacks"). Kudla made the invaders, the player's tank, sounds, and colors more closely reflect the original's. His improvements succeeded impressively.

The first step in hacking *Space Invaders'* graphics was to discover the memory address where graphic content (as opposed to the location of the game's *engine*) was kept in the machine language code. This is not nearly as hard a task as it may sound. Each invader is made up of ten "scanlines" of graphics, where each scanline matches one pass of a television's elec-

```
.byte $C6 ; |XX   XX | $FC96        .byte $A5 ; |X X  X X| $FC96
.byte $42 ; | X     X | $FC97       .byte $5A ; | X XX X | $FC97
.byte $7E ; | XXXXXX | $FC98        .byte $24 ; |  X  X  | $FC98
.byte $7E ; | XXXXXX | $FC99        .byte $FF ; |XXXXXXXX| $FC99
.byte $56 ; | X X XX | $FC9A        .byte $DB ; |XX XX XX| $FC9A
.byte $7C ; | XXXXX  | $FC9B        .byte $7E ; | XXXXXX | $FC9B
.byte $19 ; |   XX  X| $FC9C        .byte $3C ; |  XXXX  | $FC9C
.byte $25 ; |  X  X X| $FC9D        .byte $18 ; |   XX   | $FC9D
.byte $42 ; |  X    X | $FC9E       .byte $00 ; |        | $FC9E
.byte $80 ; |X       | $FC9F        .byte $00 ; |        | $FC9F
```

Figure 5.3. Original and hacked graphics, code, and memory addresses for *Space Invaders* **and** *Space Invaders Arcade.* **Images © Taito and Atari, Inc.**

tron gun across its screen. Each scanline of the 2600 invaders' graphics is eight bits, or switches, wide. It is possible to decompile the machine language code into a graphic representation of the program's switches' values, and the invaders' graphics' location in the code become obvious, in spite of appearing upside-down in the decompiled representation.

In Figure 5.3, the graphics (rotated for easy comparison with the code) for the original top-level, 2600 invader is displayed on the left next to the hacked, more arcade-faithful version by Kudla on the right. There are three columns in each section of disassembled code. The first column for each invader's disassembly shows the byte value of the eight-switch line of graphics in hexadecimal notation.[7] The second column shows the value of each individual switch in every eight-switch line, displaying an "X" for each switch that is "on" or set to "true." The last column shows the address in memory where the line is held, again in hexadecimal format.

Note that the addresses in the third column are the same for both invaders' listings ($FC96-$FC9F). The Atari 2600 does *not* rely on an operating system to abstract memory addresses like most present-day platforms, differing what happens here from the engines of "modern games" that Bogost notes are modularly "split up into software objects and frameworks" (55). These, then, are exact, static, unabstracted memory addresses in fairly monolithic code. That the addresses for the graphics are the same in the hack as the original suggests that when Kudla made his updates in *Space Invaders Arcade*, the logic of the game's original engine was not changed, and only a few switches solely related to graphics were hacked in place.

Kudla's reliance on a hack in place is also an indication of the degree to which the engine and content of this classic game are intertwined. In the byte—a collection of eight switches—located at memory address $FC96, two switches that were off were switched on and two that were on were switched off to change the appearance of the bottom of the invader. Kudla's creation of two blank lines of graphics at the top of the invader ensured the memory addresses remained synchronized in the modified content. In other words, *Space Invaders Arcade* is still using the original 2600 *Space Invaders* engine to provide the enforcement of its world's rules.

A crucial characteristic of the definition of a hack is that the original author of the game did not intend for a third party to change the game's content. *Space Invaders Arcade* can be safely considered a hack through a number of pieces of evidence. First and foremost, *Space Invaders* was initially released on a cartridge. Its code was permanently burned into Read Only Memory (ROM) and this hardwiring could not be changed, similar to the music on a commercial compact disc. Second, the game continues to be under copyright, legally forbidding just this sort of modification. Third, the author of *Space Invaders* did not provide documentation identifying the memory address of the content that Kudla changed, and the tools that now enable a hobbyist to disassemble and reassemble Atari 2600 games easily did not exist at the time of *Space Invaders'* release in 1980. Bogost described a similar situation with *Tank* and *PONG*, as well as *Combat* for the 2600, a home version of the former arcade game. The shared codebase in *Tank* and *PONG*, like that in *Space Invaders* and *Spaces Invaders Arcade*, served as a proto-engine, tying the games together in a manner that could be discovered only by a digitalistic critical approach. "[T]heir common gameplay properties relied entirely on the same codebase . . . *Tank*, *PONG*, and *Combat's* relation to one another is far stronger than interpretative notions like intertextuality or new media concepts like remediation allow" (58). Kudla's modification is different from the one Bogost describes in that Kudla's code-sharing was unauthorized. From the medium of the game's release to a complete lack of documentation on providing new or altering old content, it is safe to say *Space Invaders Arcade* is an unsanctioned hack.

There is another species of game alteration that works in a similar fashion, but where the hackers' addition of new content is anticipated and encouraged by the games' designers. Rather than a hacker finding a memory address through subversive code disassembly, in these cases designers expose a standardized memory address (usually abstracted by a folder location) where new content can be placed and read by a game's engine. This content can be as simple as a new skin for an avatar's frame that gives the player a different color or set of clothes or as complicated as a full modification, including new maps, textures, player models, and even rules for in-game scoring or physics.

Taken together, hacks and the addition of new code show that games are never done. From the very first games released on a home console to

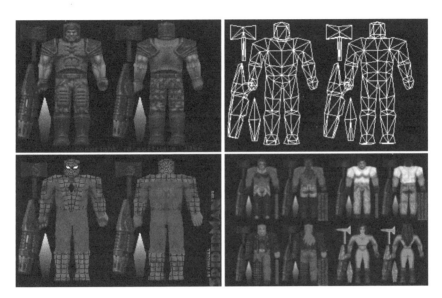

Figure 5.4. From *Quake 1*: (*top left*) default skin; (*top right*) model wire frame outline; (*bottom left*) *Spider-Man* skin; (*bottom right*) female skins, marine model. Images © id Software.

the latest games to hit market shelves, every one is open to alteration and additions in the digital age, with the Internet enabling mass consumption even of hobbyist releases.

Engines and Intentionality: Easter or Fossilized Egg?

Hacks, skins, and modifications are means for technically savvy gamers to coauthor the games they play. Another important concept in the video game that deserves close attention is the Easter egg, a portion of a game that is not added by savvy players but hidden by author(s) in the original. If found, an Easter egg provides a metalepsis similar to what Montfort describes in Infocom's *Planetfall* (30), but the effects are usually much more innocuous. Like literal Easter eggs, Easter eggs in video games *are meant to be found*. Determining whether a hidden portion of a game is a fossil (an unintended leftover from earlier development) or a true Easter egg waiting for discovery can be difficult. Distinguishing between the two and understanding how they affect the interpretation of digital artifacts is the goal of this portion of this chapter.

The most famous Easter egg in a video game can be found in Warren Robinett's Atari 2600 game, *Adventure* (1980). Game authors were

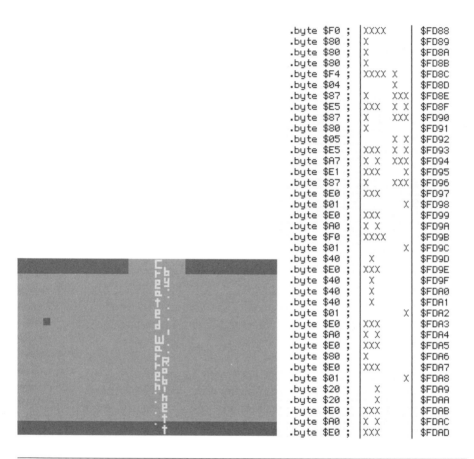

```
.byte $F0 ;  XXXX         $FD88
.byte $80 ;  X            $FD89
.byte $80 ;  X            $FD8A
.byte $80 ;  X            $FD8B
.byte $F4 ;  XXXX X       $FD8C
.byte $04 ;       X       $FD8D
.byte $87 ;  X    XXX     $FD8E
.byte $E5 ;  XXX  X X     $FD8F
.byte $87 ;  X    XXX     $FD90
.byte $80 ;  X            $FD91
.byte $05 ;       X X     $FD92
.byte $E5 ;  XXX  X X     $FD93
.byte $A7 ;  X X  XXX     $FD94
.byte $E1 ;  XXX    X     $FD95
.byte $87 ;  X    XXX     $FD96
.byte $E0 ;  XXX          $FD97
.byte $01 ;         X     $FD98
.byte $E0 ;  XXX          $FD99
.byte $A0 ;  X X          $FD9A
.byte $F0 ;  XXXX         $FD9B
.byte $01 ;         X     $FD9C
.byte $40 ;  X            $FD9D
.byte $E0 ;  XXX          $FD9E
.byte $40 ;  X            $FD9F
.byte $40 ;  X            $FDA0
.byte $40 ;  X            $FDA1
.byte $01 ;         X     $FDA2
.byte $E0 ;  XXX          $FDA3
.byte $A0 ;  X X          $FDA4
.byte $E0 ;  XXX          $FDA5
.byte $80 ;  X            $FDA6
.byte $E0 ;  XXX          $FDA7
.byte $01 ;         X     $FDA8
.byte $20 ;   X           $FDA9
.byte $20 ;   X           $FDAA
.byte $E0 ;  XXX          $FDAB
.byte $A0 ;  X X          $FDAC
.byte $E0 ;  XXX          $FDAD
```

Figure 5.5. *Adventure's* Easter egg with code disassembly. © Atari, Inc.

not credited in games released for the 2600 by Atari, and Robinett decided to circumvent this rule by burying his name in a secret room of the game. That Robinett intended players to find the secret room can be deduced from three clues. The first and most obvious is that the message is visible when playing the game. As will be shown, the game's code clearly holds his name, but Robinett provided a means for gamers to read the message on their television screens without sifting through its digital code. The second is that the graffiti reads, "Created by Warren Robinett." This message expects interpretation: it does not simply hold the author's name but unambiguously tells the gamer that the game was indeed made by the named individual. The last comes from the method by which the room is discovered. The room is accessed when the gamer's avatar places a "dot" Robinett hid in the game near the wall of a specific, easily accessed room. Robinett had programmed the game's engine to flash objects when more were on the screen than the 2600's hardware could easily support. The 2600 will only easily display a maximum of two complex objects called "sprites" (called "player graphics" on the 2600) on the screen with each frame. When more needed to be present, Robinett circumvented the 2600's limitation by making *Adventure*'s frames flash quickly enough (with two different objects displayed per frame) to let the gamer understand that more objects were there, though with the side effect that the items would seem to strobe constantly. Robinett put an extra object into the room that contained the secret dot to ensure that the room would flash when the player entered.[8] A perceptive player would notice the flashing in spite of there apparently being fewer items than what caused flashing elsewhere and be curious enough to eventually discover the existence of the dot. Not only does *Adventure* allow a gamer to read the message on his or her screen, it also provides hints for the player to discover those means.

That the secret message was not discovered by Atari during the game's development testifies to the way games could be, in the classic era, created by a single programmer without much oversight. A simple disassembly today, as shown in Figure 5.5, displays Robinett's message as easily as the same method finds the invaders' location in *Space Invaders*. Yet *Atariage.com* lists five more games released by Atari that included some sort of Easter egg containing "Programmer Credit" ("Tips, Cheats, and Easter Eggs").

San Francisco Rush: Time-Delay Easter Eggs and the Sophisticated Gamer

Not all digital Easter eggs are created to resist a parent corporation's attempts to dehumanize programmers.[9] *San Francisco Rush: Extreme Racing*, created for one of Nintendo's home consoles, the N64, found itself in a particularly precarious position. The N64 had enough power to approach very closely the game play and experience of the coin-operated original,[10] released the previous year. Gamers were also expecting the home version to contain content from the more recent arcade update, *San Francisco Rush: The Rock*. The arcade sequel's title headlined a new track for the racing game, which went to great pains to intricately recreate the streets of San Francisco; the extra track was one created on the landscape of Alcatraz, "The Rock." When *San Francisco Rush: Extreme Racing* was released, however, not only was there no Alcatraz, *Extreme Racing*'s project lead, Ed Logg, quashed any reports of plans to bring *The Rock* to the N64 (IGN Staff "Rush").

There was a rumor, propagated online, that claimed that *Extreme Racing* had the Alcatraz level hidden on the cartridge. A number of myths regarding how to access the track sprouted, including winning a race on each track in record time, using a manual transmission in those races, and even using a specific car while racing. None of these in-game methods unlocked the track (Stevefel et al.)

The Alcatraz track was unlocked no later than January of 1998, when a player posted his or her successful discovery of a code to hack the game to Usenet (bunivfan). The code worked with a device called a GameShark, which allows gamers to change values in their console's memory, much as Kudla did with the *Space Invaders*. Instead of changing bit values, the hack pointed the game's engine to the secret memory address that held Alcatraz, tricking the engine into loading and playing the hidden track. On March 19, *IGN.com* published a code from Atari Games that allowed gamers to access the track without a GameShark hack (IGN Staff "You're Going").

IGN.com interviewed Logg on April 1, 1998, regarding how the track came to be hidden on the cart. In brief, Atari Games' sales department did not want Alcatraz in the N64 version so that it would not, as they saw it, compete with the arcade game, and when the level was added it was hidden so well that, short of the GameShark, no one was able to access the track. The sales department was never contacted. The motivation for hiding the level was not strictly commercial, however; Logg admitted that the level was not likely to be as well tested as the other six in the game, which is apparent when the level is played (IGN Staff "Exclusive Interview").

San Francisco Rush: Extreme Racing challenges the archetypal concept of the Easter egg, like that found in *Adventure*, in two main ways. The first is that *Extreme Racing*'s track was embedded to create a sort of time-release content rather than exist as something gamers could hunt and locate within the game. Logg and his team did not provide a hint like Robinett's flashing objects. At the same time, it was content that the game's authors intended for the gaming public to experience if and only if they were in some way in contact with the circles that provided codes, be it Usenet, *IGN.com* and other Internet sites; gaming magazines; or friends who could access one of those outlets. In effect, they hid part of the game *outside* of the physical media of, in this case, the cartridge. Alcatraz was to be a multimedia Easter egg.

Multimedia Easter eggs have become the rule in video games, and the means of their distribution mark a sharp change from Robinett's in-joke for perceptive players. Lists of newly released codes that almost certainly could not have been guessed are standard in the back of magazines dealing with video games in what has become a somewhat codependent state of affairs. The publishing of video games' codes amounts to free game advertisements at the same time that the anticipation of new codes sells each new magazine issue, turning Montfort's metalepsis into an industry.

The second way that *Extreme Racing* helps to redefine the Easter egg is the way that it deprivileged the work's authors. Alcatraz was discovered without its authors' consent and contrary to the authors' design by GameShark hackers. Gamers are now savvy enough to search for hidden content that is not accessible solely using the game's traditional interface. Alcatraz was meant to be found. With its *early* discovery, however, gamers proved they had the means to find unintended "eggs" as well. GameSharks, disassemblers like that used by Kudla, model viewers like Pakrat (Naughton), and utility software that allows file inspection like hex editors allow gamers to break from the intended interfaces and creatively search for hidden content. These tools provide new directions for a player or "reader" to access digital works.

Fossils: Unintended Easter Eggs

If a programmer creates a subroutine that may not be used in a later version of their program, there is no technical requirement to remove it. If Warren Robinett had decided to hide his secret message from gamers, he could have deleted the extra room where the message was displayed and left the data with his message in *Adventure*'s code, only to be found with a thorough disassembly. Unlike text that has been struck through, unused code does not create any noticeable effect for its end users. It simply remains, fossilized.

In fact, there is often good reason to leave unused code in a program. If a later version needs a similar function, the code is already integrated with the codebase and is ready to be called. In some respects it can be an extra tool in the toolbox for an anticipated need, but one that is currently not required. There is also a potential advantage for fossilized code when testing an application. If the fossilized code has been cut out but not removed, perhaps for expediency's sake, and the program makes its way through user testing, completely removing the code later would require more testing to ensure a sloppy removal did not accidentally introduce new errors. Either reason can produce fossilized code in any digital work. Fossilizing code is a uniquely digital process. One switch might be changed (a Boolean expression that, if "true," would have caused a subroutine to be called is set to always evaluate as "false," fossilizing the subroutine) and the end user's experience is, in theory, *exactly the same* as it would have been had the code never existed.

Tomb Raider: The Angel of Darkness (2003) is an example of a video game with fossilized content. Whereas the first five entries in the *Tomb Raider* series shipped like clockwork, one coming out before each year's holiday buying season, *Angel of Darkness* was released over three-and-a-half years after *Tomb Raider: Chronicles* (2000). One *Tomb Raider* fan, upset by *Angel of Darkness*' errors, created a list called the "AOD Bugs definitive list" in which sixty-two bugs were listed (Dragoncarer). Bug 1.1, "The Secret Garden," describes fossilized content: *Angel of Darkness* opens with a training level that allows users a chance to become familiar with the complicated controls of the game. Much of the level was scrapped, presumably to allow the game to be released more quickly. The fossilized content is still within the game, and parts of it can be seen from conventionally accessible portions of an extant level. Entering the fossilized content requires either hacking the game or loading a saved game where Lara Croft, the game's protagonist, begins at a location in the fossilized area. As Figure 5.6 shows, in the fossilized area, large parts of the surrounding cityscape are missing and training instructions are displayed for the player. One safe assumption from the archeological evidence is that the training section of *Angel of Darkness* was originally intended to be much more elaborate.

Hot Coffee and Possible Piltdowns

The skull planted in Piltdown, England, may be the greatest scientific hoax, and is certainly the greatest in physical anthropology.[11] No more than an orangutan jaw placed next to a human skull, the false fossil tricked anthropologists for more than four decades. The Piltdown concept is a useful one for video games, especially when trying to evaluate rhetorical intent with respect to apparently fossilized content. Are programmers cunning enough to disguise Easter eggs in their games as fossils to trick the gaming public into believing they were accidents?

Rockstar's *Grand Theft Auto: San Andreas* raises just this question. *San Andreas* contains what appeared to be a fossil: a portion of the game that is inaccessible without some sort of hack or download. Here, the ostensibly fossilized content allows a gamer to have limited control over relatively graphic sexual scenes between the player's avatar, named "CJ," and

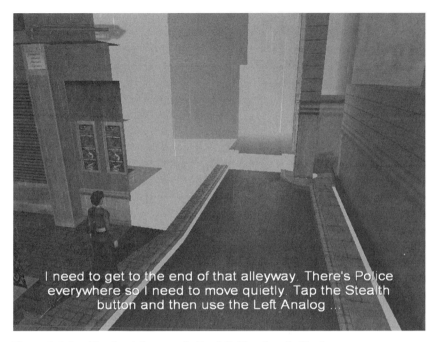

I need to get to the end of that alleyway. There's Police everywhere so I need to move quietly. Tap the Stealth button and then use the Left Analog ...

Figure 5.6. Fossilized training area in *Tomb Raider: Angel of Darkness*. Image © Eidos Interactive.

his girlfriend(s). After dating, CJ's current girlfriend may invite him into her house for coffee. For a player without the "Hot Coffee" modification, the camera shakes suggestively (like CJ's car when he picks up a prostitute) after he is invited into his girlfriend's home, but for a player with the modification, the camera follows CJ inside.

Patrick Wildenborg, who discovered the "fossil" and created a modification that allowed others to access it easily, says the following about the modification on his website:

After reading various discussion [*sic*] about this mod around the internet, I would like to make the following statement:
*All the contents of this mod was already available on the original disks. Therefor [*sic*] the scriptcode, the models, the animations and the dialogs by the original voice-actors were all created by RockStar. The only thing I had to do to enable the mini-games was toggling a single bit in the main.scm file.* (Of course it was not easy to find the correct bit). (Wildenborg, emphasis in the original)[12]

After Hot Coffee's discovery, Rockstar quickly became trapped in a controversy, and the Federal Trade Commission investigated how the game received a "Mature" rating, which *recommended* its sale to people seventeen years old and older, and not an "Adults Only" rating, which would have *restricted* its sale to those able to prove they were eighteen years old and up. An "Adults Only" rating was then given to *San Andreas* due to the apparent fossil discovery, and the game was pulled from mass retailers' shelves. A revised version without the Hot Coffee content was written and re-released, and an update was provided online to erase the content from personal computers with the game already installed.

Rodney Walker, a Rockstar spokesman, quickly attempted to fashion a metaphor for Hot Coffee's inclusion favorable for his company:

> An artist makes a painting, then doesn't like the first version and paints over the canvas with a new painting, right? . . . That's what happened here. Hackers on the Internet made a program that scratches the canvas to reveal an earlier draft of the game. (Schiesel)

While it is true that fossilized content can "reveal an earlier draft" of a game, the metaphor is flawed due to Walker's inattention to digitalism's influence on the rhetoric of the *San Andreas* minigame. A copy of a painting does not include an embedded history. Owners will not discover a sketch of Mary with her left hand to her breast in their copies of mass-produced prints of Leonardo da Vinci's *Virgin on the Rocks*. Every copy of *Tomb Raider: Angel of Darkness* has the unfinished portions of the training level, every copy of *San Andreas* has the hidden sex game, and infrared reflectography is not required to discover the content ("The Hidden Leonardo"). It is also possible to erase unused code from a digital product's final version, whereas it is nearly impossible to remove an unfinished draft from below a masterpiece's last layers of paint. Walker's metaphor may have been one of the best of the quick attempts to understand Hot Coffee's inclusion, yet it is one that unjustly favors the publisher in its depiction that ignores digitalism.

The Lessons of Digitalism

Studying virtual realities dependent on digital hosts requires an emphasis on digitalism, which in turn enables readings that would otherwise be missed. Conjoining what are now multidisciplinary concepts is required to question complex works, like *Grand Theft Auto: San Andreas*, on a footing equal with authors, whether those authors are sanctioned or unauthorized. These approaches help remove the limitations of legacy methods, and instead of losing many of those tools, the integration reinvigorates them.

This chapter's quick survey, moving from nostalgic to contemporary digital artifacts, does little more than scratch the surface of a digital approach, as it concentrates on the contested fringe of the representation of virtual worlds. Articles like Carolyn Miller's "Writing in a Culture of Simulation: Ethos Online" have opened the door for analyzing the next wave of virtual reality, where great characters are created not simply by great writing, but by skillful writing combined with convincing artificial intelligence. The time and tools for integrating digitalism with cultural studies are here, and the field awaits.

Notes

1. Even more stark a break from the "black box" approach is Montfort's characterization of BASIC as a particularly difficult language with which to write IF and one he has tried using himself. Here, *Twisty Little Passages* has clearly moved from the accessible approaches of IF-as-narrative and riddle and on to the third—complex computer programs.

2. An interesting study would be the history of video games based on analog computers. I am only familiar with William Higinbotham's *Tennis for Two*, created in 1958 (US Dept. of Energy). Regardless, this claimant for the title of the first video game offers an intriguing alternative to the metaphors of digitalism.

3. There is always an exception that proves the rule. In Visual Basic 6.0, once arguably the most popular programming language for the Microsoft Windows operating system, "true" is represented by "-1." To make things even more convoluted, once the Visual Basic code is translated into machine language, the "-1" becomes a "1" again (Bailey et al.).

4. The is reminiscent of Captain Kirk's answer to the Kobayashi Maru simulation in cadet training, recounted in *Star Trek: The Wrath of Khan*. When presented with a "no-win"/always "false" trial in training, Kirk, after failing the simulation twice, reprograms/hacks the computer to create a winning solution.

5. Though the explanations given for these terms herein are arguably accurate, a much better—and extremely accessible—primer text is Richard Mansfield's *Machine Language for Beginners*, which explains assembly language programming and the operation of a series of chips found in the Atari 2600, Commodore 64, Nintendo Entertainment System, and the Apple II. These chips are simple enough to allow a beginner to achieve a reasonable understanding of their operation and complete enough in their design that the conceptual lessons learned easily extend to contemporary processors.

6. "Port" comes from "portable" and is something of a misnomer, as most early "ports," like *Space Invaders* for the 2600, were more precisely *rewrites* on alternate hardware. Other arcade ports that did not fully exploit the 2600's hardware

include the infamous *Pac-Man* (see *Ms. Pac-Man* on the 2600 as an example of what the game could have been), *Zaxxon*, and *Popeye*.

7. Hexadecimal is a base-16 numbering system that allows eight binary switches to be displayed in two digits. In the "ones" place, *A, B, C, D, E,* and *F* represent *10, 11, 12, 13, 14,* and *15,* respectively. An *A* in the "tens" place represents ten sixteens, or *160.* For this study's purposes, all that is required is an understanding that these are numbers and that the "$" preceding each hexadecimal number is a signpost that we are using base-16, not base-10.

8. In this room, the "darkness" was technically an object. The darkness, the dot, and one extra item were enough to create the flash.

9. An engaging introduction to the topic of the dehumanization of the programmer is Edward G. Nilges's "PRACTICAL DECONSTRUCTIVE CODING."

10. *Extreme Racing*'s project lead mentions that tracks were shared between the arcade team and the N64 team, meaning that they were both using approximately the same format for their content, truly porting levels from platform to platform rather than rewriting the game. The levels from the original arcade game were going directly into *Extreme Racing* and three levels from *Extreme Racing* were borrowed and placed into a later arcade release (IGN Staff "Exclusive Interview").

11. This section can be found in an expanded form in "Inviting Subversion: Metalepses and Tmesis in Rockstar Games' *Grand Theft Auto* Series" in *The Meaning and Culture of Grand Theft Auto Critical Essays,* ed. Nate Garrelts (Jefferson, NC: McFarland Press, 2006), 210–25.

12. After a controversy appeared regarding the modification, Wildenborg appropriately hid this text and the locations of pictures of the modification in his webpages through the use of "html comments," a method usually used by html coders to leave messages for other coders viewing their pages' code. To read the quoted material, web users had to hack Wildenborg's page to access the trivially hidden content from within the web page's html code, a method not coincidentally similar to what Wildenborg did to hack *San Andreas.* He has, as of 13 January 2008, restored the text to his site.

Works Cited

Aarseth, Espen. *Cybertext.* Baltimore: Johns Hopkins University Press, 1997.

"Atari 2600 - Space Invaders (Atari)." *www.atariage.com* (6 November 2004). Accessed 7 August 2005.

"Atari 2600 Hacks - Space Invaders Arcade." *www.atariage.com* (19 November 2004). Accessed 7 August 2005. .

Bailey, Wm. Ruffin, Cor Ligthert, Herfried K. Wagner, et al. "Why is minus one (-1) equal to true in VB again?" *microsoft.public.dotnet.languages.vb* (Usenet, 21–23 June 2004). Accessed 13 August 2005

Barr, Roger, ed. "Hacked Rom Reviews!" www.*i-mockery.com*. Accessed 12 August 2005.

Blue Zircon. "Thompson 1928." *www.gtagaming.com* (26 July 2005). Accessed 12 August 2005.

Bogost, Ian. *Unit Operations*. Cambridge: MIT Press, 2006.

bunivfan. "SF Rush Hidden Track Code." *rec.games.video.nintendo* (Usenet, 13 January 1998). Accessed 10 August 2005.

DieselGT. "'Tumbler' Batmobile." *www.gtagaming.com* (17 July 2005). Accessed 12 August 2005.

Dragoncarer. "AOD Bugs definitive list." *db.gamefaqs.com* (9 December 2003). Accessed 7 August 2005.

IGN Staff. "Exclusive Interview: Ed Logg." *ign64.ign.com* (1 April 1998). Accessed 7 August 2005.

"The Hidden Leonardo." *www.nationalgallery.org.uk* (2001). Accessed 12 August 2005.

"History of the 11th Annual Interactive Fiction Competition." *ifcomp.org/comp05/history.html* (2005). Accessed 8 August 2005.

IGN Staff. "Exclusive Interview: Ed Logg." *ign64.ign.com* (1 April 1998). Accessed 7 August 2005.

___. "Rush: The Rock Not Coming to N64." *ign64.ign.com* (17 November 1997). Accessed 7 August 2005.

___. "You're Going to Alcatraz." *ign64.ign.com* (19 March 1998). Accessed 7 August 2005.

Mansfield, Richard. *Machine Language for Beginners*. Greensboro, NC: Compute! Publications, 1983.

Montfort, Nick. *Twisty Little Passages*. Cambridge: MIT Press, 2003.

Miller, Carolyn. "Writing in a Culture of Simulation: Ethos Online." In *The Semiotics of Writing: Transdisciplinary Perspectives on the Technology of Writing*. Ed. Patrick Coppock. Turnhout, Belgium: Brepols, 2001. 253–79.

Muckelbauer, John. Review of *The Terministic Screen: Rhetorical Perspectives on Film* by David Blakesley. *JAC* 23.4 (2003).

Naughton, Tom. *Pakrat* "About" page. *pakrat.fragland.net* (10 October 2001). Accessed 14 August 2005

Nilges, Edward G. "PRACTICAL DECONSTRUCTIVE CODING, an essay in the critical theory of computer science." *comp.lang.basic.visual.misc* (Usenet, 16 November 2001). Accessed 10 August 2005.

Pomaville, Leann, ed. *Quake Woman's Forum*. 1999. *planetquake.com*. Accessed 11 August 2005.

"San Francisco Rush–Cheat Codes & Secrets–GameFAQs." *gamefaqs.com*. Accessed 7 August 2005.

Schiesel, Seth. "Video Game Known for Violence Lands in Rating Trouble Over Sex." *New York Times* (21 July 2005).

Stevefel; Tal A. Funke-Bilu; bliss; et al. "SF Rush Alcatraz track: Relase [sic] the code Atari-Games !! (please)." *rec.games.video.nintendo* (Usenet, 18 January–18 February 1998). Accessed 10 August 2005.

"Tips, Cheats, and Easter Eggs." *www.atariage.com/hint_list.html* (10 October 2004). Accessed 7 August 2005.

US Dept. of Energy. "Brookhaven 1958 Video Game - DOE Research and Development (R&D) Accomplishments." *Office of Scientific and Technical*

Information (*www.osti.gov/accomplishments/videogame.html*). Accessed 7 May 2005.

Wildenborg, Patrick. "PatrickW GTA Modding | Home." *patrickw.gtagames.nl/index. html*. Accessed 10 March 2006.

Wolf, Mark J. P., ed. *The Medium of the Video Game*. Austin: University of Texas Press, 2001.

Games Cited

Adventure (Atari VCS/2600). Sunnydale, CA: Atari, 1978.

Descent (Windows). Champaign, IL: Parallax Software, 1995.

Grand Theft Auto: San Andreas (PlayStation 2). New York: Rockstar Games, 2004.

Grand Theft Auto III (PlayStation 2). New York: Rockstar Games, 2001.

Quake 1 (Macintosh). Santa Monica: id Software/MacPlay, 1996.

Quake 2 (Windows). Santa Monica: id Software/Activision, 1997.

Quake 3 (Macintosh). Santa Monica: id Software/Activision, 1999.

Space Invaders (Atari VCS/2600). Sunnyvale, CA: Atari, 1980.

Space Invaders Arcade (Atari VCS/2600). Atariage.com, 1999.

San Francisco Rush: Extreme Racing (N64). Milpitas, CA: Midway Games West, 1997.

Tank (Coin-Op). Kee Games, 1974.

Tomb Raider: Angel of Darkness (Macintosh). Austin: Aspyr, 2004.

Tomb Raider: Chronicles (Macintosh). Austin: Aspyr, 2000.

Zork (various platforms). Cambridge, MA: Infocom, 1979.

6

Screw the Grue
Mediality, Metalepsis, Recapture

Terry Harpold

I begin with an assertion that I consider an axiom of videogame studies: *Gameplay is the expression of combinations of definite semiotic elements in specific relations to equally definite technical elements.* The semiotic plane of a game's expression draws on the full range of common cultural material available to game designers and players, such as shared myth, conventions of genre and narrative form, and comprehension of the relevant intertextual canons. The technical plane of the expression—computational, electronic, and mechanical systems that support gameplay—is the more restricted. Its elements are more localized to a given situation of play (*this* software, *this* hardware) in ways that the semiotic elements of play seem not to be (where do relevant cultural myth and the intertextual canon start and stop? will this not vary according to the competence of the player?). Moreover, because the technical elements of play should demonstrate the consistency and stability fundamental to usable computing devices, they are deterministic and capable of only finitely-many configurations. (For the present and the foreseeable future, we play in Turing's world.) The challenge of game design is to program the entanglement of semiotic and technical elements in an interesting and rewarding way. The expression of play activates this entanglement in well-defined and predictable combinations.

The cultural-semiotic repertoire of videogame play can be measured, though the extent to which this could be limited to the videogame, strictly speaking, is doubtful. Games are cultural texts, drawing on symbolic domains well outside of a conjectured gameworld or a collection of user responses; an anthropology of gaming must reach beyond the material contexts of a specific episode of play.

My focus in this essay is on the technical end of entanglement and the points of contact between technical and semiotic elements of play. Though intuitively the player must imagine that some contact is necessary—the game's interface must engage the underlying game engine, which must engage the computer's operating system, and so on—the relation between a given technical element or elements and traits of the gameworld will not always be expressed in ways that are significant *for the player*, whose attention is, for the most part, on events and existents of the gameworld. Some technical elements may seem to have no discernible effect on the game's expression; their influences, if any, can only be conjectured. (For instance, how is playing a text-based adventure game created for circa-1980 computers different from playing the same game on a 2007 computer with vastly more memory and a many-times faster processor, when this seems not to change behaviors of the game's parser in any meaningful way?) Other elements will have determinate effects that are evident to anyone who plays or observes a game. (Playing a first-person shooter [FPS] such as *Doom* on an underequipped system is very unlike playing it on one with a souped-up videocard and a faster processor.) Yet others have effects that are no less determinate but which are only indirectly marked; their contribution to play depends in a very real sense on their not being recognized by the player. I will describe several of these below. It is precisely in the fundamental role of constraints—play is freedom within defined systems of constraints—that videogames merit being called *games* in the first place. But videogames represent a particular variant of the freedom-within-constraints model of play proposed by theorists such as Johan Huizinga and Roger Caillois, in that rules and objects that define characteristics of the gameworld are bound to states of hardware and software that have no direct correlates in other forms of play. We may say that specific aggregates of hardware and software occurring together and in relation to the semiotic plane of the game's expression constitute its particular *medial* bases—that is, the complete character of its encoding in the medium of the videogame.

In an obvious way, medial determinisms of a videogame's expression will be marked in boundaries of its computational and mechanical elements. Monitors, keyboards, mice, game controllers, etc., are capable of limited numbers of discrete electromechanical states; their affordances are constrained by the granularity of their operations. Hardware bottlenecks related to computer and video memory, processor speed, available disk storage, the latency of read-only media, and network throughput enforce upper limits on computational efficiency. Play is subject also to contingencies of its performance: keys jam, controllers fail, hard disks crash, network communications are interrupted. Program or operating system bugs that were irrelevant to one round of play may plague others or bring them to a halt. The limits of a player's abilities may be caught up in these infelicities, as fatigue, clumsiness, or unfamiliarity will compound effects of any design flaw or device error. Our auxiliary organs, as Freud observed, have not grown on to us well; they give us much trouble at times.

More subtly, medial determinisms will be marked—of necessity—in related structures of the program and the gameworld. In these cases, a structure in the gameworld or a pattern of play corresponds in a direct way to an underlying attribute of the program, representing it to the player in a form that is appropriate to the world and masks the technical requirement that it fulfills. Common threshold structures of the world—closed doors or windows, elevators, magical portals—often fulfill this dual function. Segmenting spaces of the world in a way that is easily accepted by the player, they may also mask computational latencies (the rendering engine must be given time to catch up; a new portion of code must be loaded into memory) or limits of the game's database (transporting her avatar to a new "level," an elevator also redirects the player's attention away from the fact that there is no inter-level space beyond the elevator's compartment, as nothing there is computationally defined). Crucially, the threshold matches the program trait to the gameworld trait concurrently, or with such close approximation that their difference is not noticed much.

In this and similar moments of play, the user's attention is primarily on the gameworld rather than its software and hardware correlates; there is entanglement, but its expression tends toward a reification of one plane of gameplay. We may say that by some mechanism, which may vary from game to game and in the degree of its openness, the gameworld *recaptures* traits of hardware or software, repurposing them to its own ends and masking their potential disruption of the world with information that is notionally distinct from it. The back-directed orientation implicit in the term *recapture* is appropriate to the concept because, as I understand it, recapture takes place on the cusp of a sort of crisis in representation: exactly at the moment where entanglement threatens to bring forward the game's determinism by its definite technical situation, that determinism is turned back into the gameworld, so as to seem to be another of its (arbitrary but consistent) rules. Recapture is, on the one hand, a fundamental operation of videogame expression; it is hard to see how lines of code and a box full of hardware could seem to constitute a world without it. On the other hand, it will be specifically marked when technical elements of play are particularly troublesome to the designer or the game is for that reason or another unusually self-conscious of its medial conditions.

I describe below three examples of recapture in videogames of the 1980s and 1990s. Each was designed to run under hardware and software that are by early twenty-first-century standards much constrained. *Zork 1* (1982) was developed for Infocom's Z-machine interpreters for 1980s personal computers with less than 48K of RAM (Blank; Montfort); *Virtual Valerie* (1990) was developed in an early version of Macromedia Director, for versions of the Mac OS lacking protected memory; *Bad Mojo* (1996) was developed for the 8-bit color displays and low-speed CD-ROMs typical of late-1990s desktop systems. The phenomenon of recapture will not be restricted to constrained hardware and software environments; it will occur in any definite medial object that articulates a fictional world. It is likely, however, that operations of recapture will be more clearly traced in constrained conditions such as these. Game developers working in them must attend to the meagre resources at their disposal; their solutions to technical challenges are often both plainly evident and cannily crafted. In contrast, developers working with comparably unlimited hardware and software are more free to be profligate in their uses of resources. In that circumstance, the player is likely to miss effects of recapture altogether, or to mistake them for arbitrary rules of form, such as genre conventions, rather than fundamental conditions of play. A salutary consequence of the backward glance: the seeming clunkiness of older games, seen from the present, demonstrates to us aspects of the gaming situation that the panache of contemporary games often obscures.

Screw the Grue

The player of Infocom's 1982 text adventure game *Zork: The Great Underground Empire* (Figure 6.1) is free to wander in the many "twisty little passages" above and below ground, and to interact with objects and creatures she encounters there, but at the risk of her confusion or peril.[1] Some objects are inscrutable; some are dangerous; even when the creatures are not menacing (and most are), they rarely have her best interests in mind. Her fate in the gameworld is largely determined by her responses to *Zork's* text parser, which presents her with a brief description of an object or a scene, after which she types a command in reply, after which the parser gives a little more information, and so on.[2] The goal of the game is to collect a series of "trophies" scattered throughout the labyrinths of the Great Underground Empire while fending off attackers and making use of some objects (a lantern, a box of matches, a screwdriver, and so on) to solve the game's puzzles.

Among the player's adversaries is the grue, "a sinister lurking pres-

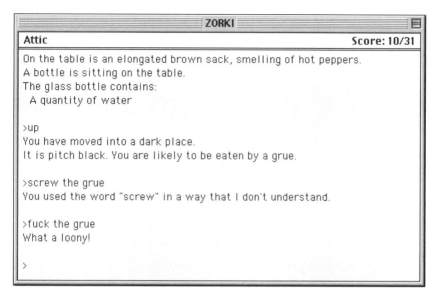

Figure 6.1. *Zork 1: The Great Underground Empire* {Attic}. Shown here is a Z-machine interpreter for Mac OS 9. Image and text © Infocom, Inc.

ence" whose "favorite diet is adventurers" and who is likely to show up whenever the player's avatar enters an unlit space. "No grue has ever been seen by light of day," the parser observes, "and few have survived its fearsome jaws to tell the tale."[3] The grue's dual *narrative* and *technical* function is obvious: to force the avatar to return to the light or find a way of illuminating the dark. A menacing grue frees the game's designers from the practical burden of representing movements in total darkness in a text-only interface. When confronted by a grue, one should flee or turn a light on it; one will otherwise be eaten and the game will come to an end. The grue is therefore a thing to which one should show some respect.

Figure 6.1 records my attempt to disrespect the grue. Upon being warned that I may be eaten, I type the response "Screw the grue." I mean by this, of course, to insult the grue, but the parser duly attempts to make sense of my command in other terms. A screwdriver is an important tool in *Zork* and the player's avatar will often have one in her possession; screwing is something you do to a screw with a screwdriver. *Screwing* a grue, however, is ill-advised or impossible, as there's no likely place on a grue to insert a screwdriver and the creatures are, in general, intolerant of being messed with. In point of fact, my figurative use of the verb "screw" has no meaning in the game's lexicon, and so the parser replies that it doesn't grasp my intention. "You used the word *screw*," it complains, "in a way I don't understand." By way of explanation, I clarify my disregard for the grue more directly: "Fuck the grue," I reply. Now the parser shows more understanding of my intent: "What a loony!" it exclaims.

Under the circumstances, this may be a reasonable estimate of my lack of decorum or anatomical probity, and given the parser's famous literal-mindedness, I shouldn't be surprised that it rejects forms of abuse that it determines extreme. Yet, I find this exchange intriguing on two counts. First, the intended audience of the parser's expressions of confusion and then dismay is, I think, ambiguous. To whom is its assessment of my mental state addressed? Like other responses it makes in the course of gameplay, its replies are putatively directed to my avatar, but they appear in this case to carry meaning beyond that relation, albeit confined to the gameworld. The grue menaces; the game will end prematurely if I don't get my avatar out of the dark. But I've used up a turn spewing insults—in effect, rejecting the contract of the game and the good will of the parser. For this *I* am judged a loony—not because I've behaved stupidly (you *can't* screw a grue), but because *to behave badly is to play badly*. The game's designers have anticipated that querulous players might resort to typing insults, so they've built into the game an ability to distinguish between valid commands (you can screw several things in *Zork*, so long as they take a screwdriver) and invective (you can't fuck anything in *Zork*).[4] Misbehavior of this kind will be rejected, and may result in your avatar being placed in peril by your fooling around—which seems strangely prim, given that the parser will not object to your commanding the avatar to kill itself by jumping off a cliff or stabbing itself with a rusty knife (which is why the "loony" appraisal must be directed to *me*, as those behaviors are arguably crazier than insulting or attempting to copulate with an invisible monster).

Second, the parser's replies in this exchange illustrate a limit to what I can accomplish in the world of *Zork*. I've undertaken two turns in a row to do something that is impossible or forbidden, and *have been warned of this in a way that is consistent with normal operations of the game*. There's nothing unusual about that; the parser works in exactly that way all the time, in that it tries to make sense of your input in terms of its very restricted vocabulary. But that's just the lesson of this episode: back-end limits of the game's database (in which movement in the dark is unrepresentable and certain verbs are undefined in relation to grues) are handled during play in ways that conform to established rules of the gameworld. Some of those rules concern the physics of the world, and some seem to be about that and perhaps something else. What remains unclear afterwards (when I am dead, the victim of my own churlishness) is the degree

Figure 6.2. *Virtual Valerie*. Image © Reactor, Inc.

to which the conformity of the parser's replies to these limits may also sig-
nal some permeability of the boundaries between the gameworld and the
situation of play. The first reply tells me, in effect, that the parser doesn't
know what I'm talking about, which is not the same thing as reporting
that my input is in error. (Compare its "in a way I don't understand" to
something like "ERROR: That verb is not defined in the game database.")
The second reply tells me that the parser understands me—though it may
not distinguish between a figurative and a literal action—*but it won't let
me play that way*.[5]

Valerie's Question

Figure 6.2 shows an image from *Virtual Valerie* (1990). I've written elsewhere on Mike Saenz's notorious 1990 "interactive erotica" for Macintosh; I won't rehash that analysis here (Harpold). However, this moment
in *Valerie* seems to me to merit another look, as some aspects of it are
akin to my exchange with the *Zork* parser.

The principal aim of *Virtual Valerie*, as one might surmise from her
invitation, is to "get down to business" with the game's eponymous hero-

ine. The player is free to wander the cartoonish corridors and rooms of Valerie's apartment, to open and close her cabinets and closets, examine the pictures on her walls and the books on her shelves, to view titles in her laserdisc collection—including, intriguingly, an abbreviated version of *Virtual Valerie*—and so on, but he (the player's avatar is male) will eventually meet up with Valerie in the position shown here.[6] If you respond to her invitation by clicking on the "Yes" button, you and she are transported immediately—no time is wasted showing the way—to her bedroom, where she enthusiastically submits to more involved advances. (Cartoon sex, limited to crudely-animated play with sex toys and predictable responses on her part. *Valerie* considerably predates the full-motion video FPS interfaces typical of later interactive adult titles.)

More than this possibly tempting opportunity hangs on your choice: if you reject Valerie's invitation and click on the "No" or "Huh?" buttons, *your computer will reboot.* No advance warning is given: the game was written in Macromedia Director, and your misplaced mouseclick simply invokes Director's rarely-used "Restart" command. In 1990, there was good reason to avoid it, as the Mac OS had limited support for multitasking and no memory protection; any application—including the operating system—open at the time you made the wrong choice was at risk of being damaged by *Valerie's* sudden exit. "The forced reboots," Saenz explains, "were my method of punishing the player for 'trespasses.' I tried to imagine how Valerie might slap the player's face, and a reboot was the closest approximation I could come up with."[7] It is to my knowledge the only showstopper of its kind in modern computer gaming.

As in my uncouth encounter with the grue, this moment of *Valerie* entangles technical and representational registers in such a way that each naturalizes the others. Also as in *Zork,* the consistency of the gameworld—the interactivity of objects in Valerie's apartment, her response to the player's choice—is subtended by an implicit contract: one plays by the rules . . . or one does not play, by the rules. But the force with which the contract is enforced in this case is obviously more extreme. My bad behavior results in a program response that transgresses with shocking effect registers of play that we might reasonably expect would be distinct. This is all the more ironic, as *Valerie* is unapologetic pornography; transgressive effects are anticipated in merely beginning the game.[8]

Saenz has given us all the information we need to understand the seriousness of our endeavor in the on-screen buttons that represent the possible choices in this scene. They compel us to show some respect for limits of the gameworld—is that heavy breathing the sound of an approaching grue?—by frankly marking their technical bases. Strictly speaking, the buttons shouldn't be here; they belong to—they address—*another place*. Everything else in Valerie's apartment resembles what you might expect there: stylish furnishings, books, vases, hanging pictures, a stereo and TV, telephones, light switches. The buttons, in contrast, seem to reside somewhere between the surfaces of the apartment and the inside of the computer screen; they are, manifestly, *buttons*: beveled edges, Chicago font, and the rest.[9] In that, they figure a more radical laying-bare of the gameworld's dependence on its mediality[10] than *Zork* could ever manage, because the Z-machine has no comparable connection to basic functions of the operating system.[11] Recapture is more effective in *Valerie* because it implicitly accounts for *its own mediality*: rejection of Valerie = system reboot = rejection by Valerie; the *frisson* of this unexpected disruption translates the pleasure forecast by her offer into a thrilling display of its precariousness. If we conclude on second or third try that the reboot is meant to be a parodic infraction of the conventions of play, its force is such that it resituates the expressive potential of the game so as to include an address of the real conditions of play.

Narrative theorists refer to level transgressions such as these as *metalepses*. As first described by Gérard Genette (*Narrative Discourse* and *Narrative Discourse Revisited*), a metalepsis occurs when the ostensible boundary between two narrative worlds is breached, as when in Joseph Conrad's novel *Heart of Darkness* Marlow interrupts his account of his voyage up the Congo river to converse with his audience, who are seated on the deck of a ship anchored in the Thames river long after Marlow has returned from Africa; when the Balzacian narrator pauses to alert the reader to facts about a scene that are not evident from its plot or dialogue (*Narrative Discourse* 134–35); or when the narrator of John Fowles's *The French Lieutenant's Woman* observes in passing that the characters of the novel "never existed outside my own mind" (Ryan 207). As is particularly clear in the examples of Balzac and Fowles, metalepses may draw attention to the fact that a story is being narrated *by someone*, signaling thus her control over elements of the narrative regardless of its appearing to be an account of things-that-really-happened.[12] Such intrusions may be so extreme or numerous that her control is shown itself to be subject to further levels of control, and these to others, etc.—Laurence Sterne's *The Life and Opinions of Tristram Shandy, Gentleman* is a model case—belying the notion that these distinctions can be made with much confidence.

Metalepses may be also effected from the domain of the embedded narrative outward, as in fictions that "break the fourth wall" when a character directly addresses her audience *as* an audience: that is, as conjectural (for her) beings who observe events of the narrative from an external vantage point. Such moments are almost always openly ironic: that is, they suggest that a character is aware that she is an agent operating for the moment in a fictional world—"*this* isn't real, it's only a charade; *you and I*, on the other hand, *are* real"—showing in this a degree of self-awareness that should be impossible. These turnabouts may be disturbing to the spectator precisely in that they subvert her presumption that her self-awareness is of a superior nature (Bertolt Brecht's "theatre of alienation" relies on this effect).

The scope and kind of metalepses are as varied as the literatures in which conditions of narration are textually marked; that is to say, pretty much every text in which we may detect the barest hint of self-awareness. That is, to be sure, a typical characteristic of twentieth- and twenty-first-century narrative arts; the print fiction, film, and new media of the last century abound in examples of level transgressions.[13] In part for this reason, the degree to which the transgressions must be considered deliberate (again, Sterne represents a model) has been questioned by some critics. Wagner, for example, has proposed that some metalepses, rather than being calculated manipulations of narrative conventions, may be evidence of historical and technical shifts in literary method or genre, in which at least some acknowledgement of the conditions of narration is normal rather than exceptional. Genette, who earlier stressed the role of metalepsis as a barometer of narratorial control, has recently (2004) described it as a sign of the "fictionality" of some literary objects, on which basis we detect their difference from those objects that purport to merely show us our world as it is.

This last emphasis, on metalepsis's marking of fictionality by disrupting narrative form, seems to me a useful point of departure for understanding the significance of medial recapture in videogames. Level transgressions, when they are accompanied by evidence of the gameworld's technical bases (*Zork*), or when those bases are forcefully marked (*Valerie*), are the plainest signals of entanglement. Metalepsis, in classical terms, is a purely narrative structure; it may be described without regard for media because it is a trait of conjectural domains that are set apart by literary conventions. Classic (i.e., structuralist) narratology insists on the separability of narrative form and medium (Chatman). But if level transgression should be enacted in such a way that the outermost boundary of the gameworld is breached and the world's rules extended to material conditions of play (*Zork* and *Valerie*, with different degrees of disruption), we confront a new turn on a familiar concept: metalepsis, whatever its degree of violence, must then have a medial basis.[14] Recapture domesticates or reorients the mediality of this sort of metalepsis by precisely extending rules of the gameworld outward, or bringing the outside into the world. The difference is not insignificant, but the results are much the same.

"It was the roach!"[15]

A final example, less wrenching than the first two. The images in Figure 6.3 illustrate adjacent segments of the gameworld of Pulse Entertainment's *Bad Mojo* (1996, 2004).[16] The image on the right shows a portion of the tiled bathroom floor of the seedy dockside bar in which the game takes place. On the left is the corresponding space behind the bathroom wall, occupied by a gruesome rat that the player's avatar, a cockroach, must kill in order to advance in the game. (As shown here, the roach has defeated the rat by pushing a pile of rusty razor blades from the edge of a wall stud behind the medicine cabinet onto the rat, guillotining it. The game's considerable popular and critical success was no doubt due in part to its unapologetic yuck factor.) The spaces are colored in hues of blue, black, and green (the tile, baseboard, and floor of the rathole); brown, black, and gray (the rat and the cockroach, the razor blades); and red (the rat's blood). The textures of the rat's fur and the bathroom floor are notably subtle, given that they are rendered using no more than 256 colors.[17]

This is not unusual for computer games published in the last decade of the twentieth century, as most were designed for video subsystems capable of displaying potentially millions of colors but no more than 256 different colors at one time.[18] Working within such a constrained palette, a talented graphic artist may create surprisingly nuanced surface textures—*Bad Mojo* is a clear demonstration of this—but she will likely have to rely on different subsets of the available color space ("color lookup tables" or CLUTs) in order to capture the nuances of different surfaces of the gameworld.[19] As the number of such surfaces is multiplied within a scene, the difficulty of precisely rendering each increases, as more of the CLUT must be assigned to it, leaving fewer colors available for other textures. If the same object must appear in scenes requiring different CLUTs (for example, the player's avatar or something that it carries), the number of available colors will be further reduced, as those assigned to the object must be reserved for it. Scenes dominated by very different textures may require entirely different CLUTs, forcing a switch as one scene replaces another. This transition must be handled with finesse, as it can easily produce momentary distortions of the image such as posterizing and moiré effects.[20]

Game designers in the 1980s and 1990s dealt with these challenges

Figure 6.3. *Bad Mojo*. Images © Pulse Entertainment, Inc., and Got Game Entertainment, LLC.

by limiting the number of textures in scenes or basing them on overlapping subsets of similar CLUTs. When necessary, changes between CLUTs could be masked by carefully-designed transitions within the gameworld. Jordan Mechner's celebrated murder mystery *The Last Express* (1997) used a rotoscoping technique to simplify the appearance of human actors, preserving much of the available palette for the ornate interiors of the Orient Express, on which most of the game takes place. Restricting avatars' movements to the explicitly closed and segmented space of the train freed designers from having to depict a more varied world (e.g., only one compartment or corridor is visible at a time, landscapes seen through the train's windows appears mostly as green and brown blurs). It allowed them, moreover, to introduce threshold structures—darkened platforms between train cars, doors, curtains—beyond which a change in the CLUT could be made in a form appropriate to the spatial logic of the gameworld. Players passing from a car dominated by one set of textures to a car dominated by a different set were stopped for a brief moment at their intersection, during which time the CLUT was shifted.

The designers of *Bad Mojo* conceived of their game as a sequence of still images representing adjacent segments of the gameworld ("islands of activity"), traversed by a small avatar with a limited range of motion: a cockroach, "driven" by the player over surfaces of a seedy dockyard bar (Figure 6.3). During play, the segments are switched in and out integrally as the roach crawls over the edge of one into the next. It appears free to move in any compass direction—the player uses the arrow keys to direct it—but barriers in the world are often strategically placed to orient the player's exploration of the world. The roach can't crawl over liquids or through flames, for example, or leap over chasms. (It does a few times fall from a height and manages in one segment of the game to hitch a ride on the back of a moth.) The dominant textures of adjacent segments may vary slightly—crossing a floor or a wall involves repeating multiple segments that look much the same—or substantially; the only colors present in every scene are the handful of browns and reds reserved for the roach's body.

This patterning of the gameworld and the actions of the avatar are, in fact, direct analogues of the game's technical bases. The roach is the simplest animated sprite, requiring minimal visual detail or animation. Its limited abilities (it can crawl, it can push small things) provide the perfect alibi for severely restricting an avatar's affordances. The barriers it encounters in the gameworld suggest that there is more to the world than must actually be defined; it's just the case that a roach can't get to those places. The segments of the world—the plainest evidence of the game's data structure—correspond to units of its textbase loaded in and out of memory from the CD-ROM. According to the game's producer, *Bad Mojo* began with a set of technical solutions to performance bottlenecks of Windows 95 and Mac OS 7—a simple sprite, a restricted gameworld, loading whole screens from slow read-only media; its darkly comic, Kafkaesque story emerged from a design *based on the bottlenecks*.[21]

We approach here what is at once the most radical and the most subtle dimension of entanglement and recapture. Where metalepses of the *Zork* or *Valerie* kinds alert us in a punctual way to the gameworld's dependence on its mediality (and vice-versa), that dependence in *Bad Mojo* is more generally marked, in that its effects appear largely unremarkable. That they can convince us that nothing much happened (the roach crawled over the edge of one space into another) when something quite significant in technical terms occurred, or convince us that there is more in the gameworld that meets the eye when there is, exactly, nothing more, demonstrates unequivocally that narrativity cannot be completely separated from mediality. Where narrative patterns leave off and technical patterns take up—the reverse is likely the more decisive direction of influence—is hard to measure. Finding their crossings may become harder as evolving hardware and software are more forgiving of their mutual limits. But we can be sure that the two patterns are at a basic level homologous, and that the playability and very likely the pleasures of a game will depend on the extent to which recapture can manage the expression of this homology. The craftiness of the best game design is that it achieves this in such a way that the player does not much notice it for the time during which it is taking place. (How often should she have to think of backend databases, OS-level functions, and logical color spaces *while playing*?) Semiotic elements and technical elements are specifically combined in the expression of a game (my initial axiom again); recapture moderates effects of combination, supplying thus their motives and their alibis. Which means, crucially, that while its potential operations may be programmed in advance—that being the crux of the game-as-program—recapture happens during play, in the complex digressions and feedback loops that are activated in actual play.

The consequences of this are, I suspect, of considerable significance for game studies. A supposed antagonism of simulation and narration has distracted much of game studies for the better part of a decade.[22] The enervating debates between ludologists and narratologists could be set aside by approaching disruptions between the simulated and the narrated at their medial intersections. In that context, I would argue, simulation would no longer be mistaken for a process in which mediality is irrelevant to play (the characterization of gameworlds as nascent holodecks is the most naïve version of this model). Instead, it could be understood as the game's moment by moment recapture of its technical elements—its way of seeming (for the player) to absolve itself of that contribution to the basic contingency of mediality. Narration is one of the primary operations by which this absolution is achieved within the semiotic plane of play, but is not (as the ludologists have shown) exhaustive of a game's expressivity; extra-narrative elements (mimesis, performance) may also come into force. Recapture opportunistically binds each to the technical plane of play and thereby to the others.

These, it seems to me, are stories we might play with for a while.

Notes

An earlier version of this essay appeared in *Game Studies* 7.1 (2007).

1. *Zork 1* is the first of five text adventure games set in the *Zork* universe, which has also generated two novels and three "choose your own adventure" books for young adults. Its enormous influence on subsequent game design is everywhere apparent. (For simplicity's sake, I do not distinguish in this essay among *text adventure games*, *interactive fictions*, and *videogames*, using in most cases the last term for all three categories of computer-based game.)

2. Here and below I follow terminology proposed by Montfort (26): *commands* are instructions by the player that should effect some change in the gameworld; *directives* effect changes related to operations of the program. Thus, in *Zork*, the verbs "take" and "open" (e.g., "take sceptre" or "open bottle") are commands, and the verbs "save" and "restore," by which the player preserves the current state of the game or restores a saved state, are directives.

3. This observation is elicited by the player typing in the question, "What is a grue?" As Montfort observes (27), the question necessarily invokes a transgressive crossing. No one in the gameworld can know the answer—every adventurer who has met a grue presumably has been eaten—so the description of the grue relayed by the parser must be based on knowledge outside the gameworld, and can only be addressed to the player, not her avatar.

4. See "Profanity Adventures" at *www.monkeon.co.uk/swearadventure* for an amusing investigation of the responses of other text adventure games to obscene commands.

5. A friendly reminder of the correct method of play would be no less transgressive of the gameworld's boundaries. "In one somewhat dramatic moment in *Zork III*, Blank and Lebling poked fun at the strict input requirements placed on users by computers, and in particular the Infocom parser's inability to understand typed input that would be clear to a human but might differ by a single character from what the computer would accept. When a player is near the end of her quest and has encountered the Dungeon Master at a door deep within the complex, the old figure says: 'When you feel you are ready, go to the secret door and SAY "FROTZ OZMOO"! go now!' He starts to leave but turns back briefly and wags his finger in warning. 'Do not forget the double quotes!'" (Montfort 134).

6. In a curiously gruish scene that breaks with the game's FPS scheme, the player is able at one point to see the avatar's obviously male shadow cast across the threshold of a door that opens into a darkened room. When the light switch is flipped on, the shadow disappears, and the avatar is nowhere to be seen.

7. Private correspondence, 1994.

8. The crashing response was removed from the second release of the game after

many players reported it as a bug (Harpold). In *Virtual Valerie: The Director's Cut*, failing to follow Valerie to her bedroom results in the player being transported to the hallway outside her apartment, followed by her slamming the door shut. Any attempt to reenter the apartment prompts disparaging remarks from Valerie, heard through the door, regarding the player's sexual abilities. The only way to reenter the apartment is to manually quit the game and relaunch it.

9. "Chicago" was the Mac operating system font designed by Susan Kare, who was also responsible for many graphic elements of the original Macintosh desktop. Between 1984 and 1997, Chicago was used throughout the Mac OS interface for text in menus, window titles, and buttons.

10. "Lay bare": cf. the related concept of the Russian Formalists, who considered the text's "laying bare of its devices" [*obnazhenie priema*] the hallmark of its literariness. See Erlich 192–97.

11. Classic Infocom text adventures such as *Zork* (and most contemporary interactive fictions) are run within a "Z-machine," a virtual machine capable of interpreting programs written in "Z-code," an especially compact object-oriented language for representing gameworld objects and operations and some system directives. Because Z-code is theoretically machine-independent, games programmed in it can be migrated to different operating systems, requiring only the creation of a Z-code interpreter for each system (Blank and Galley).

12. Genette (*Métalepse* 20–22) describes several examples of metalepses pointing to the narrator's control of the "facts" of historical discourse in the writings of French historian Jules Michelet.

13. See *wikipedia.org*'s several articles on "the fourth wall" and "breaking the fourth wall," which, though typically heavy on recent pop-cultural examples and making few distinctions between practices specific to media, list scores of examples of this species of metalepsis in (print) fiction, film, television, theatre, videogames, comics, and so on.

14. This I take to be an implication of Ryan's description of metalepsis as a stack structure resembling the layers of virtual machines comprising the modern desktop computer. "The stratified architecture of the computer is not in itself metaleptic, no more than the narrative stack of *The Arabian Nights*, but it creates opportunities for metaleptic operations of a technological nature (viruses, programs that operate on themselves), as well as of manipulations that lead to ludic and artistic effects" (217–18).

15. Roger Samms's insane refrain in the final cut-scene of one of four possible endings of *Bad Mojo*. Samms insists that his father's death in an accidental gas explosion was the fault of the roach "driven" by the player. Samms appears to have become mad as a consequence of having had his consciousness merged with that of a roach. It is never in fact made clear that Samms *became* the roach, as the insect is always under the player's control. Samms's refrain marks a frank if subtle admission of metaleptic transgression: it was the *player* who brought about this end of the game.

16. The 2004 *Redux* release of the game differs from the first release in color depth, some full motion video sequences and a new "making of" documentary included with the game CD-ROM.

17. This is true only of the 1996 version. For the 2004 release, game graphics were converted to 24-bit color (see below), and full-motion sequences were remastered at the higher bit depth.

18. Display subsystems of desktop computers store intensities of each of the primary colors (red, green, blue) used to produce the specific color of a screen pixel as eight-bit bytes, requiring thus three bytes of video memory for each pixel (24 bits, $(2^8)^3$ = ~16.8 million different colors, substantially more than the three to ten million different colors between which the human eye is capable of discriminating). In many modern systems, a fourth and sometimes a fifth byte (32-bit, 48-bit) are assigned to an "alpha channel" that specifies pixel translucency. Prior to the 1989 introduction of the Super VGA standard, most display systems used six or fewer bits for each pixel, limiting the number of different colors that might be displayed at one time to no more than 64 (2^6). 8-bit display systems, the baseline for most of the 1990s, used a single byte (8 bits) for each pixel, raising this limit to as many as 256 (2^8). On systems with limited video memory, the pixel resolution of the display device could also determine the available color space, i.e., higher resolutions using more video memory would be limited to fewer colors. The technical bases of color display are in fact more complex than simply scaling bit depth or changing pixel resolution, as some video subsystems use special techniques to increase the apparent color space. For example, most modern LCD systems store only six bits of data for each of the three primary colors (18 bits, $(2^6)^3$ = ~ 260,000 different colors), and use a technique called *dithering* to create the illusion that the logical color space is capable of "millions" of colors. This is because display processes that rapidly change the values of adjacent pixels, such as on-screen video playback, tend to show undesirable artifacts at higher bit depths.

19. A color lookup table matches numeric values specifying the color of each pixel to the levels of red, green, and blue displayed by the monitor. When the number of discrete values is fewer than the maximum number of different colors that may be theoretically displayed, the colors are said to be *indexed* to the CLUT. The term is generally reserved for CLUTs of 256 or fewer colors.

20. These effects may be desirable in some situations. Zach Whalen has brought to my attention the use of color lookup table cycling in some 4-bit color games to create certain visual effects and simple animations.

21. "How do you load these graphically-rich scenes and not have really long load times for the player?" Vinny Carrella, in "The Making of *Bad Mojo*" (on the *Bad Mojo: the Roach Game, Redux* CD-ROM).

22. For recent examples of the terms of this debate, see the essays collected in Wardrip-Fruin and Harrigan, and Harrigan and Wardrip-Fruin. Ryan offers a persuasive rejoinder to the more extreme criticisms of narratological methods.

Works Cited

Blank, Marc, and S. W. Galley. "How to Fit a Large Program Into a Small Machine." *Creative Computing* (July 1980). 80–87.

Caillois, Roger. *Man, Play, and Games.* Trans. Meyer Barash. Urbana: University of Illinois Press, 2001.

Chatman, Seymour. *Story and Discourse: Narrative Structure in Fiction and Film.* Ithaca: Cornell University Press, 1978.

Erlich, Victor. *Russian Formalism: History-Doctrine,* 4th ed. The Hague: Mouton, 1980.

Genette, Gérard. *Fiction et diction.* Paris: Éditions du Seuil, 1991.

___. *Narrative Discourse: An Essay in Method.* Trans. Jane E. Lewin. Ithaca: Cornell University Press, 1980. Trans. of *Figures III* (Paris: Éditions du Seuil, 1972). 65–282.

___. *Narrative Discourse Revisited.* Trans. Jane E. Lewin. Ithaca: Cornell University Press, 1988. Trans. of *Nouveau discours du récit* (Paris: Éditions du Seuil, 1983).

___. *Métalepse: De la figure à la fiction.* Paris: Éditions du Seuil, 2004.

Harpold, Terry. "The Misfortunes of the Digital Text." In *The Emerging Cyberculture: Literacy, Paradigm, and Paradox.* Ed. Stephanie B. Gibson and Ollie O. Oviedo. Cresskill, NJ: Hampton Press, 2000. 129–49.

Harrigan, Pat, and Noah Wardrip-Fruin, eds. *Second Person: Role-Playing and Story in Games and Playable Media.* Cambridge: MIT Press, 2007.

Huizinga, Johan. *Homo Ludens: A Study of the Play Element in Culture.* Boston: Beacon Press, 1971.

Lebling, P. David. "*Zork* and the Future of Computerized Fantasy Simulations." *Byte* (1980). 172–82.

Montfort, Nick. *Twisty Little Passages: An Approach to Interactive Fiction.* Cambridge: MIT Press, 2003.

Ryan, Marie-Laure. *Avatars of Story.* Minneapolis: University of Minnesota Press, 2006.

Stalker, Douglas, ed. *Grue! The New Riddle of Induction.* Chicago: Open Court, 1994.

Wagner, Frank. "Glissements et déphasages: Note sur la métalepse narrative." *Poétique* 130 (2002). 235–53.

Wardrip-Fruin, Noah, and Pat Harrigan, eds. *First Person: New Media as Story, Performance, and Game.* Cambridge: MIT Press, 2004.

Games Cited

Bad Mojo. San Francisco: Pulse Entertainment, 1996.

Bad Mojo: The Roach Game, Redux. Weston, CT: Got Game Entertainment, 2004.

The Last Express. Novato, CA: Brøderbund Software, 1997.

Virtual Valerie. Chicago: Reactor, 1990.

Virtual Valerie: The Director's Cut. Chicago: Reactor, 1992.

Zork I: The Great Underground Empire. Cambridge, MA: Infocom, Inc, 1983.

Part II

Playing *and* the Past
Understanding Media History and Video Games

7
Unlimited Minutes
Playing Games in the Palm of Your Hand

Sheila C. Murphy

You Have One New Message

First off, I have a disclaimer or two. Talking on the phone, whether to accomplish a task or to "keep in touch" with a remote friend or relative, is often an onerous chore. Some people love the phone—Andy Warhol spent much of his adult life on it. He even "wrote" his diary by placing a daily phone call to employee Pat Hackett, who transcribed Warhol's daily activities and expenses into a log that was posthumously published as *The Andy Warhol Diaries*. With the rise of cellular or wireless phone services, people throughout the globe have fallen in love with their phones—buying custom ring tones, expensive phone accessories, or elegant and multifunctional phone devices. Yet, when the phone rings, some—myself included—are filled with a slight dread. Who is calling? Why? How does one cope with the constant interruption and embarrassing ring tones that inevitably play in inopportune times and places? Yet wireless phones are today used both in global capitalist zones, like the United States and Japan, and in developing countries, where mobile phone technologies are easier to disperse among the rural poor. This means that people the world over are walking, talking communications nodules—accessible nearly all the time and, perhaps more crucially for this discussion, rarely without a handheld mobile device. If E.T. were to phone home today, surely his family would have gotten the call more quickly—perhaps on a Bluetooth headset—and they could have text-messaged him to let him know where and when they would pick him up. In mid-2005, as I write this chapter, bands have released albums only as ring tones (in Germany), phones perform a multitude of tasks that go beyond voice transmission, and phone fashions—from pony-hide holsters to fun fur pouches—are ubiquitous if not tasteful. Wireless phones and other handheld technologies like digital music players and personal digital assistants (PDAs) are now fully incorporated into contemporary experience. Literally, phones have become part of our physical existence—a small but palpable presence we carry and wear. This essay explores how these devices function as gaming platforms when their primary functions are not in use, such as during the seemingly unlimited minutes one finds unexpectedly but routinely while waiting out traffic, for an appointment at the doctor's office, or at the bus stop. How can we play our way through the banal and mundane aspects of daily experience? How and why would one play these graphically simple, small-screen games?

The very fact that mobile devices include video games as features speaks to how the telecommunications and computing industries see some continuity between mobile data devices like phones and PDAs and handheld gaming platforms like Nintendo's Game Boy or Sony's PlayStation Portable (PSP). The titles and types of games that are readily available and/or bundled in with phones and PDAs often summon up memories of popular or groundbreaking video games from various moments in the history of video games. Like free, web-based video games that evoke the basic structures of arcade hits (the numerous variations on Taito's *Space Invaders* [1978] come to mind), phone and PDA-based mobile games are intended to reach a wide audience familiar with but not deeply invested in video games. Yet the very inclusion—however cursory—of video games into these non-gaming, handheld, small-screen new media devices indicates how video gaming has become a routine part of early twenty-first-century technologically-enabled living, there to help one occupy "down times" or tune out and mediate one's surroundings, right in the palm of one's hand.

Frequently, the games bundled into palm devices like phones and digital assistants recall the early days of the gaming industry, when simple, iconic colors, shapes and sounds dominated game design. Whether as an explicit remake, like my LG 400's *Pac-Man* port, or in original styles based on early styles, handheld games share the video game visuals and sound from an earlier era (the 1970s and early 1980s) when game aesthetics and interactivity were largely born out of technological necessity: games were efficient in their use of a machine's limited resources. The resulting iconography—*Pac-Man*'s yellow circle with the missing triangle/slice, *PONG*'s acerbic "you lose" tone, *Breakout*'s boldly striped wall—shaped the industry's and the public's imagination of what a video game was to such a strong extent that, in our era of hyper-realistic three-dimensional graphics, a nostalgia has emerged for the flat, monotone, 2D worlds of these early games.

Today, games that are secondary features on a handheld device must share memory and processors with its primary functions. In this sense, then, nostalgic titles and gameplay styles dovetail quite nicely with the dedicated resources that a game takes up on a device with ostensibly more mundane purposes (communications, a calendar, online browsing, etc.) And yet, as I attempt to play *Pac-Man* on my mobile phone while stuck on a train, I can't help think that the experience is a mix of both nostalgia for *Pac-Man's* bright colors and fun soundtrack and the frustration of gaming on a phone—I am all giant thumbs playing my game on tiny, tiny phone keys.

A Confession

While I am a digital media scholar who has mostly studied computers and the Internet—video games are a new area for me—my approach to handheld and phone gaming is informed by my own do-it-yourself media ethics and, quite frankly, by my own "Scrooge McDuck" cheapskate mentality towards technology acquisition. My first mobile phone was a "pay-as-you-go" model purchased mainly as a safety measure when I was driving from Orange County, California, to Seattle in 2001. Once in the land of ample WiFi, I quickly abandoned my low-end cell phone. A few months later I found out I qualified for an AT&T Wireless "employee/family" phone because my roommate worked for the company. This phone was the ultimate "unlimited minutes" model, with free minutes galore (except for AT&T Wireless's then-new upscale mMode mobile Internet services) for about $8 a month. Soon I was using my phone all the time. When I moved to Ann Arbor, that phone service was cancelled, and I later gave the phone away.

Finally, in 2003, I broke down and became an actual wireless customer, but I could not bring myself to buy a high-end phone with multiple capabilities (camera, PDA, gaming), for fear that my new mobile telecom umbilical device would prove even more addictive than my cheap-o employee phone had been. Perhaps my own economic approach to mobile services colors the questions I want to address, but—despite my reluctance to become a mobile media user myself—I have been continuously intrigued by mobile gaming. When I first became curious about mobile game companies, it was a result of conversations I had had with software developers at Seattle-area start-ups like UIEvolution that were hoping to translate Japanese mobile gaming to the US market.

The Device That Ate Everything

Since my initial interest in mobile phone multifunctionality and gaming three-and-a-half years ago, the industry and technology have changed dramatically. Recent reports in *The Economist* and elsewhere have claimed that mobile phones, unlike computers or Internet technologies, are poised to close the "digital divide" between poor nations that lack a technological infrastructure and first-world countries that drive techno-logical development. "Mobile phones," reports the *Economist*, bridge the technological gap because they "do not rely on a permanent electricity supply and can be used by people who cannot read or write" ("The Real Digital Divide" 11). Furthermore, users' attitudes to mobile phones are significantly different from attitudes towards other digital media. Again quoting the *Economist*, "Mobile phones are a uniquely personal form of technology, thanks in large part to their mobility" ("The Device That Ate Everything").

In recent years, the mobile phone has become "the device that ate ev-erything": phone technology has been combined with digital photogra-phy in camera phones, with handheld computers/personal digital assis-tants in devices like the Treo or Blackberry that function as phone PDAs, and with handheld gaming in high-end devices like Nokia's much hyped but disappointing N-Gage.[1] Multifunction phone devices in development include a phone/music player that Apple is co-developing with Motorola and a plug-in phone adapter that Sony is working on for its PSP handheld mobile media and gaming device. Yet, as gaming scholar Tracy Fullerton suggests, this is a kind of Frankensteinian multifunctionality.[2] Phones may be able to act as handheld games, personal digital assistants, music players, or other devices, but these functions have a push-me-pull-you relationship with phone functionality. For instance, the Nokia N-Gage phone model, designed as a gaming system and phone, functions either in game mode or phone mode but not both simultaneously. So, this is a single-channel kind of multifunctionality, since one cannot game and phone together. Instead, one function might interrupt the other, or in some cases rule out the other function altogether.

This desire for phones that can do more can be traced back to wireless developments in Japan in the 1990s, when wireless phones began to func-tion as web browsers capable of performing a multitude of tasks. Fur-thermore, Japanese consumers used their phones to buy movie tickets, lattes, and other sundries, all of which could be added to a wireless phone bill. This popular iMode service, later exported into American culture as mMode by AT&T Wireless, treats the phone as a handheld tool—a calendar, assistant, guide, and communications device. The drive to expand upon what wireless phones could do happened at the same time as the push to make those phones smaller, lighter, and easier to operate. These competing priorities and the different ways that specific local and national markets use phones result in different kinds of lifestyle phones for business, basic, and youth/teen users, as well as music phones, game phones, and outdoor phones for niche markets.

Yet this trend towards multifunctional phones should not be seen as an isolated or even exceptional model. The lure of the "all-in-one" device has been a motivating factor in technological development since at least the postwar era, when appliance manufacturers and the nascent television industry linked TV to eating (consumption) and various forms of private and public leisure. In the "new media" era, devices and software that promise to function as computers/televisions/game-units/phones are prominent and usually become collectors' items (like Apple's black-case TV/computer models of the early 1990s).[3] When the mobility and size of handheld devices are taken into account, it is unsurprising that media convergence is considered a key approach for technological development. Yet, at the same time that phones that could "do it all" hit the market, another approach has more quietly become a ubiquitous technology: the portable, handheld hard drive (also known as a flash or universal drive.[4] Here, however, the paradigm is built around a device that can *store* it all—not something that can *do* it all. As media forms become more mobile and fluid, and as they address consumers in increasingly individuated ways, surely our needs to store the media we consume and use will grow—probably at a much faster rate than our desire to access all media through one mega-device. Nokia and other manufacturers still opt to build all-in-one devices, crucially unaware of consumers' desires to have media that is both immediate and transparent and to use that media in hypermediated ways, with as much technology and content as possible.[5]

The incorporation of games into other electronic devices speaks to how video games have infiltrated our contemporary experiences of transportation, temporality (lag time, down time, found time, "free" time), and communication. These nostalgic gaming experiences draw upon a range of cultural influences but also bypass linguistic and regional differences through the iconography, simplicity, and interactivity common to mobile games.

The Next "Next Big Thing"

The launch of the PlayStation Portable, combined with the sheer numbers of mobile phone users and the investment of major video game developers like Electronic Arts and Square-Enix in handheld gaming systems and software, marked mobile phone and handheld gaming as the 2005 version of the ever-elusive "next big thing" on the technological horizon. Or, to put it in the words of Robert Tercek, founder of GDC Mobile at the 2005 Game Developers Conference: "Last year, over 170 million people downloaded games to their mobile phones. In 2005 this number will triple. Are you participating in the fastest-growing sector of interactive entertainment?"[6] Or, as one GDC attendee later told me:

> Massively multiplayer online role playing games (MMORPGs) are still showing some growth, although there are only so many gamer hours in the day and I suspect that they are already cannibalizing from each other. Mobile ad-hoc games[7] were very much in evidence, at least as far as "it's the next big thing" buzz.[8]

Yet, in my own analysis of handheld gaming on mobile phones, PDAs, and MP3 players, I find I am drawn *not* to the precisely rendered, high-end multiplayer mobile games but to the low-end ones: the games prepackaged in with other devices and games played by casual gamers rather than aficionados in search of the next big thing. In short, games whose major function is killing time and defeating boredom.

These are games that, through elegant design and often abstract imagery, allow users to "tune out" their surroundings. In doing so, they necessarily shift their relationship to the space surrounding them in much the same way that the Sony Walkman created urban nomads. In his analysis of the spaces where one encounters video games, Raiford Guins discusses what he calls "threshold gaming." He describes threshold gaming as "the transitory, nondescript and virtually invisible space of the threshold game. Threshold games are random: in bars/pubs, in restaurants as cabinet and cocktail games, garages and laundrettes, airports, bowling alleys, cinemas, and in liquor stores" (204). Such spaces are key to understanding contemporary experience. Or, as Anna McCarthy puts it in *Ambient Television*:

> The routine implantation of screens in transit stations, banks, and waiting rooms—the precise arenas in which these banal and repetitive gestures take place—would seem to be a crucial phenomenon for

assessing the nature and direction of a politics of public space and the everyday. (7)

With mobile devices, both casual and dedicated gamers can carry this "threshold" experience with them, potentially translating any quotidian space into a gaming space and any unexpected blocks of available time into game time.

When I polled the forty college students in my "Video Game as Culture/Form" class about mobile phones and handheld gaming devices, I was surprised by their answers. While some of these students (about 40%) would willingly purchase high-end, dedicated handheld gaming decks like the Nintendo DS and the Sony PSP, virtually *all* of these students were unwilling to pay extra for a mobile phone designed to be both a gaming platform and telecommunications device, like Nokia's N-Gage. Nor would they pay much for downloadable game software titles. But the most surprising thing I learned from them was that *every* student in the class, including the casual gamers or students uninterested in console systems and PC games, regularly plays the preloaded games on their phones, iPods or PDAs.

Incoming Call: Telephonic Histories

What I argue here about mobile phone and data devices owes much to the history of telecommunications. A good deal of that history occurred prior to the personal computing revolution of the 1980s, and the large-scale changes that supercomputers and mainframes had upon the communications industry both prior to and after the end-user's experience of telephony was linked with computing technologies. In the mid-1990s, in an essay on telephone party lines in domestic environments, film critic B. Ruby Rich declared, "Today, of course, our national economy and communications systems have become totally centered upon the telephone as delivery apparatus" (225). Rich's assertion does not seem especially radical today, but compared with the work of other telephony scholars it is a reminder that one cannot overlook even the most banal and ubiquitous technologies of daily life. Critics like Jeffrey Sconce, Tom Standage, and Avital Ronell (perhaps the most famous of phone scholars) have all drawn attention to how phone use became normalized and accepted as a normative social technology (see the numerous references to phone usage in any etiquette book of the past fifty years). Yet using phones to game means leaving the direct voice and text networking capabilities aside in order to play game software. So, gaming on a phone or handheld device is an against-the-grain use of this technology: while not socially radical or disruptive, handheld gaming on non-gaming devices does repurpose the device, forcing it to function outside of its normal duties.

Just Killing Time (and Winning Games)

While my student poll is admittedly a small and informal sample, it shows that mobile gaming not only reaches a different gamer and non-gamer audiences, but also that such gaming has the distinct tactile and visual pleasures of small-screen, handheld media that serve the specific purpose of filling users' "found time." *Arkanoid* (1986), one popular title ported to a handheld operating system, has a handheld clone version that is even titled *AnotherBall: Timekiller Edition* (2003). While my comments here can only gesture toward the larger cultural impact of mobile phone (and PDA) gaming, I hope to discuss briefly the tactility of mobile gaming, along with a consideration of the miniaturized, low-end aesthetics of such games and the way these games reconfigure the pockets of unexpected, otherwise "empty" time that is part and parcel of contemporary mediated experience.

Media theorist Paul Virilio has exhaustively described the way that electronic technologies have changed our notions of time, speed, and distance. In his 1997 book *Open Sky*, a volume that ominously opens with a declaration about temporality ("One day the day will come when the day will not come"), Virilio describes at length how electronic technologies force a reconsideration of time, space, and experience. He writes that we have reached a state of a

> transapparent horizon spawned by telecommunications, that opens up the incredible possibility of a "civilization of forgetting," a *live* (live-coverage) society that has no future and no past, since it has no extension and no duration, a society intensely present here and there at once—in other words, *telepresent to the whole world.* (25)

Yet, even in our real-time, live, and technologically advanced culture, everyday experience is often punctuated by time lags and moments of unexpected "found time" (such as waiting for an appointment or between classes, sitting in traffic, or in some places, waiting out traffic). These found times are not shaped by speed or instantaneous communication, the factors Virilio contends are dominant temporal structures today. Instead, these found times often seem lengthy and empty—they are unexpected moments that don't serve a predetermined purpose. These times are, therefore, ideally suited to mobile gaming. Some game manufacturers even address this temporal aspect in their promotional materials, like this description of *AnotherBall* (2003), an *Arkanoid*-style mobile phone game:

> Not for the airport—you can miss your plane.
> Not for the boring meetings—you can miss your boss applying [*sic*] to you.
> Not for the train or in the bus—you can miss your stop. (Kyocera)

Apple echoes these sentiments in its description of the game "extras" on the iPod:

> You know what they say about all work and no play. Navigate to Extras and you'll find Games: Music Quiz, Solitaire, Brick and Parachute—four popular games you can play anywhere, like when you're waiting for the movie to start at the multiplex. (iPod)

In addition to fitting into short, unscheduled blocks of time, mobile game design is influenced by the small size of most mobile device screens and an imperative (in most cases) to make visually minimalist games with simple game controls. The elegance of such design is apparent in the iPod *Brick* game, in which one acts as a block on the screen, rebounding a pixelated ball against a wall of blocks. These limited graphics make even subtle aspects of game play seem dynamic. In awarding their 2004 Mobies (mobile game awards), *GameSpot* stated their criteria for judging games this way:

> This type of game [*Topolon*, a Japanese game] is supposedly the mobile ideal—something that's totally infectious and playable for anyone with a mobile phone (read: everyone), without being state of the art in graphics, sound, or control.

Unfortunately, this ideal has very rarely been realized in a mobile game to this point; many games aspire to the principle without actually having an idea of commensurate quality. This "mobile ideal" interestingly bypasses the constant push for 3D photorealistic game aesthetics (or convincing realism in games with stylized graphics) in favor of clear, minimal design. This kind of abstraction is well-suited to handheld devices, especially those that do not have high resolution or well-lit screens, and clearly looks backwards toward a nostalgic aesthetic of game play.

"Taco Phone" or Mobile Game Device?

While *GameSpot* recognizes the "mobile ideal" as an addictive game for all players, mobile phone companies like Nokia have attempted to define the mobile ideal as realistic, 3D game play on a device like the N-Gage or N-Gage QD.[9] The hard lesson that Nokia (and Cingular, the US distributor of the N-Gage) has learned is that a multifunctional device must do at least *one* of its functions well. One user review posted online of the original N-Gage stated, "It's the most cumbersome cell phone you'll ever use, as you're forced to hold it the slim way." In order to see and use an N-Gage, I had to go to multiple Cingular stores—the company does not even keep a demo phone on the sales floor—and I found that the price of the phone (with contract) has dropped from its initial 2003 base price of $299.99 to $49.99 (after rebate). It would seem that, despite the popularity of mobile gaming in Japan and Europe, the N-Gage doesn't quite fit the needs of US cell phone users, who are more likely to play preloaded mobile games or, for some, to download titles from the Web that are rudimentary versions of video, tabletop, or card games that one can still enjoy on the small screen of a mobile phone and in the short gaps of time one has for mobile gaming. Once again, time and size prove to be key elements of this form of gaming, and the results "look backward."

The small screen size of most mobile devices (at least in the United States) also means that mobile games are miniatures, endearing in their size and scale. In *The Poetics of Space*, Gaston Bachelard discusses the *preciousness* of smallness and the ways that miniature representations often defy logic:

> The cleverer I am at miniaturizing the world, the better I possess it. But in doing this, it must be understood that values become condensed and enriched in miniature. Platonic dialectics of large and small do not suffice for us to become cognizant of the dynamics of miniature thinking. One must go beyond logic in order to experience what is large in what is small. (150)

Mobile miniatures, then, especially those that we hold in the palm of our hand, are "condensed" games that allow users to "possess" the game world. Writing on abstraction in video games, Mark J. P. Wolf claims, "The simplified versions of situations found in video games allow players to feel a sense of order and understanding that may be more difficult to find in their own real lives" (64). Mobile games, with their miniature graphics and game play, seem to offer an immediate "sense of order" and mastery for gamers. Perhaps this is why some of the earliest video games are regularly reproduced in handheld versions? One game in particular seems to be ported to most mobile platforms in one version or another. The game, of course, is *Breakout*, a *PONG*-like video game and arcade game published by Atari in 1976.

Both Nolan Bushnell and Steve Jobs have, over the years, claimed to have invented the *Breakout* wall-rebounding concept (Kent 71). Jobs and Steve Wozniak (Woz), then developing the Apple II in their spare time, worked as developers for the original Atari version of *Breakout*. Atari founder Bushnell pushed the developers to create a game that used the smallest number of integrated circuit chips possible. Wozniak came up with a design that cut the number of chips for the game down significantly, but none of the other Atari designers were able to duplicate (and hence manufacture on a bigger scale) Woz's version of the game (Kent 71–72). Steve Jobs, representing himself as co-designer with Woz on the project, received a hefty bonus for creating a game with a small number of circuits. Jobs then misled Wozniak, giving him a small fraction of the actual Atari bonus. As former Atari executive Al Alcorn puts it, "That was the beginning of the end of the friendship between Woz and Jobs" (Kent 73).

While this bit of industry lore makes for a compelling story, another more crucial technological and aesthetic story is contained within it: from its inception, *Breakout*'s simple but addictive game play and design were motivated by a need to make a game that was cheap to produce and made economical use of the available technology.[10] Such strategies naturally breed imitation. Within its first year of distribution, *Breakout* was already being copied by arcade competitors in Italy and Japan (Kent 61, 75). This was the beginning of countless *Breakout* imitators—from Taito's popular *Arkanoid* series to *Blockbreaker Deluxe* (2004) and *Brick*. Mobile phone versions or variations on the game are many, perhaps because phones can best support a game that is simplistic in its design and requires only a limited amount of resources to run. In this instance, the retro-aesthetics of *Breakout*-style games are motivated by both technological limitations and nostalgia, unlike other emergent retro-tech trends like analog handset adapters for the hipster "Pokia" set.[11]

I now want to shift gears a bit—away from the appearance, setting, and size of mobile games—and discuss what happens when one plays a game in the palm of your hand. In her essay, "It's All about the *Fit*: The

Hand, Mobile Screenic Device and Tactile Vision," Heidi Cooley argues that mobile screenic devices (MSDs, her term for "mobile phones, palm computing devices and handheld electronic organizers") require users to develop a "fit" with the technology—a "particular relationship between a hand and an MSD, which opens onto a relation of interface through which vision becomes and remains tactile" (137). Cooley claims that a bond must develop between user and device for the technology to be functional because "a 'blending of hand and wrist movements' allows the 'hand to mold itself to the shape of an object being palpated or grasped'" (137, quoting Bejjani and Landsmeer). This theory of *fit* allows for the irreducibility of both hand and technology: once bonded through the user/technology bond of *fit*, the intentionality of the user and the task-oriented qualities of the MSD become secondary to the tactile and kinetic relationship between hand and device. Writing about cinema, film theorist Vivian Sobchack characterizes this embodied response and its visceral relationship to vision/visuality as "somatic intelligence."[12] Sobchack's arguments about the phenomenology of media are helpful in understanding how the mobile media forms we keep in our pockets, incorporate into our personhood, and personalize with names, backgrounds, "skins," hand-knit cases, and holsters are entwined with our own corporeality.[13] She argues that one must understand the embodied relationship that spectators have with cinema (or, in her other work, how computer users make sense of the screen interface):

> Subjective matter as we ourselves are, our lived bodies sensually relate to "things" on the screen and find them sensible in a pre-personal and global way that grounds later identifications that are more discrete and localized.

Both Sobchack and Cooley call for us to recognize not only the pervasiveness of mediated experience today but also to understand how users create a "fit" between themselves and their devices, and how technologies become incorporated into our sensorium as devices that we use by rote and that draw us in, even on their small and sometimes limited screens. These are not just games in threshold spaces: phones and music players allow users to create nearly imperceptible barriers between ourselves and the outside, and zones of private experience within public space—ways of turning off the world by turning on the game.

Notes

This essay is inspired by and owes much to my students in "Video Games as Culture/ Form" at the University of Michigan. They've taught me a lot, though I still find viewing *The Wizard* an unsettling experience.

1. *The Economist* reports that "smart phone" sales outpace the sales of PDAs and camera-phones sell more briskly than digital cameras ("The Device That Ate Everything," 9). This same issue refers to wireless phones as "the device that ate everything."
2. Conversation, 18–19 March 2005.
3. See my forthcoming book, *iLook: Visuality and Experience in Digital Culture*.
4. Arguably the Apple iPod is an example of a portable drive, though its operating system allows it to function in ways that most flash drives do not.
5. See Bolter and Richard Grusin's arguments about remediation, immediacy and hypermediacy.
6. Robert Tercek, "GDC Mobile 2006 Wrap Up." Game Developers Conference, San Jose, CA, 22 March 2006.
7. Mobile ad-hoc group gaming is where players form their own wireless local network.
8. Tom Perrine, personal e-mail, 14 March 2005.
9. N-Gage was first launched in 2003 and retooled in 2004. Not all of the features on the N-Gage QD are new additions—some of the original model's functions have been eliminated in the 2004 edition: the phone no longer functions as an MP3 player, it doesn't have a built-in radio and, most significantly, the QD is a dual-band phone (the original N-Gage was a tri-band phone), meaning it is not able to operate in as many global wireless markets as the tri-band's multiple frequencies allowed.
10. The original arcade version of *Breakout* used a black-and-white monitor as a display, but the screen was overlaid with tinted transparencies, which made the bricks appear to be different colors.
11. Custom-produced adapters allow one to connect an analog phone handset to a mobile phone. Initially produced by independent outlets, the fad has grown and now Boost! Mobile, a major UK and US cellular carrier aimed at the youth market, offers retro analog handset adapters for some of its phones. See *Pokia.com*.
12. Sobchack: "However, rather than providing the mediating bridge between the image and its comprehension by the viewer's lived body, signifier and psyche just reproduce the binary split between image and body and thus they still cannot account for the *somatic intelligibility* of the film image or a *somatic intelligence* of the spectator's body that is more than primitive reflex."
13. See the broad range of products sold to contain iPods and mobile phones: rubber skins, crystal-embedded pocket-purses, and even handknit iPod "thongs" that provide a tactile holder for the device. Apple even sells iPod "socks" under their own brand.

Works Cited

Bachelard, Gaston. *The Poetics of Space*. Trans. Maria Jolas. Boston: Beacon, 1994.

Bolter, Jay David, and Richard Grusin. *Remediation: Understanding New Media*. Cambridge: MIT Press, 1999.

Cooley, Heidi. "It's All about the *Fit*: The Hand, Mobile Screenic Device and Tactile Vision." *Journal of Visual Culture* 3.2 (2004). 133–55.

GameSpot. "Mobile Game of the Year." *www.gamespot.com* (2004). Accessed 5 March 2005.

Guins, Ray. "Intruder Alert! Intruder Alert! Video Games *in* Space." *Journal of Visual Culture* 3.2 (August 2004).

Hackett, Pat, ed. *The Andy Warhol Diaries*. New York: Warner, 1989.

iPod. *www.apple.com*. Accessed 7 March 2005.

Kent, Steven L. *The Ultimate History of Video Games: From Pong to Pokémon and beyond . . . the story behind the craze that touched our lives and changed the world*. Roseville, CA: Prima Publishing, 2001.

Kyocera. "AnotherBall: The Time Killer Edition." *store.kyocera-wireless.com* (1 October 2004). Accessed 5 March 2005.

McCarthy, Anna. *Ambient Television: Visual Culture and Public Space*. Durham: Duke University Press, 2001.

Murphy, Sheila. *iLook: Visuality and Experience in Digital Culture* (forthcoming).

Pokia.com. Accessed 6 March 2005.

"The Real Digital Divide." *The Economist* (10 March 2005).

Rich, B. Ruby. "The Party Line." In *Processed Lives: Gender and Technology in Everyday Life*. Eds. Jennifer Terry and Melodie Calvert. New York: Routledge, 1997. 225.

Ronell, Avital. *The Telephone Book: Technology, Schizophrenia and Electric Speech*. Lincoln: University of Nebraska Press, 1989.

Sconce, Jeffrey. *Haunted Media: Electronic Presence from Telegraphy to Television*. Durham: Duke University Press, 2000.

Sobchack, Vivian. Carnal Thoughts: Embodiment and Moving Image Culture. Berkeley: University of California Press, 2004. "What My Fingers Knew" also available at *www.sensesofcinema.com*.

Standage, Tom. "The Mother of All Networks." In *The Victorian Internet*. New York: Walker, 1998.

"The Device That Ate Everything." *The Economist Technology Quarterly* (12 March 2005). 9.

Wolf, Mark J. P. "Abstraction in the Video Game." In *The Video Game Theory Reader*. Eds. Mark J. P. Wolf and Bernard Perron. New York: Routledge, 2003. 47–66.

Virilio, Paul. *Open Sky*. Trans. Julie Rose. London: Verso, 1997.

Games Cited

AnotherBall: Timekiller Edition (mobile). San Jose, CA: Paragon, 2003.
Arkanoid (arcade). Tokyo: Taito, 1986.
Blockbreaker Deluxe (mobile). Paris, France: Gameloft, 2004.
Breakout (arcade). Sunnyvale, CA: Atari, 1976.
Brick (iPod). Sunnyvale, CA: Apple, 2001.
Pac-Man (arcade). Tokyo: Namco, 1979
PONG. Sunnyvale, CA: Atari, 1972
Space Invaders (arcade). Tokyo: Taito, 1978.

8

Visions and Revisions of the Hollywood Golden Age and America in the Thirties and Forties

Prince of Persia and *Crimson Skies*

Andrew E. Jankowich

Games such as *Crimson Skies: High Road to Revenge* (2003) and *Prince of Persia: Sands of Time* (2003) are strongly informed by the spirit of Hollywood Golden Age films of the 1930s and 1940s. Employing the nostalgic conventions of films of the period like their "breezy" tone, *Crimson Skies* and *Prince of Persia* explore potentially controversial situations unusual to gaming. Furthermore, the use of Hollywood tropes and conventions in the video game format help broaden the game medium by supporting new subject matter and new genres. Although developers tend to focus on increasing realism in play and graphics, it is significant to see that including elements of unreality such as those taken from Golden Age films can improve gameplay and allow developers to explore unusual subjects and forms.

In the 1930s and 1940s, Hollywood film was in what has been described as its "Golden Age" with the studios releasing numerous titles each year (Thomson 198–99). Notable films of the era include titles that have become staples of American culture such as *Dracula* (1931), *Frankenstein* (1931), *Duck Soup* (1933), *King Kong* (1933), *Snow White and the Seven Dwarfs* (1937), *Stagecoach* (1939), *Gone with the Wind* (1939), *His Girl Friday* (1940), *The Maltese Falcon* (1940), *Pinocchio* (1940), *The Wizard of Oz* (1939), *Citizen Kane* (1941), *Casablanca* (1942), and *My Darling Clementine* (1946). Many of the typical and still-influential genres of Hollywood films developed in this period: Westerns, gangster movies, film noir, Hollywood musicals, screwball comedies, and Disney cartoons. Yet filmmaking in the period was also constrained by the enactment of moral restrictions like the Production Code (Thomson 142–43). Despite moral restrictions, a number of highly successful films were developed within those constraints, as the list above suggests. While Hollywood's Golden Age is now itself a historical genre, the film genres developed during this period continue to exist, being imitated, subverted, analyzed, and deconstructed in later American films and in the films of other countries. For example, Roman Polanski reexamined film noir's private detective in the context of 1960s cynicism and paranoia by making *Chinatown* (1974) a historical film rather than a contemporary fantasy. Francois Truffaut also recast the noir film through the French New Wave in *Shoot the Piano Player* (1960). A similar investigation of genre is effective in using film elements in games. In particular, the genre of historical adventure films, as exemplified by a film like *The Adventures of Robin Hood* (1938), is refigured in *Prince of Persia* and *Crimson Skies*. *Prince of Persia* and *Crimson Skies* gain power and scope by engaging and employing elements of Golden Age film.

Ubisoft's *Prince of Persia* employs a variety of indirect but highly evocative references to Golden Age film. Period works are evoked through the use of visuals and character actions as well as through narration and tone. Significant episodes of the game involve the Prince engaging in acrobatic feats to travel through a ruined palace, which reference swashbucklers like *The Adventures of Robin Hood*, *Captain Blood* (1935), and *The Thief of Baghdad* (1940). Furthermore, the Prince's superior social standing is established through his calm, bemused narration of the game, flavored with an aristocratic British accent that suggests the Hollywood trope of British "refinement." A classic cinema romance supports the adventure as the Prince finds and loses and finds the Sultan's daughter amidst the chaos of a potentially apocalyptic event. By using these traditional narrative devices, the game is able to immerse players in an unusual setting for video games, a Middle Eastern world, albeit an ancient one.

The player in *Prince of Persia* follows the quest of the eponymous prince to halt the destruction that he has unwittingly unleashed when he is manipulated into using the mystical Sands of Time. The Sands of Time are a fantasy element, creating the apocalyptic crisis that drives the game by turning almost all the living things in the castle to monstrous sand creatures. However, the Sands also give the Prince mystical visions and the ability to manipulate time. Through the course of the game the Prince must travel through the Maharajah's sprawling castle, overcoming traps, fighting with people and creatures that have been horribly transformed by the Sands, and gradually developing an alliance with the maharajah's daughter Farah.

Microsoft's *Crimson Skies* sets its story explicitly in the 1930s era while employing a Hollywood Golden Age tone. In *Crimson Skies*, the United States has fragmented into competing, autonomous regions that have severed ground ties like railroads between each other, encouraging a greater emphasis on flying than existed in the actual United States of the period (Huseman). Territories are "ruled by gangs of air pirates and militia and their planes and zeppelins" (Cieniawa). The player takes the role of Nathan Zachary who, having lost his fortune in the 1929 stock market crash, becomes a roving air pirate in conflict with other gangs and groups (Knudson).

In *Crimson Skies*, the alternate history 1930s United States is repeatedly reinforced by combining elements from period movies and serials to create a visually persuasive fantasy. The game's collage of movie elements produces a film that has never been seen before but that recalls and draws an archetypal authority from a variety of cinematic predecessors. With its pilot's eye view of cities and landscapes, *Crimson Skies* focuses the player on the cockpit perspective that most people will only have encountered in movies. The use of persuasively detailed images of unlikely aircraft like autogyros draws on classic movie tools: by using realistic presentations of fanciful aircraft, the game brings the player into the filmic world of special effects that endeavors to present impossible or improbable objects in a realistic manner. Realistic surface presentation helps to suspend disbelief over the airworthiness of the autogyros and rear-propeller fighter planes. Throughout the game, new environments are presented that recall movie sets from genres of the period: an Old West mine that alludes to Westerns, a mysterious tropical island typical of adventure and horror tales, and skyscraper-filled cities out of film noir. The game allows the player to tour around the sets, providing opportunities to appreciate the vistas and settings that the coding has achieved and extending the range of the film set to an immersive world.

The setting of this game's world is interesting because it makes use of the common science-fiction subgenre of alternate history, which appears infrequently in video games. While games set in near-future dystopias or in post-apocalyptic settings are almost as common in video games as in science fiction literature, alternate history is a far less frequent theme.

Prince of Persia and *Crimson Skies* can be considered exercises in indirect nostalgia. Their references are indirect in that they refer to past works and consist of fairly inconcrete characteristics such as style and tone but also employ elements of direct reference that have been noted by critics. For example, in *Prince of Persia*, the traps in the maharajah's castle have been described as "reminiscent of designs in old movies" (Xbox Solution) while *Crimson Skies*' soundtrack employs "orchestral tunes that fit like a glove for a 1930s-esque setting" (Cieniawa). Other references and comparisons, such as the use of an acrobatic hero reminiscent of the physically adept protagonist of a historical adventure film like *The Adventures of Robin Hood*, provide interesting visions and re-visions of Hollywood films of the Golden Age. Compared to more explicitly violent games like *Grand Theft Auto: Vice City* (2002), these games employ a more indirect or playful approach to violence that can be seen as reminiscent of the post-Code propriety of Hollywood. While *Crimson Skies* uses a version of a 1930s setting, *Prince of Persia* uses more indirect methods to refer to films of the era, adopting visual styles and signals from its movies without directly imitating a particular title.

Cinematic Visual Cues in Prince of Persia

The most immediately apparent reference to film in *Prince of Persia* comes through the visual presentation. The player in *Prince of Persia* is immediately introduced to the cinematic perspective. As in other games, movie-like cutscenes that set the storyline and advance the story outside of gameplay are prominently used in *Prince of Persia*, but what is especially noticeable is the cinematic quality of the graphics throughout, resulting in "silky-smooth motion" for the Prince's actions (Casamassina). The choice of third-person play makes the Prince's movement through the game like that of an actor moving through a set, captured with a cinematographer's eye and designed with the visual flair of a film art director. Light is used effectively, not only providing game cues and setting mood but also creating the rich visual environment of film.

The visual environment is grounded in the use of persuasive detail and dramatic vistas present throughout the gameworld that make it seem as much like the product of movie set design as computer code. The elaborate palace with its mixture of opulence and menace seems to become a character in its own right in the way that emblematic movie sets can, like that of Xanadu in *Citizen Kane*.

The simultaneity of visual realism and fantasy can be seen as derived from film's continuing attempt through special effects to make the fantastical persuasively real. The level and extent of the detail in the palace provide a particularly realistic setting for the fantastical elements that occupy the player-protagonist. Palace walls feature bas-relief carvings, rugs have geometric patterns, windows have wrought-iron screens, and mosaics decorate walls even in seemingly out-of-the way corridors. In addition, the plethora of details provides rich visual cues that firmly establish the mythical Eastern world of the game. Each element works in conjunction with the others to provide a well-established foundation that immerses the player in the game world.

The artificial light of computer code flickers and shines with a cinematographical fluency throughout the game world. As the player leads the Prince through game time, the sky turns from day to pink sunset to night, providing another subtle indication of cinematic realism. Light also provides clues and visual drama in its varying treatment. Light from different sources is treated differently. The light shining in through a window creates a different mood in the room than that from a flaming brazier hanging and swaying above a hall. Light pouring down from an unseen overhead source is used to provide atmosphere and a sense of direction within the labyrinthine palace. The light leaking out of arched stone windows across a dark courtyard of the palace is just one of many ways in which light is used as a visual cue to encourage the player to move dynamically through the landscape.

Multiple and cinematic perspectives are frequently used to provide powerful and filmic scenes in which the player can act. The sense of a robust game world is established by camera-like shots showing battle scenes at angles that maximize dramatic perspective for the player. The angled shots serve multiple purposes by emphasizing the visual appeal of the palace's large opulent chambers while reminding the player of the tactical advantages of movement. Yet elsewhere the visual beauty of the palace is established seemingly more for aesthetic than functional grounds. When the Prince makes his way into the open air, the views of the expansive palace and grounds are so striking they seem to encourage repose in the player so that the scenes can be maintained on screen rather than receding into the past.

In addition, game play is presented in scenarios with clearly established perspectives that emphasize the visual nature of the scene with the care of a film. *Prince of Persia* uses setting cinematically, moving from the confined passages of the palace out to the exuberant and dramatic palace grounds that provide richly visual layers of landscape backgrounds. *Prince of Persia* creator Jordan Mechner is also a documentary filmmaker who attended film school; renowned game designer Will Wright noted the cinematic feel of Mechner's early work (Keighley). *Prince of Persia*'s relationship to film has continued with its designer's commission to write a screenplay based on the game (Bramwell).

The game also treats time in a way that supports a cinematic feel by giving the player a sense of directorial control. *Prince of Persia* extends time up to and beyond the passive experience of time for the viewer in film, where time is controlled by the authority of the director. The game allows the player a degree of control through an hourglass device that measures the Prince's developing ability to manipulate and reverse time by replaying events and, in a sense, supplying an alternate cut. *Prince of Persia* also allows the player to glimpse the future through flash-forward quick-cut prophetic films that help to guide strategy by providing a storyboard of sorts for the upcoming level.

Indeed, the emphasis on a cinematic feel is so strong that it sometimes undermines the gameplay. The forced camera angles at various points in the game, such as when the Prince must enter confined spaces, require a disconcerting adjustment of the player's orientation to the game controls in order to continue moving on the same plane once the forced viewpoint has shifted. Similarly, the forced perspectives necessary to maintain cinematic distance can induce eyestrain and obscure details, leading to player mistakes. Furthermore, the player can take advantage of the cinematic camera by choosing to switch perspectives manually from a close-up first person to a more long-distance view, but the default view that the game offers tends to emphasize climactic moments in the narrative and suffuses the game with a film-like sense of epic grandiloquence that is reinforced through the game's use of voice-over narration and witty dialogue.

Part of *Prince of Persia's* charm comes from its skillful use of narration and dialogue, a feature that in many games is not an asset. *Prince of Persia* employs extradiegetic narration as the Prince introduces the player to the game, sets the tone, establishes the character prior to gameplay, and continues to comment on action and events throughout the game. By explicitly framing the game as a story, the Prince's narration suggests metafictional playfulness, but it also succeeds in gaining a firm control of the game tone by establishing an authoritative dominance. *Prince of Persia* even successfully extends this control to the regretful tone of the narrating Prince pleading with the player not to end the game. The Prince's narration even seeks to control the player's errors in gameplay. The Prince will complain, "Wait, that's not what happened," when the player's bungling ends the "story" of the game prematurely. In order to "hear" the whole tale of the game, the player must submit to the Prince's control of the narrative.

The Prince's voice is also used effectively in the dialogue between the Prince and the primary female character, Farah, which is reminiscent of 1930s and 1940s cinema. Critics have acknowledged the superior quality of the writing and acting in *Prince of Persia,* noting its playfulness (Casamassina). The dynamic between conflicting threads of suspicion and romance in the relationship between the Prince and Farah can be traced to the sparkling, dialogue-heavy examples of sophisticated male-female interaction in Hollywood films of the era of different genres like *Bringing Up Baby* (1938). In this capacity, Farah moves beyond the typical representation of a female character in historical adventure, which often presents the heroine as more passive (Taves 122–24).

This comparison is important in considering the nostalgic rendering of *Prince of Persia* because the primary connections between *Prince of Persia* and the Hollywood film come through the game's allusions to the genre of historical adventure films popular in the 1930s and 1940s. Historical adventure films like *The Adventures of Robin Hood* and *The Mark of Zorro* (1940) are part of a genre that reached its apex during this period. Historical adventure shares some qualities and general themes of another genre that developed during this period, film noir. In both historical adventure films and film noir, individual protagonists find themselves trying to rectify problems in an indifferent or even hostile world. However, historical adventure films typically allow for more optimistic endings, which the historical settings of such films tend to support. Setting a film in a historical period precludes the question of whether an individual's action can be historically significant. For example, the viewer is unlikely to question whether Zorro's actions in *The Mark of Zorro* have any impact beyond his immediate area or beyond his lifetime. In contrast, film noir frequently demonstrates the impotence of an individual in the face of a corrupt or uncaring society. In this sense, the two genres can be seen as complementary in their propositions but different in their conclusions.

The Prince can be compared to the historical adventure heroes from films in the 1930s and 1940s in a number of ways. The setting of *Prince of Persia* is clearly historical, but it is history at a fictional remove. The game sets its story in variations of Persia and India that are equivalent to the England of *Robin Hood*, where social justice motivates the plot but even the most downtrodden peasant wears clean clothes in exuberant Technicolor hues and has received excellent dental care. The elements of castles, knights, kings, and peasants are used to create a romantic environment derived distantly from the historical reality of England's feudal system. In comparison, the gritty hands-on realism attempted in *Splinter Cell* (2002) is not present. As in *Robin Hood*, the Prince's success depends as much, if not more, on physical ability than intellect or cunning. Puzzles are present but physically navigating them is essential. This suggests that *Prince of Persia* is clearly in the realm of the historical adventure, where physical skill is linked to heroism, rather than film noir, where cynical intelligence is frequently necessary for success, as is the case in films like *The Maltese Falcon* (1941). In addition, the setting of *Prince of Persia* is Romantic in the sense that it is both societally and historically remote from the typical gaming experience. Historical adventure films similarly favor a remote location, such as a pirate ship or the England of centuries ago, whereas film noir concentrates on the contemporary city.

The clearest links to Hollywood Golden Era films, therefore, come through the exuberantly athletic Prince's adventures and historical adventure films of the period like *The Mark of Zorro* and *Robin Hood*. Roger Ebert notes that Errol Flynn's stardom can be traced to the "lighthearted exuberance, the good cheer with which he embodies a role like Robin Hood." The Prince's narration and characterization establish his exuberance and good cheer in the face of the cataclysmic dangers of the palace and invoke the physicality of films like *Robin Hood*. By focusing on individual action in a historical setting, *Prince of Persia* emphasizes the ability of a human body that is at the fore in combat and in movement throughout the environment of the game. The Prince's acrobatic abilities are only relatively realistic as in *Robin Hood*. The Prince moves with an ease and grace beyond the purely realistic and executes acrobatic leaps beyond the ability of any actual person. The Prince's ability to run along walls is somewhat beyond the normal bounds of human agility but is a relatively real movement extended to be pleasurable for the player. The Prince's abilities are, however, limited to a relatively realistic system of physics. The Prince cannot fly, for example, but he can do just enough to advance the story, just as Robin Hood successfully performs in the context of the movie. Roger Ebert has suggested that the thrills of *Robin Hood* endure because the stunts look real, noting that the action is "thrilling precisely because it is mostly real." This feeling is often present in *Prince of Persia*, although reality's rule, and that of gravity, is diminished enough to allow for fun and exciting gameplay.

In terms of physical action, *Prince of Persia* represents a middle ground between the labored realism of a film-noir-derived game like *Splinter Cell* and the cartoon-like exaggerated physical violence of titles like those in the *Mortal Kombat* (1992) series. Commentators have noted how the intuitive controller system works in concert with the "silky smooth motion" of the Prince to create a sense of acrobatic ease (Casamassina). Even in the apocalyptic setting of *Prince of Persia*, the Prince's bemused voice creates a controlled narration that charts a path between exaggerated extremes. A noir-derived game like *Splinter Cell* places its character in a hostile, contemporary environment, suggesting a sense of the challenges that the noir protagonist faces in terms of the indifferent universe he is up against.

This contrast also applies to the characters themselves. Superficially, the Prince is fairly anonymous, known only by his fairy-tale like title and status, and the game thus taps into archetypal connections that the character's narration expands into a personality. In contrast, *Splinter Cell's* Sam Fisher is a stoic mid-career professional going about his business methodically rather than exuberantly, and coping with his daughter's worries alongside the challenges he faces in the line of duty. The game design in *Splinter Cell* discourages extravagant play; rather, it encourages the player to skulk in the shadows to avoid confrontation at all, as opposed to the acrobatic swordplay of *Prince of Persia*. Even Sam Fisher's actions are frequently accompanied by grunts of effort, and his actions suggest the endless hours of physical training of the marathoner rather than the effortless, inexplicable joy in physical activity of Robin Hood or the Prince.

The physical abilities available to the character in *Prince of Persia* and the ease of controller usage help make physical action pleasurable to the player. Much of the gameplay of *Prince of Persia* consists of guiding the Prince through acrobatic routines. As play continues and the Prince's abilities increase, the ease with which he runs along walls and swings from bars suggests the abilities of a circus performer more than a superhero. The Prince's actions seem only remotely possible. Disbelief is suspended but not abandoned, and the Prince's abilities seem to be an extension of human abilities rather than the total lack of realism implied in the metahuman power of a superhero. Because *Prince of Persia* retains this connection to the human, the game's relationship to historical adventure rather than science fiction or horror becomes more apparent, even while fantastic elements drive the game's action. The Prince's swinging on poles and jumping between ledges can be compared to historical adventure action such as the acrobatic motion of Errol Flynn's Robin Hood fighting a roomful of soldiers in the banquet scene. Some of the pleasure for the filmgoer and gameplayer takes place in accessing the joy of physical action exhibited in games like *Prince of Persia* and films like *Robin Hood*. In the scene where Robin Hood disrupts the barons' meeting in the banquet hall, he displays just this level of blithe physicality. He flips over his chair, fights multiple opponents simultaneously, and then jumps from a torch holder up to a balcony. Later, when escaping from his own execution, Robin Hood rides down a rope holding up the portcullis gate before darting down the other side of the gate. Similar to the many climbing tasks in *Prince of Persia*, Robin Hood climbs ivy to reach Maid Marian's room. At other times, Robin's movements up and down curving flights of castle stairs seem so effortless that they suggest the weightlessness of a video game character.

Specifically, historical adventure films frequently emphasize vertical movement, and characters are often shown moving quickly up walls and jumping down from heights. Robin Hood's men swing down on vines and jump from tree branches to attack the Sheriff's men. Abu, in the *Thief of Baghdad*, swings across his jail cell on a rope rather than walk, and later clambers up and down through a market before moving onto the roofs. Later, he must climb up an idol and dodge mechanical traps to retrieve the Eye of Truth, which is similar to an early level of *Prince of Persia* in which the Prince must climb to get the Dagger of Time. In *Captain Blood*, the pirates ascend into the rigging to attack, and Zorro frequently moves up and down walls to establish his reputation for elusiveness. Similarly, the Prince must explore the environment of the game thoroughly but in a fairly constrained order to succeed. While one may explore imaginatively, there is little capability to step out of the quest narrative and range along a horizontal space in the way allowed in games like *Grand Theft Auto*. The linearity of the gameplay then connects to the fairly circumscribed goals of the historical adventure.

There is a symbolism in this powerful but constrained physical action. Historical adventures frequently take place when the hero has suffered a reversal that must be overcome. Peter Blood is enslaved by the government of an uncaring king, Zorro finds colonial California run by a corrupt government, Robin Hood finds corruption in a kingless England, and Ahmed in *The Thief of Baghdad* loses his throne. Frequently, the hero is brought low from a high social status. The narrative of the films revolves around reversing the temporary societal problems that have disrupted the proper order. Corrupt governments must be removed and the proper rulers restored, whether they are Richard the Lion-Hearted in *Robin Hood* or Zorro's father in *The Mark of Zorro*, but there is no question of a broader societal change. Feudalism remains in the world of *Robin Hood* as does the system of peonage in the world of *The Mark of Zorro*. Even Peter Blood, after being enslaved and abused by his society, takes the post of governor of Jamaica upon the succession of a new English king. Just as the characters in these films embrace only a limited degree of change, so too does their physical action suggest extraordinary effort and ability that is limited by the prevailing realities of the environment.

The Historical Adventure, Video Games, and Colonialism

With *Prince of Persia's* emphasis on narration, the voice of the Prince becomes a prominent part of the game and an interesting subject for analysis. The use of an aristocratic British accent for a Middle Eastern narrator immediately suggests a colonialist approach, but the treatment of the character comes to be more complex. Specifically, the Prince's accent can also be seen as an attempt to reference the timeless arena conjured by the seeming authenticity of the historical adventure film.

Prince of Persia can be regarded as open to charges of Saidian Orientalism in its depiction of the magic-infused Eastern setting, even while this approach further connects the game to Hollywood films. Peter Lamont has recently examined the appeal of this magical vision of Eastern cultures in *The Rise of the Indian Rope Trick,* exploring how a fraudulent story about the exploits of Indian street magicians had such lasting influence. Films like *Gunga Din* (1939) demonstrate the interest in this vision by appealing to the wonder of the alien and colorful. Films of the Hollywood Golden Age frequently emphasize exotic settings and characters— as in, for example, *Lives of a Bengal Lancer* (1935)—and a striking number of films used colonialist subjects in the 1930s and 1940s. Although there is a connection to the films of the era in *Prince of Persia*, the game generally employs a different approach. The appetite for the unusual in movie audiences of the 1930s and 1940s is understandable given the increasing importance of international affairs and the relatively few outlets for information. However, an Orientalist critique of video games seem less persuasive in a medium where English and other Western cultures are depicted as equally suffused in magic and exoticism, as in the *Lord of the Rings*-inspired fantasy genre that is so dominant in gaming. Set in a precolonial period, the cast of characters of the *Prince of Persia* does not include Europeans to serve as heroes or villains, relying instead on a range of Persian and Indian characters. Only the Prince's accent might be considered an attempt to make the non-Western element of the game more approachable to a North American game player.

Instead, David Cannadine's class-based response to Said's critique of Orientalism seems equally, if not more, appropriate and in keeping with Hollywood films. Cannadine's *Ornamentalism* argues that British attitudes toward colonial possessions in the British Empire were strongly affected by British attitudes toward social hierarchy in dealing with class-based leadership figures like maharajahs (11). Historical adventure films of the 1930s and 1940s like *The Scarlet Pimpernel* (1934), *Captain Blood*, and *The Mark of Zorro* frequently feature a protagonist of high social status who is forced by circumstances to adopt a violently adventurous role. The use of a highborn hero in *Prince of Persia* is unusual in video games, which more commonly focus on the struggles of ordinary characters in an unusual situations, as in *Half-Life* (1998), or almost characterless professionals, which are more often the case, as in *Splinter Cell* or *Halo* (2001).

Crimson Skies

While *Prince of Persia*'s use of an "exuberant" tone and a charming character utilizes historical adventure themes, *Crimson Skies* treats characters in a manner reminiscent of Golden Age Hollywood films alongside more explicit references to the 1930s while dealing with disturbing historical undercurrents. The alternate history of *Crimson Skies* portrays a 1930s America that has shattered into warring regions following Depression-era stresses, yet the blithe picaresque tone to *Crimson Skies* is established in the first cutscene, in which the protagonist, Zachary, steals back a plane he had lost gambling the previous night. Zachary's roguish adventures take place in a collapsed but liberating environment, such that the breakdown of society in *Crimson Skies* is also an invitation to escape from societal pressures. Zachary, as an alternate-history historic adventure character, creates escapism of a doubled type: removed in real years and in contingent historical events.

The game expresses its exuberant tone in its approach to the main activity of the game: flying. Zachary makes use of a wide range of vehicles from an era preceding the modern standardization and centralization of flight. The improvisational nature of the way Zachary creates and repairs his flying machines helps convey the tone. In addition, the relative freedom the player has in the game to travel throughout the world creates an environment supportive of the engaging tone.

In its evocation of the pleasure of flying, *Crimson Skies* is clearly reminiscent of early twentieth-century attitudes. The early twentieth century was a period of extensive experimentation with the possibilities of flight. Adventurous pilots like Charles Lindbergh and Amelia Earhart were popular public figures, and numerous aviation companies tried to prosper in a developing industry. This "garage" style, indicative of a new technology industry, is evident in the range of real-seeming but fanciful contraptions available for use in the game's stable of vehicles. Similarly, 1930s and 1940s films frequently displayed a cheerful and innocent interest in developing technologies like aviation before World War II demonstrated the destructive potential of technology. Films of the 1930s frequently focused on peaceful aspects of aviation, with heroes performing as barnstormers or in air circuses, competing in air races, or working for air mail companies, before the emphasis became more military by the end of the decade (Paris 58–61, 65–69). In comparison, post-war horror films of the late 1940s and 1950s deal with the power of technology to create problems sufficient to disrupt the natural order (Telotte 98). The connections to use of the atomic bombs in World War II in films like *Godzilla* (1954), *Them!*

(1954), and *The Thing From Another World* (1951) are frequently noted by critics (Telotte 98). In contrast, technology in *Crimson Skies* remains relatively decentralized, with a tendency toward less warlike attitudes. Technology is something to be embraced and enjoyed, and in the virtual eternity of the video game that enjoyment can appear costless.

While flying in video games is fairly common, the ebullient attitude present in *Crimson Skies* is relatively unusual, suggesting a 1930s approach to the technology. Flying is presented as powerful but innocent. *Crimson Skies* uses a system of physics that is relatively realistic, with simplified pleasures of flight but without the requirements of skill and knowledge, whereas many video games dealing with flying, such as complicated flight simulation games like *Microsoft Flight Simulator* (2006) or *IL-2 Sturmovik* (2001), are focused on realism and emphasize the complexity of flying. Other games employ flight as an element of a largely fantastical world. For example, in *Panzer Dragoon Orta* (2002), the protagonist rides through a post-apocalyptic world on the back of a modified dragon. There is something disturbingly unsettling about the bizarre world where *Orta* is set that undercuts some of the pleasures of flight. Interestingly, *Crimson Skies* mixes these genres of realism and fantasy (through the use of alternate history) to recapture successfully some of the pleasures of flight associated with the 1930s.

That this approach must look to the past can be emphasized by a comparison with contemporary attitudes. Planes are now seen as a nuisance and a danger. Most people's experience of commercial flying only seems to underscore this. Rather than remembering the glamour of Pan Am, most people seek out the economies of Southwest Airlines and EasyJet, and the major airlines are widely regarded as doomed to eventual extinction (Maynard). Air travel is closer to mass transportation than ever but characterized by a combination of tedium and fear that makes affection or fascination difficult to sustain.

Many more contemporary films dealing with air flight increasingly focus on flight as it is manifested through corporatized commercial aviation or military flight. *Airport* (1970) and its sequels present flight disasters as a societal and bureaucratic problem as much as a pilot problem. In these films, the daredevil spirit of the pilot is frequently controlled by the hegemonic organizations that control access to flying. The pilot is capable of individual heroism, but only in dire circumstances when the normal need for obeisance to bureaucratic authority can be suspended. Consider, for example, more current treatments of airplanes and air travel in film. Films like *Bounce* (2000) and *Fearless* (1993) suggest that commercial air travel is remarkable primarily in its ability to wreak death on a diverse group. Air travel is a unifier of danger and discomfort, and it is threatening because the individual has no possibility of control over the plane. The potential for heroism in piloting can only be seen in the military or government-authorized context of films like *Top Gun* (1986) or *The Right Stuff* (1983). Interestingly, even *The Right Stuff* itself explores the decline of the heroic pilot from a Chuck Yeager, individualist figure to passive astronaut.

By looking backward, *Crimson Skies* seems to suggest not only a look back at a politically oriented alternate history but a partly fantastic situation in which the predictions of *Popular Science* and *The Jetsons,* where we would each have our own air-car, have come to fruition. Historical films of the 1930s like *Hell's Angels* (1930) celebrated flight and film's ability to record the experience (Paris 38). Howard Hughes's success in conveying flight was such that some critics regard the non-aerial scenes of *Hell's Angels* as tedious interruptions (Paris 38). Even the life of Howard Hughes himself, packed with dramatic and noteworthy events, was recently filmed as *The Aviator* (2004), focusing on his own aviation achievements.

In exploring the individual potential for aviation, *Crimson Skies* summons up a disturbing backdrop and in doing so makes a relatively unusual foray for video games into the genre of alternate history. Gaming has comparably few examples of alternate history, although one of gaming's primary influences, science fiction, is rife with them. *Uchronia,* a database of alternate history, lists more than 2,600 works dealing with alternate history. *Crimson Skies'* suggestion of a fragmented America presents a particularly disturbing subtext, because its violence is inevitably directed at erstwhile fellow Americans. A number of games like *Conflict: Vietnam* (2004) do allow a certain degree of exploration of historical contingencies but not in the same way as the refracted view of alternate history.

Alternate history in this respect creates a disturbing subtext. Unlike *Prince of Persia*, the opponents in *Crimson Skies* are essentially fellow Americans but for a historical turn. The violence is internecine and reminiscent of Civil War conflict if not the same level of carnage. *Crimson Skies* does allow the player a visual distance from the objects of violence inherent to onscreen aerial combat. However, *Prince of Persia* distances the player from violence more profoundly by making only fantastic creatures the objects of violence. For the Prince, his opponents are dead, mystically reanimated human forms, appearing to lack much in the way of genuine humanity. The fact that they are reanimated ghouls makes it possible for the destruction of the once-human creatures to seem like a moral act. The protagonist of *Crimson Skies* faces human opponents and human opponents who might, but for a quirk of historical fate, have been friends or neighbors. This is a particularly powerful undertone for a gameplayer existing in the physical reality where the historical quirk never occurred. For the gameplayer, those opponents never actually became opponents but exist as friends and neighbors of relatives.

The superficial exuberance of flight celebrated in *Crimson Skies* is also undercut by this subtext. In this respect, the 1930s setting emphasizes the disconcerting aspect of the conflicts in *Crimson Skies*. The 1930s are now frequently regarded as a prelude to the triumphal achievements of the United States' last "good" war, World War II. The internecine conflicts of *Crimson Skies*, then, can be seen as a precursor to and variation on the aerial war of World War II. Instead of fights against Nazi pilots, however, the pilots of *Crimson Skies* kill each other. The talented pilots of *Crimson Skies* would not only have been fellow citizens but likely allies in the armed struggle against the Axis powers.

The potential of the despair and unrest of the 1930s United States is fertile ground for historical divergences and has even disrupted literary genre lines, such as in Philip Roth's *The Plot against America*, where a well-known "literary" author has brought science-fiction tropes into more mainstream literary arenas. Interestingly, in crafting an alternate-history dystopic 1930s America, Roth uses Lindbergh as an aviator who is able to leverage his fame from flying to become President, with dire results for American Jews (53–54). Roth's novel can be seen as a variation on Sinclair Lewis's own speculation from 1936 on the possibility of a fascist president, in *It Can't Happen Here*. The potential for things to have gone even more disastrously wrong in the 1930s seems to be both a contemporary and a historical concern. The internal conflict suggested by the *Crimson Skies* scenario creates an unavoidable parallel with the chaotic events of the 1930s. The picaresque tone makes the unsettling background of the game ironically more accessible.

Crimson Skies' use of an alternate 1930s US setting for its fragmented and violent vision also compares to intriguing cinematic views of this era. The image of the thirties as a time of anarchic disorder is a frequent theme in films depicting this period. Arthur Penn's *Bonnie and Clyde* (1967) presents an image of what J. Hoberman has described as the "righteous outlaw" crossing the desperate landscape where deadly bank robbers could be reimagined for the socially chaotic 1960s (177). *Raiders of the Lost Ark* (1981) reinterpreted movie adventure serials of the thirties and forties to present an era where individual adventure still seemed possible and consequential before the mass international historical forces of the Second World War, and *Tomb Raider* (1996), in some manners, reinterpreted the *Indiana Jones* films for contemporary contexts. Comedies of the 1930s, while often presenting benign escapist fantasies, could also present narratives that hinted at the fragility of the existing social order, such as William Powell's Boston Brahmin "forgotten man" in *My Man Godfrey* (1936).

Specifically, film in the 1960s tends to present a vision of the 1930s as a time of chaotic freedom and violence. The violence in *Bonnie and Clyde* was widely noted by critics (Kael 55) and often seen as an attempt to depict a missed opportunity by the suffering rural poor during the Depression to seek profound societal change against the existing social structure (Hoberman 174–78, 185). The explicit violence in the film is mixed with a comic tone, but it is also unsettling in that it is in some sense the brother-against-brother carnage of revolution or civil war. The violence is especially striking because it is directed against neighbors and low-level functionaries of the government. Of course, given the civil-war-like nature of the violence, there is also something true about the converse, which makes it chilling when the bank robbers' car is perforated with machine gun bullets by police officers. The Barrow gang doesn't kill robber barons but locals trying to simply make a living. A similar undercurrent subverts the superficially blithe tone of *Crimson Skies*. The breakdown of the United States into competing mini-states forces each conflict to be one of civil war, and inevitably this brings to mind historical facts about the destruction of the Civil War in which more Americans died than in all other wars involving the United States combined (McPherson 854).

In comparison, the approach to violence and technology in *Crimson Skies* is relatively indirect. The use of guns and planes as weapons creates an inevitable visual distance for the player from the violence they transmit. The bullets and bombs travel away from the player so that explosions are only visual effects. In this approach, some of the disturbing aspects of the alternate history treatment can be set at a visual remove from the player that also allows psychological separation. This strategy allows the game developers to create a provocative setting of internecine conflict with sufficient mental distance to make it acceptable to the mainstream gameplayer.

The vision of the 1930s in Penn's *Bonnie and Clyde* is also instructive in the way it envisions social organization in the absence of the nation-state as a viable model. The Barrow gang is similar to the clan-based organization of *Crimson Skies*. In the absence of strong ties to society and societal institutions, the breakdown seems to lead to familial and fraternal organization. The breakdown of national identity and institutionalism shows this to be a particularly bleak scenario—not as initially off-putting as the post-crisis world of *Half-Life 2* (2004) but with an insidious sense of the skull beneath the skin.

Conclusion: Remixing the 1930s

The connections to Hollywood films in games like *Prince of Persia* and *Crimson Skies* suggest new sources of inspiration for video game development. At a recent conference, a game developer suggested that the emphasis on graphics is pricing small and innovative developers out of the market (Doctorow). While graphics will continue to be important—and both games examined here employ high quality graphics—cost-effective narrative development and the ability to tap into established cultural genres and archetypes in *Prince of Persia* and *Crimson Skies* suggest new possibilities for game development. The "magic" in games like *Prince of Persia* and *Crimson Skies* derives its power from archetypes developed by Hollywood adventure films and works to support gameplay while helping to expand game audiences. Game development has traditionally looked to science fiction and Tolkienesque fantasy for much of its inspiration. *Prince of Persian* and *Crimson Skies* reimagine Golden Age movie adventurers in historical settings, bringing with them the charm and wit of a Hollywood picture and suggesting a refreshing change for the medium. In addition, by using the mediating references to Golden Age archetypes, developers can explore unusual or provocative subjects by looking at Eastern subject matter and alternate history. A possible path for the medium of games to develop in new and original directions is to seek models not only in future scenarios derived from science fiction and fantasy literature but in art forms of the past like the Golden Age movie. If investment costs force developers to explore only the most conservative ideas (Doctorow), then gaming may find itself struggling with the same creative drought and dwindling audience of cost-burdened contemporary Hollywood (Epstein). *Prince of Persia*'s own sequel, *Prince of Persia: Warrior Within* (2004), suggests some of the problems of this conservative path. Instead of the interesting and charming character of the Prince in *Prince of Persia: Sands of Time*, developers attempted to create a darker and more contemporary character that resulted in a character that is "more generic than before" (Goldstein). Looking to the past rather than the present suggests one path for developers to create innovative designs in the game context, confront new issues, and develop new audiences.

Works Cited

Bramwell, Tom. "Bruckheimer Films Buys Prince of Persia Film Rights." *www. eurogamer.net* (3 April 2004). Accessed 19 July 2005.

Cannadine, David. *Ornamentalism: How the British Saw Their Empire*. New York: Oxford University Press, 2002.

Casamassina, Matt. "Prince of Persia: The Sands of Time: This Is How You Make a Sequel." *xbox.ign.com* (10 November 2003). Accessed 19 July 2005.

Cieniawa, Lee. "Crimson Skies: High Road to Revenge." *www.armchairempire.com* (25 November 2003). Accessed 19 July 2005.

"Crimson Skies." *wikipedia.org*. Accessed 19 July 2005.

DeMaria, Rusel, and Johnny L.Wilson. *High Score! The Illustrated History of Video Games*, 2nd ed. Emeryville, CA: Osborne/McGraw-Hill, 2004.

Doctorow, Cory, "Game Developers' Amazing Rants on the State of the Industry." *www.boingboing.net* (11 March 2005). Accessed 19 July 2005.

Ebert, Roger. "The Adventures of Robin Hood." *Chicago Sun-Times* (17 August 2003).

Eliot, Marc. *Cary Grant: A Biography*. New York: Harmony, 2004.

Epstein, Edward Jay. "The Vanishing Box Office: A Terminal Condition." *slate.msn. com* (5 July 2005). Accessed 19 July 2005.

Goldstein, Hilary. "Prince of Persia: The Warrior Within." *xbox.ign.com* (23 November 2004). Accessed 19 July 2005.

Hoberman, J. *The Dream Life: Movies, Media and the Mythology of the Sixties*. New York: New Press, 2003.

Huseman, Charles. "Gaming Nexus Review: Crimson Skies: High Road to Revenge." *www.gamingnexus.com* (3 November 2003). Accessed 19 July 2005.

Jonric. "Interview with Raph Koster." *www.raphkoster.com*. Accessed 19 July 2005.

Kael, Pauline. *Kiss Kiss Bang Bang*. New York: Little, Brown, 1968.

Keighley, Geoff. "The Final Hours of Prince of Persia." *www.gamespot.com*. Accessed 19 July 2005.

Knudson, Michael. "Crimson Skies High Road to Revenge Review." *xbox.gamezone. com* (28 October 2003). Accessed 19 July 2005.

Lamont, Peter. *The Rise of the Indian Rope Trick: How a Spectacular Hoax Became History*. New York: Thunder's Mouth, 2005.

Lewis, Sinclair. *It Can't Happen Here*. New York: Signet, 1936.

Maynard, Michelle. "Delta's Tough Sell." *The New York Times* (11 March 2005).

McPherson, James. *Battle Cry of Freedom: The Civil War Era*. New York: Oxford University Press, 1988.

Paris, Michael. *From the Wright Brothers to Top Gun: Aviation, Nationalism and the Popular Cinema*. Manchester, UK: Manchester University Press, 1995.

"Prince of Persia." *wikipedia.org*. Accessed 19 July 2005.

Roth, Philip. *The Plot Against America*. New York: Houghton Mifflin, 2004.

Schmunk, Robert B. *Uchronia: The Alternate History List* (*www.uchronia.net*). Accessed 19 July 2005.

Taves, Brian. *The Romance of Adventure: The Genre of Historical Adventure Movies*. Jackson: University Press of Mississippi, 1993.

Telotte, J. P. *Science Fiction Film*. New York: Cambridge University Press, 2001.

Thomson, David. *The Whole Equation: A History of Hollywood.* New York: Vintage, 2006.
Tolkien, J. R. R. *The Fellowship of the Ring.* Boston: Houghton Mifflin, 1965.
___. *The Two Towers.* Boston: Houghton Mifflin, 1965.
___. *The Return of the King.* Boston: Houghton Mifflin, 1965.
Turner, Benjamin. "Prince of Persia: The Sands of Time." *xbox.gamespy.com* (7 November 2003). Accessed 19 July 2005.
Xbox Solution. "Prince of Persia: The Sands of Time" (review). *www.xboxsolution.com* (29 November 2003). Accessed 19 July 2005.

Games Cited

Conflict: Vietnam (Xbox). New York: Global Star, 2004.
Crimson Skies: High Road to Revenge (Xbox). Redmond, WA: Microsoft, 2003.
Doom II (PC). New York: GT Interactive, 2002.
Grand Theft Auto: Vice City (Xbox). San Diego: Rockstar Games, 2002.
Half-Life (PC). Bellevue, WA: Sierra, 1998.
Half-Life 2 (PC). Los Angeles: VU Games. 2004.
Halo: Combat Evolved (Xbox). Redmond, WA: Microsoft 2001.
IL-2 Sturmovik (PC). San Francisco: Ubisoft, 2001.
Microsoft Flight Simulator 2004: A Century of Flight. Redmond, WA: Microsoft, 2003.
Mortal Kombat (arcade). Chicago: Midway, 1992.
Mortal Kombat: Deadly Alliance (Xbox). Chicago: Midway, 2002.
Panzer Dragoon Orta (Xbox). San Francisco: Sega, 2003.
Prince of Persia: Sands of Time (Xbox). Montreal: Ubisoft, 2003.
Prince of Persia: Warrior Within (Xbox). Montreal: Ubisoft, 2004.
Splinter Cell. (Xbox). Montreal: Ubisoft, 2002.
Tom Clancy's Splinter Cell (Xbox). San Francisco: Ubisoft, 2003.

9

Toward a New Sound for Games

Thomas E. Gersic

To advance the state of video game sound, there is a need for a theoretical framework of sound design for interactive media. While the application of sound to other forms of multimedia—such as film or television—has had years of scholarly theoretical assertions and empirical study, to date there is a surprising dearth of literature that concerns the use of sound in games, and though many empirical studies have been completed regarding the role of sound in film, very few have considered sound within the construct of an interactive environment such as a video game. As the possibilities for video game sound have evolved away from the "beeps and boops" of early games, video game sound designers and composers have taken cues from film sound because of the similarities between the media. These similarities allow for a starting point for the development of a sound design theory for interactive environments, but there are significant issues that must be considered. For the purposes of this chapter, film, video games, television, and computer animation are all considered to fall under the heading of "multimedia," about which there is an abundance of scholarly research to consider. The definition of multimedia requires only the simultaneous presence of two or more forms of media—by convention, visual stimuli are paired with sound. Additionally, for the sake of simplicity, there is no distinction made here between video and computer games, and the term "video game" is used throughout.

The relatively short history of music composition and sound design for interactive multimedia has been fast-paced and ever-evolving. While today it is considered a necessity in a sound designer's studio, the Digital Audio Workstation (DAW) had yet to be invented in the early days of game development. In fact, while the video game revolution of the 1970s could not have occurred without the advent of digital electronics, analog tape was still a staple of the recording industry, and the first digital medium for music, the compact disc, was just entering development through a joint venture between Philips and Sony. Working with vast orchestral sample libraries and effect plug-ins had not yet entered the realm of possibility, and the thought of playing back digital recordings of acoustic instruments from within an interactive environment was nothing but a dream. A composer who wanted to make music for games had to be incredibly creative given the very limited set of musical possibilities. To complicate the situation further, an early game composer did not have the luxury of inputting into the system a traditionally notated musical score, but instead had to be able to describe a composition in a variety of specialized command languages developed for each game system's audio hardware. Some systems had even less to work with. In an interview with Alexander Brandon, game composer Hip Tanaka recalls that "most music and sound in the arcade era was designed little by little, by combining transistors, condensers, and resistance" (Brandon). Even given these improbable odds, much of the music written for vintage games is still regarded as some of the best video game music ever written. Composers and sound designers of the time had to know the inner workings of the various audio chips embedded in each different game system, and the very best searched for ways to exploit minor flaws in each chip in order to coax out every last inch of sound. On some game systems, such as the Commodore 64, sound was synthesized on the fly by a combination of digital and analog components, giving early game audio a distinctive low-tech flavor. Since recording sound digitally was either a complete impossibility or extremely limited by the state of the hardware at the time, game sound effects were closely paired with music for the simple reason that they were both being created using the same synthesis techniques, on the very same chip, and were forced to share system resources with each other. This close relationship between sound and music was exploited by some game composers to heighten the impact of game sound and music by intentionally blurring the distinction between the two. For instance, in designing the music and sound for *Metroid* (1986), instead of following the trend at the time for happy, upbeat musical scores that may or may not fit with the subject matter of the game, Tanaka "wanted to create the sound without any distinctions between music and sound effects." He did this in order to make the music and sound work together as a single organic audio entity to enhance the game, as he says, to make the "players feel as if they were encountering a living creature" (Brandon).

Over the years, video game soundtracks have evolved extensively in many different directions. While many games continue to push hardware resources to the max, technology is no longer a major limiting factor in game audio. Today, some soundtracks license music from pop bands, some use entirely novel compositions, and some of these compositions have become nearly indistinguishable from Hollywood film scores. Now that there are almost limitless possibilities for game audio, how do we determine the best way to complement a given game with music and sound effects? Is the Hollywood film score the true holy grail of game audio, or is there something that fits with interactivity better? When compared with the extensive academic literature written about sound for film over the course of the past century, written theory for video game sound design is practically nonexistent. While several books exist on the topic of game sound, most focus on the technical aspects of sound design or on the role of the sound designer and composer in the game industry, but there is very little written about what it is that makes a great game soundtrack.

While there are many similarities between the various forms of multimedia, there are also some significant differences, especially when considering the role of sound within the setting of an interactive game. The most essential characteristic of a game—in fact, the characteristic that makes it a game—is that game play is nonlinear by nature. This is not the case with film, where timing is absolute and events will always happen in precisely the same order every single time. In a game, it is frequently impossible to know how long a player will remain on any single task, or to which task she will choose to move next. Because of this uncertainty, a static, precomposed, linear orchestral score will often fall short of having a strong emotional impact in video games. Musical loop points can be very distracting to the player because the loop will likely not occur at a time that makes sense within the context of the game space, but simply when the loop file reaches the end and is forced to restart. A great emotional swell in the precomposed score can seem absurd when the player's character is merely standing in an empty room, considering a puzzle. The best video game sound designs rely on the principles of multimedia theory without trying to explicitly mimic any linear form of media.

Sound Theory

Sound theory for multimedia is multifaceted, but the earliest thought regarding the combination of sound and image started with notions that mimicked synaesthesia, the physiological mixing of the senses that causes those afflicted to hear colors or see sounds. Synaesthesia is commonly attributed to drug use, but it is also a naturally occurring and well-documented phenomenon. According to Nicholas Cook, author of *Analysing Musical Multimedia*, "Historically . . . it is synaesthesia proper that has stimulated and, by way of a kind of rationalization, been invoked by the pioneers of multimedia" (29). In 1704, Isaac Newton first proposed a mapping of colors to musical keys, and there has been no shortage of followers who have proposed their own mappings in an effort to combine music with visuals (Collopy). Some of the earliest examples of multimedia, such as Scriabin's fifth symphony, *Prometheus,* which in 1910 employed the use of a *tastiera per luce* (a rudimentary "color organ"), were based on artistic interpretations of the synaesthetic condition. Later, in the 1920s and 1930s, Oskar Fischinger created a number of abstract animations that were accompanied by music. According to William Moritz, Fischinger "held the abstract imagery to contain qualities parallel to the ones found in music, and the actual soundtrack used as means to attract the attention of the audience to recognize this" (quoted in McDonnell).

As a formal basis for the creation of multimedia, synaesthesia was considered to be inadequate by Russian filmmakers Sergei Eisenstein, Vsevolod Pudovkin, and Grigori Alexandrov, who published their treatise entitled "Statement on the Sound Film" in 1928 (257–60). In this paper, the authors state their belief that further development and perfection of film can only be accomplished through the contrapuntal use of sound in relation to visuals. While there are similarities between synaesthesia and multimedia, the differences are far too important to ignore. To consider multimedia from a synaesthetic position, a sound designer has to consider there to be certain intrinsic relationships between imagery and sound. With the early multimedia artists, "speculation about the correspondences between color and music, in particular, tied in with a tradition deriving principally from Newton, which attempted to link the two directly as parallel manifestations of universal laws of vibration" (Cook 26). However, even among synaesthetes, there is disagreement as to how the senses mix. Synaesthesia does not afflict everyone in exactly the same way. For instance, composer Alexander Scriabin considered the key of C major to be red, but "his fellow countryman Rimsky-Korsakov considered it to be white" (Cook 35).

Since the general population has little to no experience with synaesthesia, and since there are no reliable synaesthetic correspondences between sound and sight, if an artist's goal is to encode meaning into artwork that an audience will be able to decode reliably, then a more productive way of relating sound to visuals is to create associations between the media within the context of a given work. While the use of the word *counterpoint* has perhaps confused more people than it has helped, Eisenstein's "basic model of cross-media relationships seems to be triadic: picture and music are related not directly, but by virtue of something that they both embody" (Cook 57). In fact, instead of trying to define sound design for multimedia by virtue of intrinsic media relationships, or out of opposition to them, Cook presents a design model that considers the relationship between music and picture to be one of metaphor, in which "the very fact of juxtaposing image and music has the effect of drawing attention to the properties that they share, and in this way constructing a new experience of each" (73).

The Role of Music in Multimedia Applications

That music can influence and even alter the perception and comprehension of visuals, not to mention increase the intensity of a person's response to them, is no secret. Film composer Bernard Hermann states:

> I feel that music on the screen can seek out and intensify the inner thoughts of the characters. It can invest a scene with terror, grandeur, gaiety, or misery. It can propel narrative swiftly forward, or slow it down. It often lifts mere dialogue into the realm of poetry. Finally, it is the communicating link between the screen and the audience, reaching out and enveloping all into one single experience. (Quoted in Cook 66)

This is not merely a belief held within the realm of artists and musicians, either. Theoretical and empirical writings in academic literature offer irrefutable evidence. Julian Thayer and Robert Levenson have recorded evidence of physiological responses to music accompanying a stressful industrial safety film, and their "results indicate that musical scores can alter electrodermal responses to a stressful film" (50). Electrodermal response, a measure of Skin Conductance Level (SCL), is considered to be a significant indicator of the internal stress being felt by a participant. Richard Lazarus, J. Speisman, A. Mordkoff, and L. Davidson had previously reported that, in a study of film stressors, "electrodermal measures were the most likely to show effects" (Thayer and Levenson 50). Even more interesting is that Thayer and Levenson were able to measure the degree of change of their subjects' SCL in various situations, and concluded that music played an important role in providing anticipation cues, leading to increased stress levels in the subjects. By altering the amount of time between the introduction of suspenseful music and the resultant accidents, they were able to observe increases in SCL that were directly proportional to time. Specifically, of the three workplace accidents shown in the film, "accident three had the longest anticipation period (30 seconds) and the largest increase in SCL" (Thayer and Levenson 51).

Additionally, Sandra Marshall and Annabel Cohen have shown that music is able to affect the perception and interpretation of a film made up of simple animated geometric figures. In the experiment, they made use of an abstract film by Fritz Heider and Mary-Ann Simmel in which "three figures, a large triangle, a small triangle, and a small circle, move in and about a rectangular enclosure that opens and closes via a hinged line segment" (96). These moving shapes have been shown in the past to elicit predictable "attributions of personality" from most viewers. When they paired the film with musical scores chosen to be either "weak music" or "strong music," Marshall and Cohen found that "the perception of features of the film could be altered by a congruent soundtrack" (111). They also found that associations from the music were able to "'set' or 'prime' the context for interpretation of the film" (111). Specifically, the interpretation of personality attributes—such as the level of aggressiveness—for each of the three geometric figures was altered by the presence of the musical soundtrack.

Marilyn Boltz, who approaches the role of film music with schema theory, states that "most theorists agree that one of the primary functions of a schema is to provide an interpretive framework" (430). In the experiment she conducted, Boltz had similar findings as Marshall and Cohen, but instead of using a film of abstract geometric shapes, she used three different clips from traditional Hollywood films. In order to support her view that musical soundtracks play a role "in comprehension by activating a given schematic framework that gives rise to certain biases during selective attending and subsequent remembering, as well as elaborative inferences that clarify the characters' temperament and behavior," Boltz showed that music not only influences perception and comprehension but memory as well (432). One week after viewing the film clips, the subjects were asked a series of questions regarding what they remembered from each. Subjects that had seen the film accompanied by "positive music"—defined as music that "displayed a major mode, a consistent tonality scheme, and a very predictable rhythm"—were more likely to interpret a film positively, and to remember positive elements within the film. The opposite was true for films accompanied by "negative music," where subjects were more likely to interpret characters' actions negatively, and also to remember the negative elements of the film. According to Boltz, "It was the implied mood of the music at the encoding phase that activated a given schematic framework that then influenced the comprehension, selective attending, and subsequent remembering of a story" (446). This experiment shows that music can influence what we, as the audience, selectively attend to, by forcing our attention toward elements that are mood-consistent with the music within the film.

Annabel Cohen describes how music works as a source of emotion within film, and outlines the difference between the concepts of mood and emotion: "Whereas both moods and emotions may be regarded as dispositions toward appraising emotional meaning structures and a readiness to respond in a certain manner, moods do not have objects; emotions do" (250). Because music has a strong ability to represent mood in the abstract, and "the screen is strong in representing the object" (Cohen 267), the pairing of music and visuals produces a significant context for the development of emotional material. Nicholas Cook, in *Analysing Musical Multimedia*, argues that "words and pictures deal primarily with the specific, with the objective, while music deals primarily with responses—that is, with values, emotions, and attitudes" (22). Cook gives as an example a commercial for the Citroen ZX 16v by stating, "Through its association with the car, the music communicates the liveliness of its engine, the precision of its road-holding. That is, the attributes of the music are transferred to the car: the liveliness and precision of Mozart's score . . . become the liveliness and precision of the ZX 16v" (6).

Sound Is Music, Music Is Sound

There is a staggering amount of evidence that shows that music influences human perception, comprehension, emotions, and memory, both alone and when presented in a multimedia setting. However, a goal of this chapter is to argue that not only the musical score but the entire soundtrack can function as a single musical work—this includes the sound design, the dialog (if there is dialog), and the score. As a musical whole, the soundtrack is just as influential as a traditional musical score. In most multimedia examples, such as with film, it is usually quite clear which sounds are part of the score and which sounds are part of the diegesis, because of the timbral differences in typical musical instruments when compared to various diegetic sound effects. Even when an associated object for a sound effect is not seen on the screen at the moment that we hear the sound, there usually lies little doubt in the viewer's mind which sounds are sound effects and which are part of the score. However, if we are considering film, given the view that sound effects and music are two separate elements of a motion picture soundtrack, how does one explain a film such as *Forbidden Planet* (1956), where the roles of music and sound effects are intertwined throughout? Or, for that matter, how does one explain *Raging Bull* (1980), where with the exception of the opening credits and one scene in the middle of the movie, the music is entirely diegetic throughout. In their article, "The Role of Music Communication in Cinema," Scott Lipscomb and David Tolchinsky "argue for a more inclusive definition of the term *film music* than that proposed in previous publications" (384). They consider the entire soundtrack of a film to be a musical score.

If we were to want to separate music and sound effects into distinctive categories, the definition of *music* must be considered. A traditional and popular definition of *music* would perhaps include a description of the various elements of the western classical tradition: melody, harmony, rhythm, and timbre. A definition of *music* might even go further by discussing the technical aspects of music, such as often-used chord progressions and voice-leading techniques. However, even the *Grove Dictionary of Music*—the self-proclaimed "world's premier authority on all aspects of music"—shies away from offering just one all-inclusive definition of *music*, stating that "imposing a single definition flies in the face of the broadly relativistic, intercultural and historically conscious nature of this dictionary" (Nettl). Instead, Grove offers up a number of different accepted definitions of *music*, along with an etymology of the word. According to *Grove*, the English word *music* first appeared in writing during the thirteenth century in the *Oxford English Dictionary* (*OED*). The contemporary *OED* definition of *music* begins with this: "That one of the fine arts which is concerned with the combination of sounds with a view to beauty of form and the experience of emotion" (quoted in Nettl).

This dictionary definition shows why the authors and editors of the *Grove Dictionary* are wisely reluctant to offer up any one definition of *music*. The *OED* definition fails to be inclusive of entire genres of western music, let alone the music of other cultures. Not all music is concerned with either the "beauty of form" or the "experience of emotion." While concerned with the "beauty of form" more than many other composers, the serialist composers of the Second Viennese School of the early twentieth century turned their backs on "the experience of emotion." Arnold Schoenberg, the father of serial music, wrote in his book *Style and Idea* that these things should be avoided in new music: "Chromaticism, expressive melodies, Wagnerian harmonies, romanticism, private biographical hints, subjectivity, functional harmonic progressions, illustrations, leitmotivs, concurrence with the mood or action of the scene" (120). Additionally, much of the music of John Cage turns its back on the "beauty of form." The silent composition *4'33''* is a piece utterly devoid of precomposed form, relying instead on the unscripted reactions of the audience to produce content for the piece. The only irrefutable elements of the *OED* definition are that *music* is "one of the fine arts" and that it is "concerned with the combination of sounds." Depending on what pieces one considers music, even the latter portion is open for debate. In fact, in *Analysing Musical Multimedia,* Cook states, "In the most inclusive sense, music is anything that somebody decides to call music; there is no *priori* need to be judgmental about it" (24).

If the definition of *music* can be reduced down to "concerned with the combination of sounds," or even "anything that somebody decides to call music," how do we separate the combination of sounds in the musical score from the combination of sounds in the rest of the soundtrack? If traditional music is capable of influencing our emotions, and influencing our perception and memory of visual events, what stops the rest of the soundtrack from doing the same thing? A collectively composed sound-track—one that is considered to be inclusive of the music, sound effects, and dialog—is one that has the potential to influence the viewer greatly regardless of the particular form of multimedia in question (for the purposes of this chapter, "the viewer" being the player of a video game). To ignore the potential for a collective sound design to work together as one large musical score, and to influence the player as such, is to ignore one of the most powerful elements of the multimedia experience.

A Case Study—*Resident Evil 0*

Resident Evil 0 is a survival horror game released in 2002 for the Nintendo GameCube. It is a game where the sound designer, Atsushi Mori, and composer, Shusaku Uchiyama, clearly put a great deal of thought into sound design for nonlinear media, and achieved an excellent result by recognizing the opportunities for sound that are presented with such a game rather than attempting to treat the game as if it were a film. While the interactivity of a game must be taken into account during the sound design process, as an analysis technique it is beneficial to compare this game to the sound design of a media with a more established theoretical background. The survival horror genre is one that has many close conceptual ties to cinema, so it provides a good basis of comparison between film and games. The "camera" in *Resident Evil 0* is mostly fixed, which creates some significant game play issues that the sound designer is left to resolve. Without sound working to create a significant feeling of a virtual environment, the visuals would feel flat, and the presence of off-camera action (such as an impending attack by a creature of which we are un-aware) would seem unfair to the player. The benefit to this situation is that sound has ample opportunity to work in counterpoint with the visu-als, creating a sonic environment that is not merely dictated by what we see on the screen. What we are listening to and what we are looking at are not always the same, and there is a constant interplay between on-screen and off-screen spaces throughout the game. This soundscape cre-ates an atmosphere of suspense that adds to the tension felt by the player. Sound is utilitarian to the game play because the player is made aware of things which he cannot see, but it also has substantial influence on the emotional effect that the game has on the player. Sound in this game is paramount to its success. It helps to place the player mentally within the game's environment, involving her directly with the action.

Alfred Hitchcock's *The Birds*, a Comparison

Alfred Hitchcock, whose career was marked by a constant search for ways in which he could best manipulate his audience, never overlooked the possibilities inherent in the use of sound. Through careful oversight of the sound design process, he was able to ensure a constant tension between on-screen and off-screen action. He used sound to involve the audience directly and to give them a feeling of constant terror. As Elisabeth Weis states in her article "The Evolution of Hitchcock's Aural Style and Sound in *The Birds*," "It is one thing to feel threatened when under attack; it is another to be frightened at all times, to feel that life is a permanent state of siege" (308).

The Birds, directed by Hitchcock, was released in 1963. It is a story about flocks of birds attacking the small town of Bodega Bay, a port town north of San Francisco. The film begins with a series of incidents where birds are seen in an increasingly ominous light. By the end of the movie, the birds have carried out a multitude of attacks and have gained control over the town, forcing its residents to leave. *The Birds* is notable for a number of technical achievements, but one point of interest is the com-plete lack of a traditional musical score. Hitchcock often chose to limit traditional scoring in his films because it gave him more control over the aural aspects of the film. The sound effects for the film, especially those associated with bird sounds, are largely electronically generated, and are frequently orchestrated as if they were the principal instruments of a score. Throughout the movie, instead of employing scored musical selections, Hitchcock uses these electronic bird sounds in order to manipulate the audience. Because he is able to make subtle suggestions by way of sound that he would be unable to accomplish with visuals, the soundtrack plays an important role in the psychological suspense created by the film. The sound of a bird may be introduced at any point in the movie to remind the audience that they are constantly at risk of being attacked. Because of this, "Hitchcock has a means of controlling tension that is effective and unobtrusive—even less noticeable than music would be" (Weis 305).

In *The Birds,* Hitchcock seems to be manipulating two variables in order to keep his audience in a state of constant terror (Weis 307). The first variable is whether the birds are initially introduced aurally or visually, and the second is whether the attacks are relatively noisy or relatively silent. The first variable keeps us constantly wondering if we are going to be attacked because our expectations are constantly being broken. At the start of the movie, we begin to identify with the main characters, and we learn that we will see an attack coming, at least shortly before it occurs. As the movie progresses, and as we are subconsciously manipulated into identifying our own fate with those of the characters, we are sometimes attacked without warning; sometimes we'll see an attack coming even though the characters onscreen do not, and sometimes we'll see the birds watching over us, but no attack will come. We begin to believe that we may be attacked at any time, so the film's times of relative tranquility begin to feel all the more suspenseful. The second variable, the noisiness of the attack, suggests to us that the birds are gaining power over the town as the movie progresses from start to finish. In the beginning, the birds are clearly angry when they attack, cawing loudly. As they wreak more and more destruction on the town, they no longer have a need to cry out. As with many of Hitchcock's films, a silent attacker is one with absolute power over his victim. The birds control the town, and their attacks are no longer out of anger—they are out of simple necessity.

One of the chief elements of terror present in *Resident Evil 0* is similar. Attacks switch between aural and visual introductions, and throughout the game, background ambience and music are manipulated either to suggest safety prior to and during an attack, or to suggest an attack at times when none will come. At the onset of the game, the only thing that we hear is the rain beating quietly against our train car. There is no music present in the game at this point, and the rain sound is easily looped, which lends itself well to the nonlinear nature of the game. Upon moving to the second car, we experience our first attack sequence. This first attack is accompanied by the first musical motive of the game, a danger theme. The rain that we previously heard gives way to a suspenseful musical theme, which fades away again only after the attacking zombies have been put to death. Through this, we have learned that music is a signifier of danger. The second attack of the game has no danger theme associated with it—only the off-screen sounds of our attacker moaning—and so we quickly learn that we cannot always expect a danger theme when we are attacked. The next time that we hear a danger theme is when we're attacked from the outside of the train by two dogs that jump into the car through its windows. Once we have killed the first dog, we expect and wait for the second one because the danger theme continues to play. We begin to associate music with not only current but also unseen, potential danger. Because of the nature of these attacks, we begin to associate the unseen, outside world with especially deadly attacks. An open window or the sound of rain coming in through a hole in the wall begins to be more terrifying than the sight of an attacker. The rain sound begins to carry emotional material in a way in which music could not. While music has implicit emotional content apart from its context, rain does not. However, through our developed associations with the outside world, we begin to attach emotional content to the sound of rain. Since many portions of a room may be just as impossible to see as the outside is, we begin to believe our life is—to use Elisabeth Weis's words—in a "permanent state of siege" (308). What is important is that we are not merely being surprised by our attackers, as surprise alone would not be suspenseful. We are being constantly manipulated into believing that we can expect attacks at certain times when that is not the case. As our expectations are set and broken, we begin to feel the suspense of the game.

The next major attack also comes from outside, but we hear it coming long before we experience it. As we move through the upper conductor's room, we are greeted with a segment where we hear something quite large pounding on the roof, but we cannot see it. At the end of this hall, the camera and microphone perspectives shift to the outside of the car, and we can only see our character through an open window. This starts to give us the feeling that we are actually present in the game as an onlooker. We begin to be not just frightened for the safety of the characters onscreen, but also for our own safety. The current location of the camera, and thus our location, is now in approximately the same space as the large attacker whom we have just heard pounding on the roof of the car.

This fact starts to make us feel uncomfortable. Once the attacker (a large scorpion) does finally come crashing down through the ceiling, we are left with a gaping hole in the ceiling and the sound of rain coming into the room. We continue to associate the sounds of the outside world with especially dangerous attacks, and we also begin to be concerned that our surroundings are not quite strong enough to protect us. As the game progresses, the sound designer can manipulate our sense of fragility by introducing sounds from the outside world to remind us that we are not quite as safe as we think we are. This is much the same as Hitchcock introducing bird sounds throughout *The Birds* in order to maintain the needed tension of a thriller.

The aural introduction of attacks adds to the suspense of the game. However, if all attacks are first introduced aurally, the player grows to expect attacks, and the time between the aural introduction of an attacker and the ensuing attack ceases to be suspenseful. When this occurs, we simply know that it might be a good time to stock up on ammo and make sure that our gun is fully loaded. This is a downfall of the otherwise excellent survival horror game *Silent Hill* (1999). The radio that we have with us at all times warns us of the proximity of attackers throughout the game, but after the first few attacks, we start to wish for the occasional surprise attack. To keep us off-guard, attacks in *Resident Evil 0* can come completely by surprise. In the first section of the game, we are attacked by a zombie hidden in a refrigerator at the back of the train. We have grown to expect some form of aural warning prior to an attack, so when we have no warning that an attack is imminent, we are shocked and potentially unprepared, breaking our expectations of how attacks will occur throughout the game. Other attacks of this sort happen sporadically throughout the game, but they are infrequent enough that we don't grow to expect surprise attacks either. A delicate balance is maintained throughout the game between suspenseful attacks and surprise attacks, and this balance is largely the result of the sound design throughout.

We are also sometimes introduced to a situation with an ambiguous danger level. Shortly after the surprise attack from the refrigerator, we fall through the roof of the train into an upstairs passenger cabin. We find ourselves in a mostly silent room with a relatively normal-looking man standing in it, facing away from us. Our initial response is to wonder if he is actually a friend, and not an enemy. There are no sounds to make us suspicious of this man, nor is there an immediate attack. As we approach the man, wondering if he might be of some help to us, the ensuing attack demonstrates otherwise.

Music as a Signifier, Pseudo-Diegesis, and Generative Music

In *Resident Evil 0*, music is initially only used as a signifier of danger in order to indicate an attack. For the entire first section of the game, which takes place on the train prior to the train crash, the background sounds are made up entirely from environmental sounds. These range from various rain sounds, to fire, to the "squishing" sound of leech zombie eggs piled in a room, to the sound of the train moving and the tinkle of the chandeliers. These environmental sounds work well in the game because they contain no dynamic emotional content, which helps to make the loop points less noticeable. Music is used sparingly to indicate danger, but the loops are long enough that most attacks are over with before the end of the track is reached. Once we progress from the train into the next stage of the game (The Training Facility), we are met with the first musical material that is present while we are not under attack. "Safe" music is distinctly different in feel from "danger" music in this game, and many of the rooms in the house use music to indicate subconsciously that the room is a safe zone, where we can expect not to be attacked. These rooms are important because they provide a place to leave items that we have no room to carry and are also frequently the location of save points throughout the game. By now, we have started to associate danger music with attacks, safe music with safety, and outside ambience with potential danger. What keeps us on edge is the constant breaking of the rules that have been set up for us. We are usually safe in rooms with "safe" music, but from time to time we are attacked in these spaces. Conversely, we can frequently expect an attack in rooms that have outside ambience, but sometimes no attack comes, making us doubt our assumptions about the outside and other unseen areas. We are left constantly in a state of unease, because we are unsure when and where we will be attacked.

Elements of certain diegetic sound effects are added into the music to heighten the tension. In *The Birds*, the bird sounds make up what would otherwise be the musical score, and certain segments are orchestrated as if the bird sounds were actually the instruments of a musical score, such as the house attack near the end of the movie. The music in *Resident Evil 0* employs the same technique, albeit in a more limited fashion, with a blending of pseudo-diegetic elements into the music causing some of the "safe" music to seem more menacing. The music in the cage room is an example of this, where we hear reverberant banging sounds that are understood to be a part of the music but still feel somewhat diegetic.

This concept could have been expanded to include generative music, also referred to as *stochastic music*. A relatively contemporary movement in academic music has been the composition of music that is based on sequences of probabilities, so that each performance of a piece is somewhat different. One pioneer of this form of music has been Iannis Xenakis, who writes in his book, *Formalized Music,* "The laws of the calculus of probabilities entered composition through musical necessity" (8). Similarly, these laws can and should enter video game composition and sound design out of the necessity for game audio to reflect accurately the action on screen.

The generative creation of music, based on a system of probabilities such as Markov Chains, has been relatively unexplored in the realm of game sound design, but it opens up significant possibilities for the live interaction among music, sound effects, and action on screen. For instance, in *Resident Evil 0*, as with most games, a particular room's score is made up of static looping music. With a generative musical score, a particular room's score could have a number of possible elements to choose from, some of which would play in certain situations, and some of which would not play depending on a list of probabilities determined by other elements throughout the game. The live generation of music could be based on a set of stored samples and ambiences and would not need to be particularly processor-intensive, and it could easily do away with the problems of a looping musical score. Loop points would become nonexistent, as various elements would be introduced and removed at alternating times, and the tension and emotional quality of the music could be altered unobtrusively throughout particular scenes in reaction to on-screen action merely by adjusting the list of probabilities of which elements would be played back at any given time. Sonic elements could conceptually be either a part of the musical score or a part of the diegesis, or they could blur the line between the two. If the audio engine has synthesis capabilities, an even greater realm of options would be presented, as an even greater level of detail could be added to the score.

Direct Audience Involvement

In *Resident Evil 0,* the shift outside the window prior to the scorpion attack is one instance where we are made to feel as if we are actually a part of the game. One of Hitchcock's constant goals in *The Birds,* and in many of his other movies, was to attempt to dissociate the audience from the characters just enough so that the viewers not only feel terror for the characters, but also for themselves. In *The Birds,* "the bird sounds are all the more abstract and terrifying when they come from unseen sources" (Weis 306), and Hitchcock is able to break down the barrier between audience and screen by building tension between what we can see and what we cannot see, and by keeping a constant menace through sound.

The fixed camera angle of *Resident Evil 0* makes the game perfect for this sort of tension. We are constantly in situations where we cannot see all of our surroundings, and frequently an attacker occupies some portion of those surroundings. Sometimes the attacker is silent until we move part of the way into a room, and sometimes the first thing that we hear is the attacker, such as the case with the cockroaches in the cage room of the Training Facility. What we hear during perspective shifts from third person to first person becomes important in this respect. The characters' footsteps are ever-present throughout the game, and our attention is frequently drawn to them because of their continuously changing sound. Whether we are walking through water, on a tile floor, over broken glass, or on squishy carpet, we are constantly noticing the sounds of the characters' footsteps. When the camera perspective changes to first-person during the cutscenes, the sounds of footsteps (or, depending on the cutscene, some other movement) are still present, which make us begin to form an association between the footsteps of the characters on screen and our own. Some of the cinematic sequences, such as the "killing villagers" sequence, also seem to switch to a first-person perspective. In the "killing villagers" sequence, we never see our attackers, we only hear them. Frequently, cutscenes and cinematic sequences will have elements where we only hear what is happening and cannot see it. This is most likely due to the fact that the visuals are still loading, but it also has the effect of suggesting that our eyes are momentarily closed. One instance is where we hear the train fire before we see it, and another is where we hear the sound of our hook-shot before we see the cable that we are climbing.

In *The Birds,* not only is there tension between on-screen and off-screen action, there is also tension between inside and outside spaces. Some of the more frightening attacks take place almost entirely unseen, such as the house attack near the end of the movie. As the movie progresses, the characters are forced repeatedly into small, fragile enclosures in an effort to find protection from the birds. During the schoolyard attack, Melanie is forced to hide in a car, and later during the gas station attack she hides in a phone booth. Interestingly, as the characters are forced more and more into enclosed spaces, the sounds of the birds are processed more and more heavily with reverb. With the exception of the sparrow attack and the final attic attack, the birds remain largely in out-side spaces, but the sound of their wings flapping begins to be reverber-ated heavily as the movie progresses. This seems to be done in order to remind us subconsciously of the enclosed spaces that the characters are being forced into. By the end of the movie, the birds have taken over the inside world as well as the outside, and the family is forced to flee their house and the town. The audio processing of the birds' wings highlights two different emotions—both the feeling of claustrophobia associated with being trapped, and the feeling of fragility associated with knowing that our surroundings aren't quite strong enough to protect us. The same forces are at play in *Resident Evil 0*. Because we are attacked sporadically from the outside, the sound designers can add outside ambience to any room in order to set the player on edge. Whether a specific reason exists for the outside ambience, such as a broken window or a hole in the wall, is unimportant.

Conclusion

The role of sound in multimedia and specifically in video games is power-ful. There is ample evidence that music and sound design can be used to alter the visual elements attended to by a viewer, how a viewer perceives those elements, and what is remembered after viewing. Music and sound design in video games have long been underappreciated—considered somewhat less important than other elements such as the graphic design, the number of polygons on the screen at any given time, or the physics engine—but that should not be the case. In the introduction to *The Fat Man on Game Audio*, George Sanger (The Fat Man) states, "Audio is al-ways the lowest priority for game developers. Always has been. Probably always will be. It's all too tragic to think about" (23). The all too common belief that the quality of the audio in a game is less important than other aspects of game design is perhaps the result of the subconscious role played by audio in multimedia, and of the constant need for game de-velopers' marketing departments to boast impressive graphical achieve-ments. However, it is no secret that flashy graphics do not make a great game; they can only add to or detract from the rest of the game's design. There are countless examples of games that have pushed the envelope of what is possible with graphics in games but have failed to win over the hearts of the gaming community.

As with film and many other forms of multimedia, unless the sound design is overtly intrusive, the player of a game will not notice the game's audio on a conscious level, nor is the player likely to notice the emotional effect. More often than not, the emotions felt by the player are intrinsically attributed to narrative elements even though the emotional power of the narrative would be greatly reduced if the audio track were to be removed. In *Resident Evil 0*, it is clear that the game creates a sense of terror in the player, but the important role of the sound design in creating that sense is not always immediately obvious. However, the effects of audio in a multimedia setting are very real and powerful. The sound design in *Resident Evil 0* takes many cues from multimedia theory, and that design is similar to that of psychological thrillers like *The Birds*. There are many similarities between the game and this movie, and there are even some places in the game that seem to allude directly to the movie, such as the occasional attacks by flocks of crows. In creating a sound design for a game such as this one, it is important to work within the construct of nonlinearity, not against it. It is also important to ensure that sonic elements work in counterpoint to visual elements. This game is especially terrifying because the sound design is successful in manipulating the experience of the player. Through careful planning, the designer and composer have set up sequences of events that make us begin to assume that certain rules will always be true. The suspense of the game is increased when those rules are broken. The constant tension created by the sound design is largely responsible for the success of the series, and the psychological terror the games are able to impart on the player.

Works Cited

Boltz, Marilyn. "Musical Soundtracks as a Schematic Influence on the Cognitive Processing of Filmed Events." *Music Perception* 18.4. 427–54.

Brandon, Alexander. "Shooting from the Hip: An Interview with Hip Tanaka" *www.gamasutra.com* (25 September 2002).

Cohen, Annabel. "Music as a Source of Emotion in Film." In *Music and Emotion: Theory and Research*. Ed. Patrik Juslin and John Sloboda. New York: Oxford University Press, 2001. 249–72

Collopy, Fred. "Color Scales?" *www.rhythmiclight.com* (2004). Accessed 18 July 2005.

Cook, Nicholas. *Analysing Musical Multimedia*. New York: Oxford University Press, 2000.

Eisenstein, Sergei M., Vsevolod Pudovkin, and G. V. Alexandrov. "Statement on the Sound Film." In *Film Form*. Sergei Eisenstein. New York: Harcourt, 1949. 257–60.

Lipscomb, Scott, and David Tolchinsky. "The Role of Music Communication in Cinema." In *Musical Communication*. Ed. Dorothy Miell. New York: Oxford University Press, 2005.

Marshall, Sandra, and Annabel Cohen. "Effects of Musical Soundtracks on Attitudes Toward Animated Geometric Figures." *Music Perception* 6.1. 95–112.

McDonnell, Maura. "Colour and Sound." *www.soundingvisual.com* (2002). Accessed 1 May 2007 at *www.paradise2012.com.*

Nettl, Bruno. "Music." *www.grovemusic.com* (July 2005). Accessed 1 May 2007.

Sanger, George. *The Fat Man on Game Audio*. Indianapolis: New Riders Publishing, 2004.

Schoenberg, Arnold. *Style and Idea: Selected Writings of Arnold Schoenberg*. Berkeley: University of California Press, 1984

Thayer, Julian, and Robert Levenson. "Effects of Music on Psychophysiological Responses to a Stressful Film." *Psychomusicology* 3.1. 44–52.

Weis, Elisabeth. "The Evolution of Hitchcock's Aural Style and Sound in *The Birds*." In *Film Sound: Theory and Practice*. Ed. Elisabeth Weis and John Belton. New York: Columbia University Press, 1985. 298–311

Xenakis, Iannis. *Formalized Music: Thought and Mathematics in Composition*. Stuyvesant: Pendragon Press, 1991.

Games Cited

Metroid (NES). Kyoto: Nintendo, 1986.

Resident Evil 0. (Nintendo GameCube). Sunnyvale, CA: Capcom, 2002.

Silent Hill. (Sony PlayStation). Redwood City, CA: Konami, 1999.

10

Remembrance of Things Fast

Conceptualizing *Nostalgic-Play* in the *Battlestar Galactica* Video Game

Anna Reading and Colin Harvey

> Nostalgia charts space on time and time on space
> and hinders the distinction between subject and object
> ... To unearth the fragments of nostalgia one needs
> a dual archaeology of memory and of place.
> —Svetlana Boym, *The Future of Nostalgia* (xviii)

It is ironic for a medium that is, relatively speaking, in its infancy that video games should rely so heavily on history and the past. Video game stores are replete with titles that allow players to fight wars already won or lost and visit cities and times long since gone. Yet video games can invoke the memory of the past in other ways than simply recreating historical vistas or reenacting past events. Video games can reinvent the narratives established by other media in a particular and playful fashion. It is this process that we call *nostalgic-play.*

In this chapter we conceptualize and explain *nostalgic-play* as a particular form of gameplay. We do this by exploring the operation and interrelationship of nostalgia and affect in the *Battlestar Galactica* video game, released in 2003. *Affect* refers to the drives, feelings, emotions, and motivations that characterize all human experience (Damasio 8).

We examine the disparate ways in which the video game rearticulates past ideas of the *Battlestar Galactica* mythos and aesthetics drawn from the original feature film and television series. We also analyze the ways in which new ideas of *Battlestar Galactica* are used and articulated through the video game in anticipating the new television version of the franchise.

We begin by mapping the concept of nostalgia as an area of scholarly inquiry and look at the ways in which it has come to be used as a critical tool within cultural theory. We argue that using the concept of nostalgia to analyze the game *Battlestar Galactica* usefully highlights shortcomings inherent in the dominant theoretical frameworks currently used to analyze video games.

At the same time, though, we argue that the current dominant model of nostalgia employed by cultural critics is itself problematic. In particular, we suggest the need to critique Svetlana Boym's study *The Future of Nostalgia* in which she establishes nostalgia as a new area of enquiry. We challenge Boym's assertion that new media and especially "the Virtual" operate independently of affect.

In contrast, we contend that it is the simultaneity of body and mind in video game play that suggests the need for a conceptualization of *nostalgia* that draws on its etymological origins embracing the physiological. We argue that video gameplay is affective. A player is influenced both in terms of his or her physical body and the wider "body of relations"— that is to say the ways in which he or she is both culturally and socially situated.

We proceed to demonstrate how a reworking of nostalgia as a conceptual tool in the form of nostalgic-play enables a complex understanding of nostalgia in relation to video games. We show this through an analysis of how the digital game *Battlestar Galactica* invokes and reinvokes the nostalgic through the body of relations that constitutes gameplay. We begin by giving some context to the game itself.

Game Context

Battlestar Galactica was originally a television series. It was made by ABC, distributed by Universal, and first broadcast in 1978 in both the United States and the United Kingdom. A feature film version, also entitled *Battlestar Galactica*, was released theatrically in 1978, prior to the television show's airing in Britain (Lewis and Stempel 15). The feature film roughly equated to the first three episodes of the television series, which were entitled *Saga of a Star World, Parts One, Two and Three*. The film and the television series utilize much of the same footage, though the narrative differs in some aspects. This is perhaps most notable in that the Judas Iscariot figure, Baltar, is killed by his Cylon masters in the feature film whereas in the television version the character becomes a recurring villain.

Two television movies subsequently appeared. As with the first film, *Mission Galactica: The Cylon Attack* (1978) utilized footage from two episodes of the television series. The subsequent film, *Conquest of the Earth*, released theatrically in 1980, used footage from the short-lived *Battlestar Galactica* sequel series, *Galactica 1980*. In 2002 the Sci-Fi Channel made the decision to commission a new television miniseries remake of the original *Battlestar Galactica* (Weller). This remake evolved into a fully-fledged series, which began production for its fourth season in 2007 (SFX).

The 2003 video game version of *Battlestar Galactica* (Figure 10.1) was developed by Warthog and published by Vivendi and is available for Sony's PlayStation 2 and Microsoft's Xbox consoles. In some respects the narrative of the game and the audiovisual elements of the game adhere to the mythology and aesthetics constructed by the original television and film versions of *Battlestar Galactica*. In other respects, however, narrative and audiovisual elements have been refashioned to complement the newer miniseries and newer television series versions. This adherence to some elements of the original mythos and introduction of elements from the newer mythos is evident both in terms of the non-interactive cutscenes of the game and the interactive, playable elements of the game.

Why Nostalgia?

Certainly within the medium of the video game, invoking nostalgia is a key factor in game construction and marketing, extending beyond simply fulfilling a player's desire to (re)visit and interact with times, places, and characters from the past. At face value, *Medal of Honor: Frontline* (2002) appears to invoke the memory of an historical event—fighting in Europe as an American GI in World War II—that many video game players could not possibly have experienced. In that sense it is not nostalgic, because for most players it is not an event they can remember, a key criteria for what constitutes nostalgia. However, *Frontline* refashions the famous Omaha beach landing from the 1996 film *Saving Private Ryan* for the purposes of gameplay, as well as riffing off numerous World War II films.

Similarly, the video game *Grand Theft Auto: Vice City* (2002) is doing something other than simply allowing players to visit the 1980s: *Vice City* draws on a plethora of gangster films, notably the Brian de Palma remake of *Scarface* (1983), as well as the original television version of *Miami Vice*, often in heavily ironic fashion. In both the cases of *Frontline* and *Vice City*, existing cultural artifacts intercede with and influence the memory. This is widespread practice in relation to video games. The reinvention of existing cultural artifacts is perhaps most obvious in the repackaging of classics such as *Pac-Man* (1979), *Donkey Kong* (1981), and *PONG* (1972),

Figure 10.1. The Xbox version of the 2003 *Battlestar Galactica* **game. Image © Vivendi Universal.**

all of which invoke memories of the original game and of early video gaming.

Cultural theory already has a number of established concepts to understand how past elements from an older medium may be reinvoked within a newer medium. So why use the lens of *nostalgia*? As Zach Whalen suggests, *remediation* could equally describe how one medium may adopt the strategies or formal elements of another. However, with remediation the analysis can become too diffuse and subsequently confused. Thus Fredric Jameson's conception of nostalgia (which he explores in "Postmodernism") is, according to Whalen, a clearer way of understanding "the roles each media form plays in relation to the other."

As we have just discussed, nostalgia is a yearning for something that tends to have been within living memory rather than distant historical memory—hence, a key feature in terms of what is yearned for is its proximity to the present. Textual analysis approaches, in separating out text from player, tend to ignore what Bergson characterizes as the "durational" nature of memory, concentrating on the moment of analysis and ignoring the player's past and ongoing experience of the world. An "affective semiotics," of the kind explored by Henry Jenkins and Matt Hills, would need to take into account the way in which the consumer of a media artifact is both constrained and liberated by their own memories (23–29).

In this respect an analysis of nostalgia in game play or what we call "nostalgic-play" in the video game can offer something new to the analysis of games in that it usefully cuts across conventional conceptualizations that separate text from player. The term *nostalgic-play* could therefore be used to describe how meaning is constituted through the reinvocation of the past in the virtual plane within a particular time-frame. This takes place through a dynamic interplay of a body of relations that includes the player, the game, and the social and cultural context of production and play.

Mapping Nostalgia

Before we can further develop *nostalgic-play* as a concept and apply it to the video game *Battlestar Galactica*, we need to unpack what is meant more broadly by *nostalgia* and its origins within cultural theory. The history of the term *nostalgia* is one that has changed significantly over time (Reading 32). Etymologically, the word originates from *nosos* meaning "return to one's ancient land" and *algosos* meaning "suffering or grief from the desire to return." *Nostalgia*, in its present and commonplace conceptualization, has come to mean a simple yearning for things past. But it is also significant that nostalgia, having been identified by a Swiss doctor in 1688, became pathologized in the eighteenth century. It later came to be seen as a debilitating disease of both mind and body that was easily provoked by exposure to familiar sights and sounds of home. In the American Civil War, for example, nostalgia was viewed as an infectious terminal illness affecting more than five thousand white troops in the North. So prevalent was it that songs and stories that might provoke an outbreak of the disease were banned.

It was not until the nineteenth century that the definition of nostalgia as a pathological disorder of memory began to disappear, though it remained an important theme and emotion in the Victorian literature (Colley; Wagner). Contemporary renderings of the term prefer instead to identify nostalgia as an anodyne, personal longing for the past.[1]

As an academic term, *nostalgia* is somewhat diffuse: within cultural theory it is used in a variety of ways, with slippage making it a problematic term to deploy as a critical tool of analysis. Stephanie Brown argues that the term *nostalgia* has "multiple and sometimes conflicting implications." Such is the confusion associated with the term that a number of recent papers have tried to clarify what is meant by it. Jennifer Delisle, for example, argues that we need to make a distinction between *experiential nostalgia*—the personal nostalgia for a place—and *cultural nostalgia*—the articulation of the past within culture. However, we would contend that the complex body of relations that constitute gameplay may involve both cultural and experiential nostalgia: thus *Battlestar Galactica* rearticulates cultural elements from the earlier television series, while invoking a yearning in the player for a lost experience of watching (or perhaps not having watched) the television series.

The more recent origins of nostalgia's usage by contemporary cultural theorists lie within key elements of postmodern theory. For example, Baudrillard has argued, "When the real is no longer what it used to be, nostalgia assumes its full meaning" (12). To Baudrillard, culture in the postmodern world is characterized by pastiche and an ability to recycle and copy different past styles and cultures. Implicated in Fredric Jameson's concept of periodization is also a concern with nostalgia. This concern has been further explored by Bryan S. Turner who argues that a predominant feature of contemporary popular culture is that it is redolent with nostalgia.

Nostalgia has since been used as a point of focus within and across a variety of academic fields. Film theorists use the concept as a way of describing and analyzing the uses and representations of the past in the moving image. For example, in *Monochrome Memories: Nostalgia and Style in Retro America,* Paul Grainge discusses the concepts of retro and cultural nostalgia in Hollywood films of the 1990s. He addresses the ways in which nostalgia has been developed and has become part of the cultural economy of branding. Pam Cook's *Screening the Past: Memory and Nostalgia in Cinema* addresses film culture's obsession with the past and the role of the cinema in mediating history through memory and nostalgia. Nostalgia has also become important within the field of sociology as a way of critiquing the development of the discipline itself: there has been a concern with the importance that nostalgia has had in the sociological imagination in its idealization of premodern societies.

Within literary and cultural studies, the term is increasingly significant. In earlier literary studies, nostalgia was viewed as "a topic of embarrassment and a term of abuse. Diatribe upon diatribe denounces it as reactionary, repressive, ridiculous" (Lowenthal 20). Yet, more recently, particularly within the study of cultural and collective memory, the conceptualization of nostalgia has moved on from being used simply to critique what were seen as conservative, reactionary narratives representative of a crisis in history and aesthetics. Instead, it is used to describe a more complex, contradictory, and provocative process in relation to elements of the past (Ladino).

For example, Holocaust memory scholars Marianne Hirsch and Leo Spitzer discuss how nostalgia as a form of remembrance for second generation Holocaust survivors operates differently from their parents' generation (85). They describe a return journey with their parents, survivors of the Holocaust who escaped from Cernowitz in Romania. Their parents experienced what they term *ambivalent nostalgia*, a desire to return to the place that was both home and the site of trauma. For the second generation, the nostalgic desire to return home incorporates a sense of needing to repair history while also being rootless, in that home is also equated with hostile territory and a fragile sense of place. The overall workings of nostalgia were understood to be multilayered and conflicted, and involved collaborative encounters between the generations where "the fracture between eras was briefly bridged" (84–86).

Nostalgia has also been used to understand the complex process of identification and rejection of the past that is a constituent part in the construction of identity. For example, Jo Moran explores the meanings of childhood nostalgia in contemporary culture. Childhood is reinvoked by the heritage industry in complex ways through the narrative construction of fantasy childhoods, as well as through everyday objects, photos, and textual fragments. The result is the production of "disjointed feelings of desire and mourning" (160). In this respect, this use of nostalgia points to how nostalgic identification with past forms and nostalgic affects might enable us to clarify our understanding of the relationship between player and game in video game studies.

This more complex usage of nostalgia is especially evident within the study of the literature of exile, the most well-known of which is Svetlana Boym's *The Future of Nostalgia*. Boym argues that, in a globalized culture in which cyberspace disarticulates people in both time and space, there is a countermovement to this process in the form of a collective nostalgia (xiv). Nostalgia, Boym contends, which has reached epidemic proportions worldwide, appears to be a longing for a place, but it is also a desire to be back in a particular time. In this respect, "nostalgia charts space on time and time on space and hinders the distinction between subject and object." Nostalgia, she believes, is "a symptom of our age, a historical emotion" (xvi). Within this, though, she argues that that there is an important conceptual distinction to be made between what she terms *restorative nostalgia* and *reflective nostalgia*:

> Restorative nostalgia does not think of itself as nostalgia, but rather as truth and tradition. Reflective nostalgia dwells on the ambivalences of modernity. Restorative nostalgia protects the absolute truth, while reflective nostalgia calls it into doubt. (xviii)

Boym adds that with restorative nostalgia two main plots predominate, "the return to origins and the conspiracy." In contrast, reflective nostalgia has more of a rhizomic plot, "inhabiting many places at once and imagining different time zones" (xviii).

Conventional Approaches to Video Games

The dominant paradigms that tend to be used within conventional analyses of video games are known as the narratological and ludological approaches (Frasca 221–35; Newman 18, 91). The narratological approach proposes that video games are best studied as interactive stories by using the same analytic strategies established in the fields of literary and film studies. By contrast the ludological approach instead suggests that video games are an experiential medium and are fundamentally at variance with the kinds of sequential narrative engagement offered by other media such as film, the novel and the theatre play. Video games, ludologists argue, need to be analyzed according to the operation of play and rules.

On face value it could be argued that in terms of nostalgia, Boym's notion of the restorative maps clearly on to narratological approaches, while reflective nostalgia with its rhizomic qualities maps better on to the ludological. Certainly within the *Battlestar Galactica* video game, whether one takes a narratological or ludological perspective, nostalgia plays a pivotal role in enabling meaning to be generated within the game. However, as we shall see, interestingly, restorative and reflective nostalgia within *Battlestar Galactica* seem to operate concurrently.

Thus, from a narrative analysis viewpoint, much of the narrative framework for the game takes its impetus from the original filmic and televisual iterations of the *Battlestar Galactica* franchise, begun in 1978. However, the game's narrative context can be seen as a prequel to both the original series and the newer miniseries, and either articulates or rearticulates many familiar elements while including many new elements specific to the 2003 television miniseries.

In terms of playing through or with the past or what we term *nostalgic-play*, the player adopts the role of Adama, a central character in the original television and film iterations of *Battlestar Galactica* played by Lorne Greene. Viewers of the original television and film incarnations of the franchise know that it is this character who must, consequently, lead the remnants of the human race to find the mysterious lost Thirteenth Tribe of Man on planet Earth. In the *Battlestar Galactica* game, as the player takes on the past-in-the-present role of the character Adama, s/he has the ability to view events from two perspectives—from within the cockpit of his or her Viper spacecraft or from outside of the craft (Figure 10.2).

At the climax of the level, the player must defend the *Battlestar Galactica* ship itself. Further, Adama is a character who the player "knows" will play a major role in "later" *Battlestar Galactica* mythology, both in terms of the old and new television series. Following an explanatory opening monologue that both reinforces and reinvents existing mythology, the first level of the game sees the player having to defend various human spaceships against attack from enemy spacecraft. The enemy craft are identified visually within the game itself, in the accompanying extra-diegetic instruction manual, and on the game's soundtrack as "Cylon Raiders." In addition to elements of plotting from the original versions, the video game features a number of familiar characters and, crucially, the same actors (Richard Hatch and Dirk Benedict) voicing some of those characters.

In audiovisual terms, the iconography reinvokes the original *Battlestar Galactica* television and film series: the representation of both friendly and enemy spaceships, their movement through the "space" of the game, and the accompanying sound effects of laser beams and explosions are all drawn from the original iterations of the television series. In purely narrative terms, however, a key point of departure from the original television and film iterations of the franchise occurs in the voice-over prologue of the game. The Cylons, the player is informed, are machines created by human beings. This contradicts a key scene in the original iteration of the franchise, wherein the character of Apollo (played by Richard Hatch) explains to the young boy, Boxy, that the Cylons were originally lizard creatures who copied the humanoid form when constructing their robotic Cylon warriors. In this version of the mythos, these Cylons then rebelled against their lizard masters.

However, the game's rearticulation of the original mythos and aesthetic fits with the *Battlestar Galactica* television remake's decision to make humankind's Cylon adversaries products of humankind's own making. In eschewing this aspect of "otherness" we can perhaps observe the post–9-11 and War On Terror themes that inform both the digital game and 2003 miniseries iterations of the *Battlestar Galactica* franchise. In the later game and miniseries versions, we humans have created our own nemesis. It consequently becomes clear that narrative elements of the *Battlestar Galactica* video game simultaneously invoke both restorative nostalgia and reflective nostalgia in Boym's terms.

At the same time, though, there is nostalgic-play in both restorative and reflective forms in those aspects of the game that we might obviously identify as ludological[2]—i.e., the gameplay itself. The player must attack those alien spacecraft indicated by the crosshairs turning red on the display screen until sufficient craft are destroyed or such time has elapsed

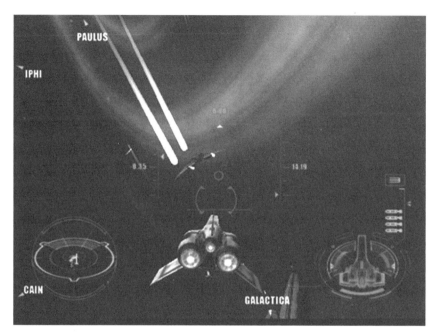

Figure 10.2. Outside view of Viper craft from the *Battlestar Galactica* game. Image © Vivendi Universal.

that a cutscene is triggered indicating that the *Battlestar Galactica* is itself being targeted by the Cylon ships. The player must then move to defend the Galactica mothership. Importantly, progression in the first level of the *Battlestar Galactica* video game is dependent not only on the success-ful obliteration of attacking Cylon spacecraft but also on the defense of the eponymous mothership. In other words, responsive, accurate senso-motor skills are rewarded on the basis of adherence to the rules, or *ludus*, of the game (Caillois). In *Battlestar Galactica* adherence to the rules then reinvokes the heroic mythos of the old *Battlestar Galactica* series whereby valiant warriors in fighters must defend the last vestiges of humanity from oblivion. In this limited sense, *ludus* could be read in terms of Boym's idea of restorative nostalgia: obedience to the rules equates to protection of the absolute truth. Equally, since it is a subversive act, freeform play—what Caillois terms *paidia*—could be read as Boym's reflective nostalgia.

However, the terms *ludus* and *paidia* do not entirely account for the widely varying experience of gameplay. The *Battlestar Galactica* video game relies on exploratory gameplay in order that the user can both orien-tate himself or herself in the environment and simultaneously track both enemy and friendly spacecraft. This could be read as both freeform play and adherence to the rules of the game. Consequently, since such gameplay can be read as both *ludus* and *paidia*, mapping these separately onto restorative and reflective nostalgia respectively is in turn problematic.

There is an additional theoretical challenge raised by analyzing nostalgia in relation to video games that stems from the fact that the conventional approaches to games studies do not currently account for all the elements that constitute gameplay. As Klevjer (191–99) has observed in his analysis of *Grand Theft Auto III* (2001), it is difficult to separate more obviously narrative elements from behavior that we might characterize as ludological. *Ludus* and *paidia* often operate within a narrative framework in which all elements are interdependent: an additional complication is that in the context of many video games, ludic elements and story elements are inextricably entwined.

Nostalgia and Affect in the Virtual Plane

In these respects, an approach that seeks to analyze video games in terms of nostalgia, focusing on nostalgic-play, can have significant strengths. It may eliminate the false dichotomies inscribed in conventional approaches to the study of video games, including those between subject and object, text and player, meaning and identity, and rule-based and freeform play. As Boym notes, "Nostalgia, like irony, is not a property of the object itself but a result of the interaction between subjects and objects, between actual landscapes and the landscapes of the mind" (354).

However, as well as the theoretical distinction that Boym makes between restorative and reflective nostalgia being difficult to distinguish in the context of interactive games, there are two additional theoretical weaknesses in Boym's conceptualization of nostalgia. This makes her approach problematic to apply to the analysis of video game play. The first weakness is that, within Boym's study of the literature of exile, computers and cyberspace are seen as independent of affect: "Computers, even the most sophisticated ones, are notoriously lacking in affect and sense of humor" (354). We would argue otherwise: affect is central to the set of relations that constitutes gameplay. Likewise, within the subset of *nostalgic-play*, the emotional, physiological yearning for a past spacetime is a key element.

The second theoretical shortcoming that can be identified with Boym's conceptualization of nostalgia and the application of her strategies of analysis to video gameplay is that her understanding of the virtual is somewhat reductivist, since it is narrowly configured through the technology of the computer. What we would suggest in relation to video game play is that the virtual, rather than being narrowly configured in relation to the computer or even the game itself, is better understood in Bergsonian terms as a plane of potential in which matter and mind are indivisible.

Conceptualizing Nostalgic-Play

So, just how should playing with the past in video games or what we have come to term *nostalgic-play* be conceptualized? In our view there are three important elements to understanding and framing nostalgia as a lens for use in studying video games and game play. These elements involve memory, time, and affect. As Andreas Huyssen observes, nostalgia is not separate from memory, but rather is part of it—a form of memory (88). Since even the most freeform example of *paidia* requires rules of some kind to operate, and since the learning and application of rules are dependent upon memory, we might therefore conclude that all games are in some way *memory* games. We are able to orchestrate ourselves within the game environment, temporally and spatially, precisely because we remember where we are within the game, or simply because we remember that we are playing a game.

The player's dexterity with the PS2 or Xbox controller in the video game version of *Battlestar Galactica* dictates how successful he or she will be in terms of the game's *ludus*. The body memory acquired from previous experiences playing this game—and to some extent participating in other PS2 games, as well as non-video games, rule-based activities, and the physical world in general—will contribute to the level of dexterity and rapidity of response the player is able to call upon during a gaming session.

Because memory is not merely a product of mind but also an element in a wider set of relations, it is necessary to employ theoretical stances complementary to ideas of affect. A properly somatic approach to understanding nostalgic-play renders conventional psychological and cultural distinctions a false dichotomy since, as Massumi argues, identifying culture and nature as separate entities is only to restate Cartesian dualism in other language (9–11). Henri Bergson's conception of memory as connected with matter enables an understanding of nostalgic-play that reconnects body and mind in the virtual plane.

Identification of the need for an affective, somatic approach to the study of video games is not new: Diane Carr and Torben Grodal have both adumbrated affective approaches. However, both these theorists have tended to present affect as an adjunct to existing narratological approaches, seeing the video game as text rather than medium. Similarly, ludology, which posits video games as experiential, still views games as texts to be read rather than elements within a set of relations (Frasca; Juul).

The player's somatic engagement in terms of nostalgic-play with the game *Battlestar Galactica* extends beyond manipulation of the various buttons and joysticks on the PlayStation 2 or Xbox controller. The body of relations governing gameplay should be understood as a complex interrelationship between the player, the game, and all those myriad factors through which player and game are constructed.

In this sense, the wider body of relations—the *context*—of nostalgic-play in which the game is played also cannot be ignored. Consequently, for some players of the *Battlestar Galactica* game, the familiarity of memories of the original *Battlestar Galactica* series and those longings—affective desires—to pilot a Viper fighter craft against opposing Cylon fighters will be invoked. Simultaneously, however, for these same players, certain aspects of the narrative and audiovisual iconography in their alterity derive from an affective desire to witness newer iterations of the *Battlestar Galactica* mythos, as provided by the 2003 miniseries and the subsequent four seasons of the new television series. The familiarity of the past and the shock of the new are conjured contemporaneously.

Further, we know that a feature of nostalgia is that it is a yearning for something "within time." In this sense, nostalgic-play can best be understood as part of memory in a Bergsonian sense in which time is understood as durational (Bergson 186). In terms of nostalgic-play this means that the past is dynamically related to the present rather than the present simply informing our view of the past, or vice versa (Deleuze 63). For Bergson, past and present are contemporaneous; they co-exist. The act of remembering is characterized by a rhizomic series of links whereby the past, present, and future are continually interlinked with one another. Thus, in terms of the nostalgic-playing of the game *Battlestar Galactica,* both the attacking and defending spacecraft recall the look and sound of the old television series while also anticipating the look and sound of the new television series. In the Bergsonian sense, past, present, and future are simultaneously and dynamically called into play.

To conclude, the lens of nostalgia is highly effective in relation to the study of video games. It cuts across established dichotomies between player and game and it highlights the theoretical shortcomings of ludological and narratological paradigms. At the same time, however, the predominant conceptualization of nostalgia within cultural analysis—such as that put forward by Svetlana Boym, for example—is problematic in relation to the analysis of video games. Thus we would contend that we need a reconceptualization of nostalgia specifically for video games in the form of nostalgic-play. Importantly, this understands gameplay itself within a wider body of relations and conceives of nostalgia as a dynamic element of memory with the virtual as a plane of potential, that includes a sense of durational time and affect.

Finally, approaching games in terms of nostalgic-play also highlights more broadly how memory is increasingly central to understanding the manifold ways in which games are produced, marketed, and above all, played. The yearning to revisit or experience some element within a past time and place through play is key to understanding the human psyche in a postmodern culture in which new technologies are central to time compression and distanciation. In a global environment in which time and space have collapsed, there is a concomitant drive to remember: fast.

Notes

1. Interestingly, the term in its negative form as a debilitating longing is not without equivalents in other cultures though it is constructed differently. Within certain elements of Chinese culture the cure for the equivalent to nostalgic longing is represented through the mythology of Old Lady Meng's Soup. When a person dies their soul may suffer agonies of pain if the past life were remembered, but after drinking the soup the soul passes over the Bridge of Pain and demons hurl the soul into waters of new life (Schwarcz 40). From this, a person who is pained by remembering too much is said to need Old Lady Meng's Soup, which obliterates their obsessive desire to call up the past. However, *nostalgia*, as we seek to use it in this paper, is best understood as having emerged out of Western cultures of migration, warfare, displacement, and exile.

2. Caillois, whose insights into non-video games and play provide a touchstone for ludological investigation, differentiates *ludus* from *paidia* (13). *Ludus* refers to more complex, rule-based play, while *paidia* is used to identify more freeform kinds of play.

Works Cited

Baudrillard, Jean. *Simulacra and Simulation*. Trans. Sheila Faria Glaser. Ann Arbor: University of Michigan Press, 1994.

Bergson, Henri. *Matter and Memory*. London: Zone Books, 2002.

Boym, Svetlana. *The Future of Nostalgia*. New York: Basic Books, 2001.

Brown, Stephanie. "On Kitsch, Nostalgia and Nineties Femininity." *Studies in Popular Culture* 22.1 (1999).

Carr, Diane. "Play Dead Genre and Affect in *Silent Hill* and *Planescape Torment*." *www.gamestudies.org* 3.1 (May 2003).

Colley, Ann. *Nostalgia and Recollection in Victorian Culture*. Basingstoke: Macmillan, 1998.

Cook, Pam. *Screening the Past: Memory and Nostalgia in Cinema*. London: Routledge, 2004.

Damasio, Antonio. *Looking for Spinoza: Joy, Sorrow and the Feeling Brain*. London: Heinemann, 2003

Deleuze, Gilles. *Bergsonism*. London: Zone Books 2002.

Delisle, Jennifer. "Theorizing Cultural and Experiential Nostalgia." Paper presented at "Nostalgia and Cultural Memory."

Frasca, Gonzalo. "Simulation versus Narrative: An Introduction to Ludology." In Wolf and Perron. 221–35.

Grainge, Paul. *Monochrome Memories: Nostalgia and Style in Retro America*. Oxford: Praeger, 2002.

Grodal, Torben. "Stories for Eye, Ear, and Muscles: Video Games, Media, and Embodied Experiences." In Wolf and Perron. 129–55.

Hirsch, Marianne, and Leo Spitzer. "We Would Never Have Come Without You: Generations of Nostalgia." In *The Politics of Memory*. Eds. Katherine Hodgkin and Susannah Radstone. London: Routledge, 2003. 79–96.

Huyssen, Andreas. *Twilight Memories: Marking Time in a Culture of Amnesia*. New York: Routledge, 1995.

Jameson, Fredric. "Postmodernism: Or the Cultural Logic of Late Capitalism." *New Left Review* 146 (July–August 1984). 53–92.

Jenkins, Henry. "Excerpts from 'Matt Hills Interviews Henry Jenkins.'" In *Fans, Bloggers, and Gamers: Exploring Participatory Culture*. New York: New York University Press, 2007.

Juul, Jesper. "Games Telling Stories? A Brief Note On Games and Narratives." *www.gamestudies.org* 1.1 (July 2001).

Kellington, Treava Ann. "Nostalgia and Pathological Mourning in Ted Hughes' Birthday Letters." Paper presented at "Nostalgia and Cultural Memory."

Klevjer, Rune. "In Defense of Cutscenes." In *Proceedings of the Computer Games and Digital Cultures Conference*. Ed. Frans Mäyrä. Tampere, Finland: Tampere University Press, 2002. 191–202.

Ladino, Jennifer K. "Rediscovering Nostalgia within Contemporary Theory." Paper presented at "Nostalgia and Cultural Memory."

Lewis, John E., and Penny Stempel. *Cult TV: The Essential Critical Guide*. London: Pavilion, 1993.

Lowenthal, David. "Nostalgia Tells it Like it Wasn't." *The Imagined Past: History and Nostalgia*. Eds. Christopher Shaw and Malcolm Chase. Manchester: Manchester University Press, 1989. 18–32.

Massumi, Brian. *Parables for the Virtual: Movement, Affect, Sensation*. Durham: Duke University Press, 2002.

Moran, Jo. "Childhood and Nostalgia in Contemporary Culture." *European Journal of Cultural Studies* 5.2 (2002). 155–73.

Newman, James. *Videogames*. London: Routledge, 2004.

"Nostalgia and Cultural Memory: A Conference for Graduate Students," Department of English, University of Victoria, British Columbia, 4–5 March 2005.

Robertson, R. "After Nostalgia? Wilful Nostalgia and the Phases of Globalisation." In *Theories of Modernity and Post-modernity*. Ed. Bryan S. Turner. London: Sage, 1990.

Reading, Anna. *The Social Inheritance of the Holocaust: Gender, Culture and Memory*. Basingstoke: Palgrave, 2002.

Schwarcz, Vera. *Bridge Across Broken Time: Chinese and Jewish Cultural Memory*. New Haven: Yale University Press, 1998.

SFX. "Galactica's Fourth Season Gets Extended." *www.sfx.co.uk* (22 March 2007). Accessed 13 May 2007.

Turner, Bryan S. "Mourning Bodies and Cultural Nostalgia." *Body and Society* 7.4 (2001). 97–102.

Wagner, Tamara S. "Nostalgia and the Victorian Novel." *www.victorianweb.org* (11 November 2002). Accessed 1 May 2007.

Weller, Mark. "History of Battlestar Galactica."*Battlestar Galactica Continuity and Timelines Site* (*members.cox.net/battlestar/history.htm*), May 2005. Accessed 1 July 2005.

Whalen, Zach. "Playing the Past." Address at "Playing the Past: Nostalgia in Video Games and Electronic Literature," University of Florida, 18–20 March 2005.

Games Cited

Battlestar Galactica. Paris: Vivendi Universal, 2003.

Donkey Kong. Kyoto: Nintendo, 1981.

Grand Theft Auto III. New York: Rockstar Games, 2001.

Grand Theft Auto: Vice City. New York: Rockstar Games, 2002.

Medal of Honor: Frontline. Redwood City, CA: Electronic Arts, 2002.

Pac-Man. Chicago: Midway, 1979.

Donkey Kong. Kyoto: Nintendo, 1981.

PONG. Sunnyvale, CA: Atari, 1972.

Part III

Playing *with* the Past

Nostalgia and Real History in Video Games

11

Just Less than Total War

Simulating World War II as Ludic Nostalgia

James Campbell

In *Homo Ludens*, his landmark study of "the play element in culture," Johan Huizinga claims that warfare has traditionally been a part of the ludic. Although bloody, violent, and often grimly serious, as long as war maintained a difference between combatants and civilians and admitted a rough parity between the combatants, war was a game. Whether implicit or explicit, it had rules. Huizinga portrays this situation slipping away during the process of colonization as Europeans turned their arms against "lesser breeds without the law"[1] and thus lost the sense of a contest between equals.

> We can only speak of war as a cultural function so long as it is waged within a sphere whose members regard each other as equals or antagonists with equal rights; in other words, its cultural function depends on its play-quality. (89)

Finally, with the introduction of the uniquely modern concept of total war, the line between soldier and civilian is blurred out of existence and all trace of war as ludic *agon* is erased: "It remained for the theory of 'total war' to banish war's cultural function and extinguish the last vestige of the play-element" (90). Waterloo may have been won on the playing fields of Eton, but the mud of Flanders buried all connection between playing field and battlefield.

Huizinga does not trace the genealogy of the term *total war*, but I think it worth doing in this context. The phrase is most fully associated with the German general Erich Ludendorff, officially deputy to the army chief of staff, Paul von Hindenburg, in the latter half of World War I. Unofficially, Ludendorff was the military dictator of the wartime German state, which he organized to the single end of winning the war. Ludendorff essentially inverted Carl von Clausewitz's famous maxim that "war is the continuation of politics by other means." War was no longer to be the seeking of political ends by military means; rather, the political state was to serve military ends. The economy was mobilized to produce military equipment, the population seen either directly as resources for war (i.e., cannon fodder) or as producers of goods in support of war, and the culture was rallied in support of the national/military cause. In such a situation, of course, all members of the population are part of the war effort, and once this assumption was established for the German state, it was easy to extend it to the condition of opponent states: Ludendorff was a devout proponent of the unrestricted submarine warfare that caused the US entry into the war, and he supported the nascent technique of strategic bombing that, however ineffectual in material terms, brought the terror of war to non-uniformed citizens in London and Paris. Thus, in Huizinga's terms, war stopped being ludic in 1916 when Ludendorff ascended to power. Looking back, it seems a likely date: the Christmas truce where professional soldiers met in mutual respect in 1914 had by this time given way to huge armies of recently conscripted civilians whose only real strategy was one of attrition. Whichever fully mobilized state first lost the ability materially to produce war would lose. History tells us that it was Germany that lost the war of production, whereupon Ludendorff exiled himself to Sweden where he began to create a mythology of an indestructible German military that had been betrayed at home by leftists, Freemasons, and Jews. He later returned to Germany and was elected to the Reichstag as a Nazi.

What I want to do in this chapter is take a look at first-person shooter games that are historically situated to represent and simulate the Second World War. I begin with Huizinga and Ludendorff to make a point: World War II was a total war from the beginning. Hitler had learned the lessons of Ludendorff's Great War, and the Western Allies would adopt them as well. Civilian casualties outnumbered military in World War II.[2] It was a war of complete economic mobilization for all of the major combatant nations. *Homo Ludens* itself can be read as a kind of requiem for the ludic in the face of the rise of Nazism. The Nazi party adopted a doctrine of total war before they even found a war to fight; in a sense, with Ludendorff's paranoid ravings forming one of many inspirations, they continued the last total war more or less where it had been left off. Improvements in technology resulted in death on a mass scale not possible twenty years before. Much of this technology, especially strategic air bombardment, was aimed at civilian targets. From the London Blitz to the firebombings of Dresden and Tokyo to the atomic strikes that ended the war, World War

II was a messy, tragic, and extended exercise in nonludic warfare—a full stop to Huizinga's cultural play-element as an aspect of armed conflict.

This presents a problem when you want to make a game, especially a first-person shooter (FPS). Economies of scale and their speeds of development are the usual stuff of resource management games. From the days of *Doom* (1993), however, FPSs have concentrated on the lone heroic—or, as often, anti-heroic—figure of the isolated marine in his epic quest for the BFG ("Big Fucking Gun"). In single-player modes, *Doom* pitted a human contestant (both in the sense of the player and his or her on-screen avatar) against a horde of distinctly nonhuman demonic opponents. Even in the first appropriation of the Second World War for FPS purposes, the now classic *Wolfenstein 3-D* (1992), enemies were barely human. (This seminal FPS provided superhuman mutant Nazis as opponents once the player had risen above the mundane task of dispatching merely human prison guards.) But if designers and players desire a game that is more realistic than the cartoon gothic of *Wolfenstein 3-D* (even if we take realism as a genre rather than a question of absolute and verifiable authenticity), then they are left with the task of making an enjoyable game out of a horrific and, in Huizinga's terms, profoundly nonludic experience.

So I contend that what the recent group of World War II FPS games (*Return to Castle Wolfenstein, Medal of Honor, Battlefield 1942*, and *Call of Duty*) does is create a sense of nostalgia for the Second World War as the last ludic war. They do this by imposing specifically what Huizinga claims that modern war lacks: rules. Civilians are entirely lacking in these games and friendly fire incidents are either impossible or, in the case of *Battlefield 1942*, controllable. Soldiers by and large do not panic; *Call of Duty* does contain a moment where a medic refuses to rescue a wounded solider, but it is a scripted event. It will play out the same every time one plays the single-player game, and it will always end with the panicked medic receiving a predestined German bullet to the head. The unpredictable, in other words, becomes predictable. Combatants face each other as equals in a controlled environment where war becomes an agonistic game, offering a grim form of play that tests their mettle—a kind of pugilism with submachine guns.

More telling than the overtly ludic elements of play, perhaps, is the lack of mistakes. I do not mean by this, of course, that it is impossible for the player to do stupid things and thus play badly: I consider my own play-level for these games to hover somewhere around the area of inept. Rather, the universe surrounding the field of play is a kind of error-free zone. I'm drawing here on Paul Fussell's book on the Second World War, *Wartime*, in which he constructs the war as basically a pageant of gruesome mistakes (17–35). In FPSs, however, weapons do not jam, grenades do not have unpredictable fuse lengths, players do not become hopelessly lost (reliable compasses and maps are part of the standard display for each game), and friendly troops do not mistake the player for the enemy. Things work, and death is a product of having done something incorrectly or inefficiently. It is not, with very few exceptions, a product of bad luck.

To return to Huizinga's terminology, I think what we have with World War II FPSs is a kind of remediated nostalgia. I am poaching Bolter and Grusin's term here: for them, remediation is the tendency of new media to incorporate the forms of older media—to present themselves as "refashioned and improved versions of other media" (15). I think this is both literally and symbolically true for these games. It is literal in that the games are not so much attempting to simulate the Second World War as they are attempting to simulate a Second World War film. Neither *Medal of Honor* nor *Call of Duty* exactly shrink from their homages to Spielberg's *Saving Private Ryan* (1998); the latter game is quite overt in its references to the HBO miniseries *Band of Brothers* (2001), as well as adding a healthy dose of *Enemy at the Gates* (2001) in its Soviet storyline. The adjective "cinematic" is consistently used in advertising, reviews, and fan sites for these games. A few of many possible examples: Infinity Ward, the developer of *Call of Duty*, touts the game's "cinematic intensity" on its website[3] while *The Adrenaline Vault's* review of the game cites (positively) its "cinematic feel" (Alam). The *GameSpy* review claims that *Call of Duty* "make[s] you feel like you were inside a World War II movie" (Accardo). *Medal of Honor*, *Call of Duty's* predecessor in the genre, also garners the epithet "cinematic feel" from *GamesSpy* (Accardo), while the reviewer for *The Adrenaline Vault* describes the feel of play as finding oneself in "an incredibly immersive interactive movie" (Mandel). These games thus illustrate ludologist Bob Rehak's observation that "video games are starting to resemble movies more than they do 'real life'" (104). It is abundantly clear that the game designers are aiming less for a recreation of the experience of combat in the Second World War (an admittedly impossible goal) and more to remediate the cinematically mediated access to such experiences that has been the dominant cultural mode of representation since the time of the war itself. More people have seen war films than have seen combat: in this sense, authenticity connotes truth to the war film more than to what the war film represents. A game will thus succeed to the extent that its electronic medium remediates cinema.

This argument need not involve rehashing the narratology versus ludology debate that has formed one of the foundational questions for game studies and the attendant issue of whether game studies has been unduly subjected to paradigms developed for film studies. I make no claim that all games necessarily remediate cinema, nor that they should do so, nor that the academically established study of film is the exclusively appropriate lens through which to view computer games (I also doubt that anyone actually believes this). My point, rather, is that both producers and consumers of these games are remarkably clear and explicit in their interpretations of what the games try to accomplish and, in the view of most gamers, succeed in doing. The goal, at least as far as *Call of Duty* and *Medal of Honor* are concerned, is immersing the player as a character in a war film. More specifically, they aim to give the player the experience of fighting World War II as represented in films dating from the late 1990s. To the extent that such films draw heavily on the WWII film as an already established genre, we thus have a layering effect: the games represent the recent movies, which represent the earlier movies, which putatively represent the war itself. The ludic rallying cry of cinematic realism is thus a form of *hyperrealism*, Jean Baudrillard's term for the funhouse-mirror effect of postmodern culture in which representations represent other representations to such an extent that the original reality becomes inaccessible. That what we are trying to represent is war adds yet another dimension to the conundrum: war has traditionally been viewed as a primary experience that remains unrepresentable to those without firsthand experience of it.[4]

Baudrillard's work is resoundingly ignored in much of game studies. When it is mentioned, it is usually in the contest of dismissal. The editors of the *First Person* collection, for instance, remind the reader that Baudrillard's version of simulation is not the one that operates in the discourse of computer simulation: "The simulation discussed by him is a cultural phenomenon, not a computational one—and as such is fully existent in old media as well as new" (Wardrip-Fruin and Harrigan 71). Similarly, Marie-Laure Ryan disparages Baudrillard's version of the virtual; she offers Pierre Lévy's *Becoming Virtual* as a more positive and useful alternative (25–47). Baudrillard's courting of controversy (most noticeably the provocation of 1991's *The Gulf War Did Not Take Place*) and his playful alternation between nostalgically bemoaning the loss of the real and playfully celebrating its demise practically guarantee that the name "Baudrillard" will conjure as much a style as a set of ideas (as well, perhaps, as the idea that style itself is an idea). Nonetheless, I think that it is precisely because Baudrillard's version of simulation is a cultural rather than a merely digital phenomenon that it has important implications for computer game studies. Ludology does occasionally fall into the trap of divorcing games from the cultures that produce them; if these cultures include simulation as a nondigital condition as well as a digital occurrence, it need not mean that discourse about the digital must limit itself to simulation as a pure feat of computer engineering. Moreover, I do not think it necessary to assume Baudrillard's entire argument, at least not in any wholesale fashion, in order to take seriously (or seriously enough to play with) his version of simulation as the basis of the postmodern condition.

I bring up Baudrillard because I want to investigate not only how WWII FPSs represent the Second World War (though I am interested in this as well), but also in how they simulate it.[5] I find Baudrillard helpful in thinking through this difference. "To simulate is to feign to have what one doesn't have . . . But it is more complicated than that because simulating is not pretending" (3). Representing war—whether in literature, film, or a game like *Risk*—allows a clear distinction between war and its representation. The first half-hour of *Saving Private Ryan* may well represent war in a particularly jarring and graphic manner, for instance, but it is nonetheless presenting us with something that is absent. A viewer may be shocked, but they will not be shot. Of course, a gamer is in no physical danger from *Battlefield 1942* either (carpal tunnel syndrome excepted), but the gamer is using the controls of the game to perform via the avatar approximately the same kind of behaviors that would occur during combat on a battlefield in 1942. In other words, the game corresponds to Gonzalo Frasca's game-based definition of simulation: "To simulate is to model a (source) system through a different system which maintains (for somebody) some of the behaviors of the original system" (223). In WWII FPS terms, the source system is mechanized mass combat between 1939 and 1945, while the different system is the game. Unlike reading about war, simulating it involves behavior that reproduces what goes on in combat (or, admittedly, a particular game's representation of combat; as we will see, representation and simulation may be separated for study but usually occur together in practice).

The game-simulation of WWII combat, in fact, simulates combat as constructed in previous first-person shooter games. Second World War shooters thus do not so much attempt a representation of the Second World War as they attempt to domesticate the chaos of violent history into a simulacrum of other games of the genre. Rather than offer a reflection, however distanced and qualified, of the reality of combat, the games produce a simulacrum of violence—a reflection of FPS gaming itself. In Baudrillard's first three "phases of the image" (6), an increasingly tenuous relationship with reality remains; in the fourth and final stage, any relationship has been lost and we have entered the realm of simulation.

Likewise, WWII shooters represent Second World War combat in terms of the established conventions of the FPS genre. Combat simulation thus means the simulation of other combat simulators: to restate the problem in Frasca's terms, the "source system" that the games model is the genre of the FPS more than it is either the reality or the representation of actual Second World War combat. FPS games as a genre reflect and relate to one another at the expense of their relation to history.

If I were to be thoroughly Baudrillardian in my analysis, I would have to deny that WWII FPS games have any relationship to the actual ground combat of the Second World War at all: the fourth phase of the image "has no relation to any reality whatsoever," in his hyperbolic phrasing (6). But, as stated above, though it is important to separate simulation from representation in theory, in the practice of playing and designing games the differentiation is never completely clean. I do think it possible to look at these games' representations of their historical subject matter and to make distinctions between them, and to do so begs the question of whether there is a reality that the critic can access in order to compare the games' representation to the critic's understanding of that reality. The US Garand rifle, for instance, either does or does not use the same ammunition as the standard-issue German carbine (it doesn't), and this historical fact either is or is not so represented in the games.

In order further to explore this differentiation between representation and simulation, I will now look individually at several examples of the WWII shooter game and ask first how they represent their subject matter. The idea here will be to critique the games' relationship to the war in a similar manner in which a film critic might question the representation of historical reality in a World War II movie. Having done this, I will then turn to the complementary matter of simulation and ask how these games' status as games makes their relationship to history and combat different from other modes of representation.

Return to Castle Wolfenstein (2001) has the oldest pedigree of the four games under consideration here. The original *Castle Wolfenstein* game was designed for the Apple II and released in 1983, but its sequel, *Wolfenstein 3-D* (1992), made gaming history as the first true FPS game. The single-player campaign of *Return to Castle Wolfenstein* remains true to the id Software paradigm of an isolated alpha-male character, in this case the Army Ranger/secret agent B. J. Blaskowicz, who must single-handedly bring down every Nazi secret weapons program, from the historical V-weapons project to a more historically spurious occult research project that aims to resurrect a medieval Teutonic warrior for the Aryan cause. Compared to *Wolfenstein 3-D*, *Return to Castle Wolfenstein* uses representations of actual weapons and differentiates between types of ammunition. Though it still relies on indiscriminate Nazi slaughtering as a guilt-free form of catharsis for the player, its rank-and-file German soldiers are portrayed as fairly ordinary in their concerns: they complain about the cold and the lack of bathing water, for instance. The involvement of occult and science fiction elements allows the game to genre-cross into horror: the player several times walks into firefights between Germans and monsters, either of whom will turn to attack Blaskowicz. The overall effect is significantly less cartoonish than the older *Wolfenstein 3-D*, but the game does not really set itself the task of representing Second World War combat.

Medal of Honor was originally released as a console game (PlayStation, to be precise) in 1999. Its PC update came out in 2002 as *Medal of Honor: Allied Assault*. Insofar as no zombies appear, it confines itself to much more realistic representation than *Return to Castle Wolfenstein*, but its missions still concentrate on covert activities and thus the isolated actions of one individual soldier operating outside of the normal boundaries of military operations. The main character, Mike Powell, is a Ranger working for the OSS, much like his *Wolfenstein* predecessor. Though there are several missions in the single-player game that involve operating as a team with other soldiers controlled by the computer AI, the game still emphasizes corridor-crawling and the unaided elimination of scores of enemy troops.

Battlefield 1942, released as a computer game in 2002, is the most uncharacteristic game of the four under consideration. First of all, it is primarily a multiplayer game. It can be played in single-player mode, but its strength lies in its attempt to represent large numbers of troops engaged in approximations of historical battles throughout World War II. Yet its battlefields are strangely unpopulated: storming a beach, for instance, whether in France or in the Pacific, is usually a matter of three or four attackers unloading from landing craft to face half a dozen or fewer defenders. This does not necessarily make the experience less lethal, but it does represent the war as something fought by very small groups of men. Compared to the chaos of the Omaha Beach episode in *Medal of Honor: Allied Assault*, with its dozens of AI-controlled soldiers running, ducking, and dying all around, *Battlefield 1942* gives us a relatively controllable situation. Moreover, *Battlefield 1942* is also the game that most directly foregrounds its status as a game: it uses a point system to determine victory and uses "spawn points" as places where dead avatars can rejoin the game. It uses a character class system borrowed from role-playing games: players choose what type of soldier they want to be from a set of preexisting types, though all types are fully capable of jumping into any available tank or airplane and operating it to the best of the player's ability.

Call of Duty (2003) is the most recent game and constitutes a kind of updating of *Medal of Honor*. It adds several touches of realism: weapon types are more carefully differentiated and sighting becomes a much more important part of the game. More importantly, however, the emphasis shifts from representing the heroic exploits of a single man operating on his own to a more ordinary soldier in the midst of trying to keep himself alive while fulfilling his military objectives. Teamwork is important: the player receives orders during battle (though significantly the player cannot issue orders) and must strive to coordinate the avatar's actions with those of the AI-controlled comrades. *Call of Duty* is also the most realistic simulation of the four, if by realistic we mean the one that will most quickly kill the avatar when he disregards seeking cover and charges straight for the enemy guns.

Thus as far as realistic representations of Second World War combat are concerned, we can rank the four games in terms of ascending realism in an order that corresponds to their chronological dates of release: *Return to Castle Wolfenstein, Medal of Honor: Allied Assault, Battlefield 1942*, and *Call of Duty*. Even granting that realism is a problematic term in this context, and that *Wolfenstein's* lack of realism is as much a matter of its genre crossing with gothic and science fiction as with choices by the game designers, it seems that the short-term trend in WWII FPSs has been to move away from the isolated, implausibly heroic soldier that characterized the early days of the FPS genre (i.e., *Doom* and its children) toward a grittier, less cartoonish representation of what Stephen Ambrose termed *citizen soldiers*: the nonprofessional Allied soldiers, many of them draftees, who won the war less through conspicuous acts of gallantry than through immeasurable amounts of hard work. In a sense, then, in less than half a decade the World War II FPS has gone from *The Sands of Iwo Jima* to *Band of Brothers*.

Yet, representation is not all there is to it. Games also simulate combat; consequently, they cannot adequately be accounted for merely by analysis of their reception. They can be read, and in this sense, they remain texts. Nevertheless, reading them is contingent on playing them, and playing them is an active rather than a passive process (I am avoiding the problematic term *interactive*—the nontrivial activity necessary to progress through a game distinguishes games from more traditional texts, whether we characterize this activity as truly interactive or not). We need, to borrow Gonzalo Frasca's terms, to look at input as well as output (224). Moreover, we need to consider the political and ideological repercussions of these games' particular renderings, through both representation and simulation, of history and war into ludic play.

Despite the gradual inclusion of such multihyphenated terms as *military-industrial-media-entertainment network* into political and cultural discourse, academic discussion of games still by and large steers clear of the games' involvement with the nongaming world. But one does not have to be Senator Joe Lieberman railing against *Grand Theft Auto* as a symptom of the decline and fall of American culture to claim that games have ideological status. Though it is probably easiest to see this in representation—i.e., to read the game for ideological content and implications along the same lines used when reading a novel or a film—simulation is ideological as well. Were it not, of course, the US Marine Corps would not have used a form of *Doom* for combat training, nor would the US Army provide a freely downloadable FPS game on its website (*America's Army*) as a tool not only for training, but also for recruiting.[6] For, in the era of simulation, training begins before recruitment, if we can still maintain a difference between them at all.

Simulation games, especially the first-person variety employed in shooters and flight simulators, place the player and the avatar in the same space. In a rejection of Aristotelian logic worthy of the most thoroughgoing poststructuralist, the player simultaneously both is and is not in the situation that is simulated. When playing the British portion of the single-player *Call of Duty* campaign, for instance, the player is both Sgt. Evans and the player himself or herself. The player thus identifies with the main character in an unprecedented literal manner: I am Sgt. Evans, and he is I. Accordingly, having a developed persona for Evans is unimportant, even distracting, inasmuch as Evans's characteristics would inevitably differ from my own. This may explain why no FPS character has rivaled in personal popularity the third-person shooter character of Lara Croft (despite the FPSs having all but entirely supplanted the third-person shooter in top-ten games lists in the last few years). Moreover, the player in a sense does the things that the character does: *I* shoot the German soldiers coming at me. More technically speaking, by so doing, or failing to do so adequately, I learn the behaviors that Sgt. Evans needs to cultivate to stay alive and remain an effective soldier. This is significantly different from representation: I do not learn about how to be an infantryman from reading Norman Mailer's *The Naked and the Dead*, but I learn much more than an FPS will ever teach me about what a World War II soldier's daily life consists of, the psychology of small groups of men in combat, the relationship between identities of characters in the war and their lives previous to the war, and many other philosophical and existential insights into the mundane lives of infantry troops in the Pacific Theater in the Second World War. I probably come away from the novel with a richer understanding of the immense and mostly unarticulated complexities of the war, along with a considerably less romanticized vision of an infantry-man's basic job, but I do not leave the book having performed behaviors that simulate any aspect of this job.

With an FPS, on the other hand, I/my avatar have repeatedly per-formed actions that bear a more than representational relationship with real-world actions. Granted, shooting a computer-generated enemy is not the same thing as shooting an actual human being (which is what keeps most gamers out of jail), but it does train the player for the real thing. If it does not, not only *Marine Doom* and *America's Army* but also the consid-erably more expensive military flight and combat simulators that are not available to the public become massive wastes of government resources. This is not a slippery slope argument; I am not claiming that playing a combat simulator makes the player more or less likely to engage in violent behavior outside of a game environment, nor even that he or she would necessarily be more effective were the training to be put to the test.[7] I am simply claiming that simulation involves training people to perform be-haviors that are designed to translate as seamlessly as possible into other, nongame situations, and that what and how the game simulates is never free of ideological content.

Ideology is less a matter of overt political content and more a matter of what goes without saying in the simulation and representation that constitute these games. One of the more interesting places where simula-tion and representation overlap is wounds—both the type that the avatar receives and those inflicted on other, AI-controlled characters. In both representing and simulating the avatar being hit, all four of these games play it rather mild. All use a variation on the hit points system, an inheri-tance from the predigital *Dungeons and Dragons* role-playing games: all damage to the player's avatar is nonlocalized and abstracted as a subtrac-tion of a certain amount of life force. The avatar does not get hit in the leg or in the head; he just gets hit, and getting hit does not affect his ability to continue in combat. The number of times an avatar can be hit and sur-vive depends on the particular game, weapon, and skill level selected, but generally, an avatar can be hit several times before dying, even if access to instantly-healing health packs is impossible. It is interesting to consider how nearly universal this mode of representation is in FPS games; despite the presence of sophisticated and speedy processors, as well as amounts of memory that were unbelievable only a few years ago, FPS games still use a blatantly simplistic method of representing the central matter of being hurt in combat: they represent being hit by bullets as a gradual bruising, and the bruising does not affect the avatar's ability to fight on.

From the simulation side, there is again a surprising amount of agreement among the games about what happens when someone is hit in combat. The pain and shock of receiving a wound is simulated by a jostling that momentarily disturbs the avatar's ability to aim. When hit several times by an automatic weapon, the avatar may be so shaken around that the player will be unable effectively to return fire (in this case, simulation disturbs the performance of a behavior by providing a kind of negative feedback: avoid getting shot because it screws up your aim). Again, this is patent understatement: being hit by a bullet, even in a non-"vital" location, generally ends the combat effectiveness of a soldier.[8] Even if a soldier can and does fight on after being wounded, it is difficult to claim that he or she suffers no ill effects after the moment of being hit. Again, this level of abstraction is certainly not due to the technical limits of processor power or memory capacity. The effects of wounds seem simply an issue that World War II FPS games are not interested in either representing or simulating.

This may be due, at least partially, to social factors—something best characterized as either tact or taste. Players do not want to see their avatars eviscerated, and they do not want to hear represented the cries of desperately wounded soldiers. Second World War shooters are more restrained than their fantasy-based counterparts, wherein taunting and being blown to bloody chunks of meat by a multibarreled rocket launcher are all part of the fun. It may also be that the games want to maximize their sales by avoiding the M rating from the Entertainment Software Rating Board (ESRB).[9] But allowing the benefit of the doubt, or at least admitting that such issues are often overdetermined, it is also possible that the games avoid the representation and simulation of wounds because of the games' relationship to history. Though the avatars are fictional, the games are all based, however loosely, on historical events.[10] The people represented by the computer-rendered figures are, or were, real people, and the graphic destruction of something that represents an ancestor or older relative, especially when such death agonies are billed as entertainment, is perhaps too much for a game.

Interestingly, though, cinema has apparently felt itself to be placed under no such taste restrictions. The World War II films of the last decade have flaunted their ability to represent modern weaponry's gory effects on the human body. In fact, the graphic portrayal of combat in such films as *Saving Private Ryan* and *Windtalkers* (2002) can be constructed as part of their homage to the war's veterans. Representing in realistic terms the suffering undergone by the soldiers results, for some viewers, in a greater realization of their sacrifice. Apparently, this rationale does not apply to games. World War II FPSs also avoid the somewhat cartoonish but nonetheless visceral representations of violence prevalent in fantasy-based FPSs like *Doom* and *Unreal Tournament* (1999). In fact, there's been some discontent among the fan base on this issue: several mod programs are available for both *Medal of Honor* and *Call of Duty* that promise more realistic gore. But if these games eschew graphic violence, it is not because of a lack of precedence in both filmic and ludic predecessors. Rather, I think it is a symptom of rendering the war as ludic: in order for the war to function as a game, it must be controllable. Surprising things can happen, but not things so unexpected that they seem illegal or unfair. Being dismembered by your own artillery through no lack of skill on your own part, for instance, though certainly part of modern war, is not part of the postmodern war game. That casualties tend merely to slump over and that their bodies soon disappear is a kind of sentimentalizing of the war and one, I would contend, that fits rather well with an era of tight government control of media representations of both combat and the bodies of US casualties, all in the face of dwindling military recruitment.

Whatever the reason, death and wounds are to some extent sanitized in these games. Whether intended or not, the result is that heroic behavior becomes relatively common because it is relatively risk free. It is much easier to charge an enemy position if the player knows that the avatar can stand to be hit two or three times and if the player suspects that the enemy is guarding a nice stack of instantaneously effective first aid kits. The fact that crippling wounds simply do not happen does as much as the absence of civilians and the lack of physical and psychological breakdowns to move the war back toward the ludic. It is central to the project of reconceptualizing the Second World War as a premodern, non-total war, and thus making it playable. It may well be the cost of fun.

When game designers set themselves the task of turning World War II, or even World War II movies, into an FPS game, it becomes necessary to represent total war as ludic, i.e., precisely what Huizinga says it could not be. In a sense, then, the process of converting violent history into game is a form of remediation. Just as much as the games remediate film, they also remediate the concept of *game* itself—what Huizinga calls the "play element." The war is represented as a contest between equals—a skill-based *agon*—and thus as supporting the notion that it fulfills a "cultural function" (to use Huizinga's language cited at the beginning of this article). The games remediate nostalgia for premodern warfare and displace it into an earlier version of the modern. They take a cultural nostalgia for the supposedly stable binaries of World War II and put those binaries to work on the battlefield. Under such a construction, the Allies generally prevail in ludic contest because they are more skilled (this resting at least partially on the hunched shoulders of the player). This conclusion is possible only with a revisionism that symbolically relocates World War II in the premodern: World War II is thus the final and finest hour of non-total war rather than a post-ludic bloodbath. It is the war that the Greatest Generation should have fought, if not the one they actually did.

In order to explore the consequences of this situation, I want to return to Baudrillard. Baudrillard's version of simulation emphasizes the replacement of reality: the simulation in its third phase "masks the *absence* of a profound reality" (6; emphasis in original). In the fourth and final phase, there is no longer a reality whose absence may be masked. Simulation represents without presence, substituting the simulacrum for the thing itself. Ultimately, for Baudrillard, there will be (perhaps there already is) no thing itself. The thing as such has withdrawn behind the curtain, leaving us only reflections without an original. To put this in terms of World War II FPS games, the games reflect other FPS games much more than they reflect the historical war. A perfect representation of World War II combat in game form is an impossibility, but it seems quite clear that when game designers are faced with a set of choices between making a better simulation (in military-industrial terms) of reality and of making a game that more easily fits into the established parameters of what an FPS is supposed to do, the latter choice wins every time. Though weapons are more accurately modeled and games are finally beginning to take account of how much stuff one person can possibly carry,[11] World War II shooters are still basically the next generation of *Doom*, only this time with uniforms.

There is a story, perhaps apocryphal, from the first Gulf War, in which a pilot returning from his first bombing mission was asked how it had gone. "It was so realistic," was his reply. The story is perhaps based on the response of a Gulf War F-16 pilot who answered the question with, "This is really tough but it's not as intense as my Red Flag missions were" (Greeley). Red Flag is the US Air Force's program for simulated air combat. It is difficult to conceive of a better illustration of Baudrillardian simulation. Real combat is not as intense as simulated combat; real combat is judged according to the extent that it reproduces the simulated experience. The most troubling aspect of World War II FPS games lies in their tendency to provide a veneer of military-historical hyperrealism to a core of digital "business as usual." Paradoxically, the more realistic they appear, especially to an audience brought up on *Doom* and its inheritors, the more likely it becomes that their simulations may substitute for the experience of combat itself.

This is the case on both a historical and a military level. Historically, because of the participatory nature of these simulations, as well as the seduction of authenticity, there is a tendency to substitute game play for history. This is true on the level of event: I trust that few players of *Return to Castle Wolfenstein* will take literally the fictional Nazi attempt to resurrect the dead, but it is not difficult to imagine players mistaking the Pegasus Bridge episode of *Call of Duty* for an accurate representation of this pivotal battle on June 5–6, 1944. This brings us to the level of scale. The actual battle for Pegasus Bridge involved just under two hundred British glider troops. The game represents these forces with no more than a dozen figures. Though the bridge itself is meticulously rendered, the numbers of men fighting for the bridge is greatly reduced. This is most probably a technical limitation: the rendering of many moving three-dimensional figures is extremely demanding on even the best computer equipment. But whether this is a concession to hardware, software, or gameplay limitations, the impression it leaves is misleading.

World War II shooters leave the player with the idea that war is a precision game featuring agonistic contests between small groups of men. These contests are resolved on the basis of the skill of the participants. Speed and accuracy with infallibly reliable weapons make the difference between victory and defeat. A post-ludic war is presented as an exercise in controlled agonism. Ideologically, the games construct the war as an exercise in marksmanship, efficiency, and heroics. Skill, not numbers or morale, wins the day.

In order to illustrate the counter-historical effects of this representational choice, I want briefly to delve into recent military history and tactical policy for the US armed forces. In 1948, the US Army began studying the results of World War II combat in order to improve its arms program and to consider the feasibility of body armor. Projects ALCLAD and SALVO produced some surprising results. First, actual combat in the war had taken place at short ranges. Second, the number of casualties a unit inflicted was directly proportional to the number of bullets it fired. In other words, accuracy had nothing to do with it. Whoever put the most lead in the air won. The eventual result of these studies declared that the best infantry weapon would be a light fully-automatic rifle firing a small bullet. Smaller bullets have less range, but that was not much of an issue: they are also lighter, so a soldier can carry more of them and fire more in combat. By the mid-1960s the US armed forces had adopted the M-16 as a direct result of these studies.

World War II FPSs do not reproduce these results. Again, they give the player a skill-based contest in which accuracy is paramount. Though it would be possible simply to critique the games as imperfect simulations because they do not reproduce the conditions of what they seek to simulate, in many ways this is beside the point. These games are not actually trying to simulate combat. Rather, they are trying to use history to produce playable games. The danger, though, is that this playing with history will produce a Baudrillardian simulation in which the experience of playing the game substitutes for a representational knowledge, however incomplete, of combat. In a sense, then, these games are so good at being simulations, and more specifically simulations of other simulations, that their function as representations becomes compromised. Moreover, the better and more involving simulations they are, the more they are likely to become replacements for representation. If simulating other simulations is more compelling than attempting to represent what it is they simulate, why bother to represent at all?

In appearing to simulate combat while neglecting to represent history, World War II FPS games give us just-less-than-total war, a representation of mass combat that is symbolically relocated to the pre-Ludendorff era to make the games align themselves more readily with such games as *Doom* and *Unreal Tournament*. Though they may overtly pay tribute to the actual people and events of the Second World War, they also domesticate the tragedy and brutality of the war. They attempt to inject the world of computer games with the reality of history, but in so doing they also make history unreal.

Notes

1. Rudyard Kipling, "Recessional," quoted in Huizinga (90).
2. Hart cites 55,014,000 total deaths in the war, of which 30,503,000 (55%) were civilians (455).
3. *www.callofduty.com*. Accessed 28 July 2005.
4. A phenomenon that in another context I have called *combat gnosticism*. For a sympathetic presentation, see also Fussell 267–97.
5. Lev Manovich presents a contrast of simulation and representation that centers on the question of space (111–15).
6. James Der Derian, whose particular designation for the military-entertainment complex I have used, takes up (and plays) *Marine Doom* in *Virtuous War* (88–89).
7. See Penny for a more detailed investigation of the links between simulation and behavior.
8. "Any soldier hit by a bullet is likely to be taken out of action" (Hedges 55).

Hedges's Chapter 4 (41–55), though focused on contemporary warfare, makes sobering reading when contemplating the realism of combat computer games
9. Admittedly *Return to Castle Wolfenstein* rates an M (Mature, defined by the ESRB as 17 or older), most probably for its gothic undead and cutscenes that allude to torture, but the other three games are rated T (suitable for ages 13 and older).
10. Even Castle Wolfenstein has its real world analog in Wewelsburg castle, the seat of Heinrich Himmler's quasi-mystical SS cult.
11. The most recent game of the four I am citing, *Call of Duty*, allows the avatar to carry only two weapons, while the earliest game, *Return to Castle Wolfenstein*, follows more established FPS doctrine by allowing the avatar to carry a truly prodigious amount of destructive material. Interestingly, *Halo*, a recent (2001) science fiction FPS, uses a *Call of Duty*-style limitation on carrying capacities. Significantly, the effects of fatigue are even more ubiquitous in war than the effects of wounds and go all but completely unrepresented in game simulations.

Works Cited

Accardo, Sal. Review of *Call of Duty*. *pc.gamespy.com* (29 October 2003). Accessed 28 July 2005.

___. Review of *Medal of Honor: Allied Assault*. *archive.gamespy.com* (21 January 2002). Accessed 28 July 2005.

Alam, M. Junaid. Review of *Call of Duty*. *The Adrenaline Vault* (*www.avault.com*, 5 December 2003). Accessed 28 July 2005.

Baudrillard, Jean. *Simulacra and Simulation*. Trans. Sheila Faria Glaser. Ann Arbor: University of Michigan Press, 1994.

Bolter, Jay David, and Richard Grusin. *Remediation: Understanding New Media*. Cambridge: MIT Press, 1999.

Campbell, James. "Combat Gnosticism: The Ideology of First World War Poetry Criticism." *NLH: New Literary History* 30.1 (1999). 203–16.

Der Derian, James. *Virtuous War: Mapping the Military-Industrial-Media-Entertainment Network*. Boulder: Westview Press, 2001.

Frasca, Gonzalo. "Simulation versus Narrative: Introduction to Ludology." In Wolf and Perron. 221–35.

Fussell, Paul. *Wartime: Understanding and Behavior in the Second World War*. New York: Oxford University Press, 1989.

Greeley, Jim. "Waving the 'Flag.'" *Airman* (*www.af.mil/news/airman*, September 2000). US Air Force. Accessed 28 July 2005.

Hart, Basil Liddell, ed. *History of the Second World War*. London: Phoebus, 1980.

Hedges, Chris. *What Every Person Should Know about War*. New York: Free Press, 2003.

Huizinga, Johan. *Homo Ludens: A Study of the Play Element in Culture*. Boston: Beacon Press, 1955.

Mandel, Bob. Review of *Medal of Honor: Allied Assault*. *The Adrenaline Vault* (*www.avault.com*, 12 December 2000). Accessed 28 July 2005.

Manovich, Lev. *The Language of New Media*. Cambridge: MIT Press, 2001.

Penny, Simon. "Representation, Enaction, and the Ethics of Simulation." *First Person: New Media as Story, Performance, and Game*. In Wardrip-Fruin and Harrigan, *First Person*. 73–84.

Rehak, Bob. "Playing at Being: Psychoanalysis and the Avatar." In Wolf and Perron. 103–27.

Ryan, Marie-Laure. *Narrative as Virtual Reality: Immersion and Interactivity in Literature and Electronic Media*. Baltimore: Johns Hopkins University Press, 2001.

Wardrip-Fruin, Noah, and Pat Harrigan. "Critical Simulation." In Wardrip-Fruin and Harrigan, *First Person*. 71–72.

Wardrip-Fruin, Noah, and Pat Harrigan, eds. *First Person: New Media as Story, Performance, and Game*. Cambridge: MIT Press, 2004.

Wolf, Mark J. P., and Bernard Perron, eds. *The Video Game Theory Reader*. New York: Routledge, 2003.

Games Cited

America's Army. US Army, 2002.

Battlefield 1942: Deluxe Edition. Redwood City, CA: Electronic Arts, 2004.

Call of Duty. Santa Monica, CA: Activision, 2004.

Doom. Shreveport, LA: id Software, 1993.

Marine Doom. Marine Corps Modeling and Simulation Management Office (MCMSMO), 1996.

Medal of Honor: Allied Assault: Deluxe Edition. Redwood City, CA: Electronic Arts, 2003.

Return to Castle Wolfenstein. Santa Monica, CA: Activision, 2002.

Unreal Tournament. New York: GT Interactive, 1999.

Wolfenstein 3-D. Garland, TX: Apogee Software, 1992.

12

Performing the (Virtual) Past

Online Character Interpretation
as Living History at Old Sturbridge Village

Scott Magelssen

Old Sturbridge Village, a major living history museum in Massachusetts, stages and interprets a 1830s New England community for thousands of visitors year round. Recently, Sturbridge developed an online program that allows students in classrooms to conduct a virtual interview with Sturbridge "villagers" from the past. For fifty dollars an hour, these nineteenth-century characters answer students' questions and talk about their lives in real time. They can supplement this dialogue with image and sound files. While other living museums have experimented with live, interactive television programming, Sturbridge is the first museum to adopt a strictly electronic medium for interaction between virtual museum visitors (users[1]) and character interpreters. The online chat format offered by Sturbridge challenges and alters traditional text-based narratives of history, while at the same time appearing to pose a counter-trajectory to the non-text-based norm of living museum historiography (i.e., offering visitors the chance to learn about history by interacting with live bodies). The program itself is an exquisite paradox—using twenty-first-century technology to produce a believed-in experience of interacting with a nineteenth-century individual. Based on research and interviews with Old Sturbridge Village education coordinators, and an analysis of my own classroom's experience with an online chat, this chapter inquires into the historiographic and performative issues that emerge when considering online, real-time character interpretation as a virtual living-history experience: How are notions of historical accuracy/authenticity negotiated in the slippage of virtual space? Can a virtual interview performance provide performer-spectator relationships as rich and layered as those created by traditional on-site museum programs? Can this mode of interpretation still be called "living history"?

Old Sturbridge Village is one of the oldest living museums in the United States. Begun as a collection of artifacts by A. B. Wells in central Massachusetts, it adopted living history programming in the 1970s, following the lead of Plimoth Plantation, its living museum neighbor to the east.[2] Now billing itself as the place "Where Early America Comes Alive," Sturbridge employs several character interpreters and third-person costumed staff (who do not speak in character), and offers year-round educational activities, including "second-person interpretation" in which visitors can dress in costume and immerse themselves in the past as some of its inhabitants. The "Discovery Camps" program, for instance, gives youths an experience of going to school, learning crafts, and doing chores as their peers would have in the nineteenth century.[3] The online chat with a nineteenth-century villager is one of Old Sturbridge Village's newest programs.

Interactive computer activities intended for classroom history pedagogy or as independent play for history buffs at home have been developing and expanding for the last three decades. My first encounter with computer-screen historiography was in my fourth-grade classroom, playing *The Oregon Trail* in the early-mid 1980s.[4] Now gamers can choose from a multiplicity of simulated historical experiences, from ancient and classic civilization games to experiences that offer simulated warfare strategizing of the last century and documentary games that recreate the JFK assassination and the terrorist attacks of 9-11.[5] Old Sturbridge Village's online chat program is one of the latest articulations of the intersection between history and simulated computer experience.

While the case may be that a given individual might not immediately place Sturbridge's online chat program into the category of "video game," it becomes quickly clear upon closer examination that obvious and explicit parallels can be drawn between the two, and at the very least it may be demonstrated that they are strongly related. On a fundamental level, as many of the essays in this volume articulate, video game interface experiences are grounded in the assumption of a mediated bodily presence—that is, the user must willingly suspend his/her disbelief and imagine an interaction with an other (a character or characters, helpers and antagonists, etc.). This assumption of a mediated bodily presence—and a concomitant strategic "forgetting" of the reminders of quotidian reality (i.e., the mediating technology)—is precisely the suspension of disbelief required for the Sturbridge chat program to seem authentic to classroom users. Players must suspend their formal acknowledgment of the structures that inform them that this is an artificial construction (the screen, the keypad and mouse, the institutional milieux of the museum and the classroom) and actively "believe in" the experience. In this manner, the Sturbridge chat is much like Alternate Reality Games (ARGs), the success of which is predicated on multiple users interacting with one another while believing in each other as "characters" through chat and other interfaces.[6] One may even go as far as convincingly arguing that the Sturbridge chat experience is a subgenre of ARGs, whereby the narrative of an imagined *past* encounter is co-produced by players on both ends of the video-game interface (vs. conventional video games in which the player interacts with the computer).

It should be said that, while online activity related to living history museums is not completely new, it has usually been limited to museum-maintained websites (for institutional publicity and tourist vacation-planning) and interpreter-only chat rooms (in which often jaded museum workers can vent their frustrations or poke fun at the dopey questions and assumptions museum visitors occasionally bring to their sites). That is not to say that the larger connections and play between the digital and living history realms are a recent phenomenon. In his seminal 1983 work, *Time Machines: The World of Living History,* Jay Anderson noted the fascinating tension between past and present that computers highlight: the computer, since its inception, has been used as a research tool by museum curators and museum scholars alike, and in his final chapter, "Computer Days and Digital Nights," Anderson tips his hat to the disconnect that happens to the living history scholar between full-immersion research in a re-created past environment and a return to the modern world to process his or her experiences with the latest technology (179–93). This disconnect may also be felt by visitors to historic reconstructions who, more recently, take advantage of the interactive computer displays these sites offer in their visitor centers adjacent to the re-created past environments. Such programs have had a degree of success keeping up with the shifting emphasis on interactive technology in popular culture sites. But, before Sturbridge, no museum had made the link between live, digital interaction technology and the museum-visitor experience.[7]

According to Abigail (Abby) Furlong, Education Coordinator at Old Sturbridge Village, the museum adopted the chat program three years ago when she joined the staff.[8] The chats are an hour long and are each shaped to fit the learning objectives of the particular participating classroom. Most chats, says Furlong, are done in conjunction with a subsequent on-site visit, and this, understandably, determines who uses the program—mostly upper-elementary or middle-school classrooms from

New England schools, and one from upstate New York a few years ago. Another factor that determines who participates in the chats is resources available to the school. Above and beyond the $50 fee for the program, schools either need to have a smart classroom with a computer, online capabilities, and an LCD projector, or individual workstations for each student or small group. By virtue of its nature, the success of a chat event hinges on the quality of the classroom facilities ("The more technology the better," as Furlong put it). Chats done as a lead-up activity for an on-site visit are usually very successful, Furlong noted, both in terms of the students' engagement with the chat and with their subsequent visit, the chat establishing a prior interest and set of expectations for the museum. One school has had such success with the program that it returns for a chat every year.

Regardless of the classroom's learning objectives, a Sturbridge chat consists of a live conversation with a historic character who shares details of daily life in the 1830s and sends pictures and sound files to accompany the dialogue. The type of character that interacts with the students depends, again, on the learning objectives discussed by the teacher in advance with museum education staff. If the teacher wants the students to learn about mills, for instance, the interpreter will play a mill owner. Or, a girl might tell the class what it is like working at a mill and share her experiences as a young woman in a New England community. The interpreter on the Sturbridge end will break character, if necessary, in order to field questions about the museum and its programs.[9]

Successful chats depend both on the museum staff, who research the period extensively, and the preparedness of the classroom using the program: teachers who prep their students beforehand get a better experience, says Furlong. If not, the conversation won't get much deeper than "What's your name? How many cats do you have? What are the names of your children?"

Furlong holds that the online chat program, while not able to take the place of an actual on-site visit, does afford opportunities not available to children at the physical museum village. In the chat, students get the "one-on-one" attention of an experienced interpreter for an entire hour. This is not possible to do in the village because the students rarely stay in one space for long and the interpreters need to split their attention among all visitors.

In order to get firsthand experience of the online chat program, I made arrangements to have my Augustana College Theatre History Seminar students participate in a Sturbridge chat (admittedly a different demographic than the usual grade-school children, who most often chat in conjunction with an upcoming visit to the physical site). Eleven students and I would be the users, taking turns interacting with the nineteenth-century character. We would share a single computer, with the screen projected to the front of the classroom so that all participants could watch the exchange.

My research questions going into this project were fourfold. First, I wanted to explore a very basic question, fundamental to my area of inquiry: can this program be called "living history"? Second, on a more complex level, do users have as many opportunities for a layered experience as do on-site museum visitors? That is, can the interaction take place on multiple levels, as is possible with an in-person, one-on-one visit with a first-person costumed interpreter? Barbara Kirshenblatt-Gimblett speaks of this multilayered interaction as a sort of "play" around—and against—the "membrane" created by heritage sites. In a keynote address to the Performance Tourism and Identity Conference in Wales in 1996, Kirshenblatt-Gimblett posited that the interaction between heritage site and visitor can be played out with a range of tourist "games" that often have to do with the visitor's playful teasing out of the boundaries of authenticity maintained by the museum interpreter, exhibit, or historic site, and seeing how permeable or watertight these boundaries are (Kirshenblatt-Gimblett, "Afterlives" 8–9).[10] Kirshenblatt-Gimblett holds that tourist games are a way to test the membrane so carefully fashioned and maintained by the re-creation. Is this playfulness, then, available through a computer? Does the membrane become a cyber-membrane, and, if so, what conventions would constitute it?

Third, on a practical level, how can the interpreter maintain a semblance of the virtual past while being accessed on a modern computer, and to what degree does slippage between tenses occur (slippage not necessarily being a bad thing, but often a provocative way to tease out the layers in the previous research questions)? Because of the different temporal qualities of the interpreter's character and chat room users, as in all first-person living history exchanges, a dialogue that bases its content on the very difference between time periods cannot fall into simple mimetic representation of a real-life conversation. Slippage can happen as a simple anachronistic aside, an accidental stepping out of character, or a "wink" to let visitors in on the joke where the punch line is a different meaning of words between then and now, but various and more complex institutional strategies of slippage are used daily at living museums to smooth the edges of the gap between times in order to foster livelier and less awkward sessions. Plimoth Plantation interpreters will often refer to visitors as travelers from far away, neatly substituting a spatial distance for a temporal one, and thus allowing for comfortable and realism-friendly verbal markers of difference rather than having to play up a science fiction narrative to explain the meeting of these two parties. I determined to keep an eye out for when and where such slippage might happen in the chat.

Finally, might living history chats offer more agency for the visitors to determine the trajectory of the conversation, and consequently the scope and depth of the history they receive—as Kevin Walsh puts it, on a more "democratic level"—rather than falling into one of several pre-planned narratives offered on-site? According to Walsh, all history museums are guilty of an attack on democracy and individuals' understanding of their "places" in it: they trivialize the past by separating it out as distant, nostalgic, and "other" than the present, and effectively neuter any possibility for visitor action in the present (Walsh 2, 4). "A true democracy," he says, "will offer many and varied forms of museum service." Walsh finds the beginning of the solution in emergent interactive video programs: "Essentially, interactive video offers the potential for greater democracy in access to information about the past and can allow people to develop their own cognitive maps and thus, a sense of place" (168–69). Might the user-directed trajectory of the chat get at what Walsh advocates?

After some amount of back and forth e-mailing for a date that worked for both Sturbridge Village and my class, we settled on the morning of February 22, 2005 (11 a.m. CST, noon EST). Furlong e-mailed how it would work: "The interpreter/museum educator who will be doing the chat takes the role of Levi Barnes, an early 19th century, prosperous New England farmer and mill owner. He can stay in role the entire hour or we can do that for half the time and devote the other half hour to museum education, for example. We're flexible."[11] Furlong asked a little about my class: the number, their age, and their interests. I told her we were studying, among other things, nineteenth-century theatre in North America, and that, perhaps, they might like to know what experience, if any, the villagers might have had with theatre and drama. I prepped my students for the chat insofar as telling them about my project and asking them to brainstorm some questions to ask the character (reminding them to try for more complex queries than "How many cats do you have and what are their names?" I suggested, for instance, "What do you think about the temperance movement?" as a possible question for discussion).

The chat itself with Levi Barnes went very well, in spite of some awkward technology on our end.[12] The conversation proceeded in a way I had not foreseen: a few times, a student would ask a new or follow-up question while Levi Barnes was still answering an earlier one. It would then take several lines of conversation to catch back up. The net effect was to have two or three staggered conversations going on simultaneously:

augieclass: Do you, or anyone that you know, either own or hire servants, and what are your feelings on the matter of slavery? and my name is Tim

Levi Barnes: Good-day, Tim. I hire day laborers for my mills. I personally belong to the anti-slavery society in Sturbridge.

Levi Barnes: There is no slavery in Massachusetts.

Levi Barnes: My wife and I have 6 children so we don't have any hired help in our home but other families do.

augieclass: This being the case, what type of action do you take against slavery through this group?

Levi Barnes: General Towne's family has an [I]rish servant girl that helps with the cooking and cleaning.

Levi Barnes: The anti-slavery society holds public debates and has petitions signed and sent to the congress asking them to abolish slavery.

augieclass: Aren't women beginning to work at this time, what jobs do they carry?

Levi Barnes: We had Abby Kelly from Worcester come speak to the community.

Levi Barnes: A woman can be a school mistress. Some younger girls go to Lowell to work in the factories. Some others do outwork from their home like sewing shoe uppers, braiding straw and spinning and weaving.

It appeared that Levi Barnes would respond to each portion of the question with a separate post. With the pauses between posts as each side took time to compose questions and answers, we often sent a new question before Barnes was finished with the previous one. By the same token, Barnes would use the pauses as we typed to send us images of his village: his mills, a schoolhouse, an abolitionist meeting, and a multiple-image demonstration of Barnes's wife making cheese. The students enjoyed predicting what the answers would be to their questions as they waited for a response ("How will he respond to our question about how frequently and the manner in which he bathed?" "There weren't slaves in Massachusetts, were there?"). The conversation was warm and engaging but somewhat superficial, as the group dynamic and turn-taking did not allow us to explore any one area in depth. The hour passed rapidly.

What perception of the nineteenth-century past came across to my students? Specificity, certainly: the students' questions and Levi Barnes's answers provided a contextualization of 1830s rural New England that would be difficult to glean from other media. To what extent had the continent been settled by whites? New England was running out of room, but Ohio offered opportunities for settling. What were the politics like? Barnes hinted at social conflict: Abolitionists had a strong presence in the community, but apparently the Congregationalists would not let them have their meeting house for an abolitionist gathering—they had to use the Friends Meetinghouse. How many generations were there between the Revolutionary War and Barnes's time? "My father fought in the revolution. I am in the local militia as all men from the ages of 18 to 40 are by law."

Returning to the research questions I posed earlier, the chat experience offers new angles on existing discussions of living history programs and poses new dilemmas for the museum and performance studies fields to consider. First of all, is the chat "living history"? The answer depends, of course, on the definition of the term. My contention has generally been that history becomes "living" with the addition of the live, costumed bodies of the museum staff. This can either be at a restored historic site, or in a venue with a modern environment in which a first-person character is a visitor to our time—what Stacy F. Roth calls *ghost interpretation* (17). I would also resolutely place this experience into "living history," though it demands a new slot in the taxonomy. While the real bodies of the interpreters are not visible to the users, the conversation is live, and in this case accompanied by visual imagery and sounds of the performed past (with costumed individuals and period settings and crafts). Even if a party were to conduct the chat without sound and picture files, the characterization of the interpreter clearly brings the program out of the realm of static exhibits with third-person docent interpretation. My conclusion, however, is by no means universal: when asked the same question, Furlong said she does not use "living history" as a term when she talks about online chats, because the students don't get the benefit of being in the historic setting (though Roth's "ghost interpretation" category would preclude dismissal on those grounds). "It *has* helped children when they do it in conjunction with a visit," she says, but it is "no substitute for a visit to the site."

With regard to the question about the complexity of play available around the constructed membrane between authentic character and visitor/user, my class's experience with Sturbridge's chat room and my conversation with Furlong would suggest that the membrane produced by the virtual dialogue is more easily torn by metatheatrical experimentation on the users' part (e.g., referring to the procedures of the enactment) than it would be in a first-person enactment on site. Show a costumed interpreter a digital camera in a first-person venue like the Parsonage Barn at Old Sturbridge Village, and she will not react. Or, at most, she will remark at what a strange device it is you have brought with you, all the while staunchly keeping in character. In the chat, however, the interpreters will wait until there is a question that allows them to break character. This can serve a number of purposes. It allows education staff to discuss the museum and its programs. Students may ask questions that would be best answered by making comparisons between the present and the past, in order to make more solid connections in the students' understanding. Such comparisons are not possible if the interpreter does not acknowledge any time after his or her own. "At Plimoth they don't break character at all," Furlong says. "It can be frustrating if a student can't get the answer they want. Our goal is to educate and not frustrate and limit the experience."

In our chat with Levi Barnes, the most we pushed the sensitive membrane of our virtual visit with an individual from the past proved to be our last question for the character. "Our time is drawing to a close. Do you have any more questions for me?" asked Levi Barnes. "Yes, actually," wrote Amy, "what kind of computer are you using[?]" This effectively ended the illusion and began our present-day conversation with the museum staff. "This is Bill and Abby," they replied. "We're education coordinators at the museum. We're using a fairly old computer. It's a [C]ompaq with Windows 98."

As for the slippage question: while live one-on-one living history interaction contains the possibility of acknowledging simultaneously different time frames (while ostensibly not breaking character), Old Sturbridge Village's educational goals limit how long this kind of playfulness can be maintained. As the above example demonstrates, Sturbridge staff would rather take the opportunity to break character and talk about comparisons between past and present in third-person than attempt to negotiate prolonged anachronistic conversations while keeping in character.

Slippage did emerge on a few different levels. A basic grammatical slip on the museum's end was one instance: Levi Barnes told us about educational opportunities for children in his village and then shifted tense in the caption that accompanied a sound file, typing "This is what a teacher may have sounded like." Such an unintended mistake can give the same little thrill as catching an actor breaking character. On another level, a student asked a question that brought this issue to the fore: "We have the same last name," she wrote. "Do you have plans to move west?"

The inquiry was predicated on the experience of two simultaneous moments: one in the 1830s, in which Levi Barnes existed, and one in 2005, where the student existed. She was asking if she could be related, but related over time: she would be a descendent of the Barnes that moved west. Here, then, past and present tense were loaded into the question. Whether the complexity of the question was picked up on their end, we couldn't tell. If there was a "wink" of acknowledgement to the response, it was as deeply layered in the answer as it was in the question—that while Levi Barnes had no intention of moving, one of his sons "was planning on heading to Ohio this summer," as farmland was "all but used up" in New England. What a new living-history medium like Sturbridge's online chat does mean, though, is that one just needs to look in different spaces to find examples of irony and play that accompany the acknowledging of simultaneous times. The comment about the Compaq with Windows 98 being "fairly old" was made by the present-day museum staff, but with a wink that embraced the illusion we had been mutually sustaining up to that point.

Was the chat program more or less democratic in allowing my students and me to form our own "cognitive maps" of our understanding of the past, versus getting the institutional "party line" about it? Because of the nature of the chat, and especially the preparation for it, I imagine that we were able to shape the trajectory of our experience of this virtual past in a more direct manner than if we were simply to visit the site. This had much to do with the museum's commitment to addressing the learning objectives of the classroom. A good example is the answer to the question posed by Cecilie: "Do you have a piano in your home, and how much exposure do you have to the arts such as music and theatre?" Barnes responded that indeed he did have a "pianoforte" in his home:

> **Barnes:** My wife and daughters play. We attend balls and at church we have the singing choire [*sic*]. There are occasionally some traveling musicians that come through town. This is really [our] only exposure to music.
>
> **Barnes:** We don't see plays, but there are some in New York and Boston. Shakespeare is one of the favorites. We hear about these in the newspaper.

Cecilie followed up by asking if he had an organ at his church. Barnes said that they had an organ in their meetinghouse, that it was built in 1817, and that most Congregational churches (and Baptist churches) have an organ. He included a picture of their meetinghouse organ. The museum educators were, perhaps, more equipped to answer Cecilie's specific questions because Furlong and I had discussed the classroom's learning objectives beforehand. Letting her know that we were students of theatre history and might like to know about villager's exposure to the dramatic arts had given them an indication that such a question would be forthcoming and allowed them to have the answer and appropriate picture file ready to send. While we might have been able to determine some of the trajectory, though, the narrative we received was still written by the museum.

The agency we possessed in our own consumption of past narratives, then, was more powerful than that which we would have had with a static exhibit, and arguably more than we might have had had we visited the site without the prior discussion with museum staff. The trajectory of the narrative, if anything, was shaped by a mix of impulses and agendas. Partially determined by the students' inquiry, and partially by the information the staff was able and willing to provide in the limited time, it was certainly also affected by my pedagogical maneuvers as the students' instructor (and my own agenda for the research project).

Above and beyond these elements is the idea that, by experiencing the museum outside of the museum's space, our behavior was shaped not by the museum environment but the previously established rules of our own classroom. As Timothy W. Luke writes in *Museum Politics,*

> History exhibitions formalize norms of how to see without being seen inasmuch as the curators pose as unseen seers, and then fuse their vision with authority. In the organization of their exhibitions' spaces, the inscription of any show's textual interpretations and the coordination of an exhibit's aesthetic performances, curators are acting as normative agents, directing people what to see, think and value. Museum exhibitions become culture writing formations, using their acts and artifacts to create conventional understandings that are made manifest or left latent in any visitor's/viewer's personal encounters with the museum's normative practices. (3)

Divorced from the Foucauldian panopticon of the actual museum space, our movement through the virtual terrain of the chat room was less regulated. Certainly, the institution still provided the signposts in the landscape, but our itinerary could have been allowed a range of play not available under museum surveillance (our behavior in this case was decidedly reined in, and had we transgressed decorum, the museum educators could have simply ended the chat cold).

Is it possible to suggest that students may have had an easier time willingly suspending their disbelief and imagining they were talking to an actual denizen from the past than if they were to have a real costumed body in front of them (which might not match their perception of a historic individual in physicality, appearance, odor, etc.)? It was not the case, especially for my group of performance-savvy theatre students, that the chat could offer a simple, "believed-in" moment of talking to a character. The students did, however, "play the game" of being an audience in a way that suggested that they were appreciative and excited about the performance. There were some surprises to be had: since we could not see our actual interlocutor, there was no need for him or her to dress in character.[13] By extension, then, the staff at the computer need not resemble their characters in other ways, either: a female staff member might take on the role of a male mill-owner, for example. During our chat, the students took for granted that they were interacting with a man, since that was his character. I imagined it might be a woman, since all my phone conversations leading up to this event had been with female education staff only, but I didn't let my students know this. We were all surprised in the end, when Levi Barnes broke character, that we were actually talking to two people: Abby and Bill, museum educators. Such a surprise hinges on the expectations that accompany, at least on a basic level, a willing suspension of disbelief.

Long before Alvin Toffler's diagnosis of the American psyche as suffering a state of "future shock," open-air history museums offered sites of escape from technology—their equivalents of today's computers and chat rooms. Rich in nostalgic images of the past, and sometimes downplaying the events of the industrial revolution and the class politics that emerged with it, living museums have been accused of disseminating pristine and utopian versions of America, far from the reach of invasive modern machines—places that never existed. At the same time, living museums have steadfastly continued to offer virtual environments that seem to complement the development of history museums' emphasis away from artifacts and collections toward interactive media exhibits. The Sturbridge chat room occupies a strange and complex middle ground between the two. Embracing the technology eschewed by self-proclaimed technophobes and troglodytes comprising a percentage of living history museum staff and hobbyist population, the chat seems to be heading in a fresh new direction for the new millennium. On the other hand, for all its new technology, the chat may simply replicate positivist and nostalgic representations of the past that have always been *de rigueur* at living history sites. The limitations of user-interpreter play on more than one or two levels indicates that the chat, while very modern, might not offer the kind of postmodern multilevel experience that increasingly defines popular culture activity. In the end, though, it offers the living history field, its practitioners, and its consumers an enticing and inventive new nexus of performance, digital media, and historiography.

Notes

This project has approval from the Augustana College Human Research Review Committee.

1. *Users* is the term preferred by museum scholar David Carr. Carr maintains that the *user* is not merely a visitor but an "actor and thinking receiver" who is "embedded in an environment" (xiv, 3–4). *User* fits nicely with this project, as it is a common term for an individual who uses computer technology.
2. See Jay Anderson, Baker and Leon, and Abing.
3. *www.osv.org*. Accessed 17 December 2007.
4. The Learning Company has recently released the fifth edition of *The Oregon Trail*. Disturbingly, my clearest memories of playing this game as a fourth-grader are of circling the wagons and shooting Indians, while fellow students (awaiting their turn on the Apple II) gathered around and cheered. The concept of Manifest Destiny was still clearly unproblematized at the time, at least in my small school district in northern Wisconsin (and I had a large number of Native Ojibwe classmates from the nearby Lac Courte Oreilles reservation). The graphics of this simulated encounter, looking back, were not necessarily realistic. I can still picture my blob of buckshot agonizingly inching toward each target as the Indian galloped across the screen at an equally laborious pace.
5. James Campbell suggests that these games offer largely nostalgic conceptions of war as "ludic" activity that have become increasingly anachronistic. See Campbell and Fullerton's chapters in this collection. See also Gee and Johan Huizinga.
6. Many thanks to Zach Whalen for suggesting this very appropriate parallel, and for helping me think through some of the wording. It must be said that ARG participants go to great lengths to downplay even the structures of the game itself, subscribing to a "This Is Not A Game" (TINAG) aesthetic, resisting the formalized rules and playspace of video games as traditionally understood (see *en.wikipedia.org/wiki/Alternate_reality_game*).
7. Colonial Williamsburg in Virginia offers distance-learning "electronic fieldtrips," which it bills as "standard-spaced interactive-history-learning-environment(s)" as well as live PBS television broadcasts and Internet-streaming programs in which students phone in their questions (*www.history.org*).
8. Personal telephone interview, 29 November 2004.
9. Another option, says Furlong, is to chat with a museum historian rather than an interpreter.
10. See also Kirshenblatt-Gimblett, *Destination Culture* (189–202).
11. E-mail correspondence, 31 January 2005.
12. The single keypad we used had to be aimed at the back of the room, where the technology closet was located, so that the infrared remote matched up with the

computer/projector unit. The screen, however, was in front of the room. So, we had to type with our backs to the chat as it appeared on screen, which resulted in some typos and clicking "send" a few times by mistake).

13. As a theatre person, I had asked Furlong if the staff dresses in costume anyway, as a way to help them get "into character." Not so, says Furlong. Since there's no video feed, there's no need for costumes (Sturbridge considered video conferencing as an option in early stages of program planning, says Furlong, but it was "not as attractive" to them: "too complicated [and] not worth spending the money"). The characters are played by staff in the office—usually program coordinators—and not the staff that usually works in the village. Most of them are experienced interpreters (meaning, I assumed, they don't need costumes to help create their roles).

Works Cited

Abing, Laura. "Old Sturbridge Village: An Institutional History of a Cultural Artifact." Doctoral dissertation, Marquette University, 1997.

Anderson, Jay. *Time Machines: The World of Living History*. Nashville: American Associates for State and Local History, 1983.

Baker, Andrew, and Warren Leon. "Old Sturbridge Village Introduces Social Conflict into its Interpretive Story." *History News* (March 1996).

Carr, David. *The Promise of Cultural Institutions*. Walnut Creek, CA: AltaMira, 2003.

Gee, James Paul. *What Computer Games have to Teach us About Learning and Literacy* New York: Palgrave MacMillan, 2003.

Huizinga, Johan. *Homo Ludens*. Boston: Beacon, 1971.

Kirshenblatt-Gimblett, Barbara. "Afterlives." *Performance Research* 2.2 (1997). 8–9.

___. *Destination Culture*. Berkeley: University of California Press, 1998.

Luke, Timothy W. *Museum Politics: Power Plays at the Exhibition*. Minneapolis: University of Minnesota Press, 2002.

Roth, Stacy F. *Past Into Present: Effective Techniques for First-Person Historical Interpretation*. Chapel Hill: University of North Carolina, 1998.

Toffler, Alvin. *Future Shock*. New York: Bantam, 1981.

Walsh, Kevin. *The Representation of the Past: Museums and Heritage in the Post Modern World*. London: Routledge, 1992.

Games Cited

Oregon Trail (Apple II). Novato, CA: Brøderbund, 1985.

Oregon Trail, 5th Edition (CD-ROM). San Francisco: The Learning Company, 2004.

13
Documentary Games
Putting the Player in the Path of History

Tracy Fullerton

The referential power of games—both visually and in terms of their underlying simulation—has grown dramatically in recent years. Where once games played primarily in the realm of abstract or exaggerated scenarios, we are now beginning to see game scenarios that attempt to represent and/or re-create historical events and situations. The modeling of real-world systems and interactions in games is nothing new, of course—simulation is at the heart of most game systems—but the specificity of these particular models is what makes them interesting. No longer are we looking at a generic battlefield filled with anonymous soldier units, or even a block of properties "representing" the streets of Atlantic City in only the loosest manner. These new games—if we can still call them games—simulate historical events as tragic and momentous as the Japanese attack on Pearl Harbor, the assassination of John F. Kennedy, and the September 11 attack on the World Trade Center, and as infamous and topical as the tragedy at the Waco complex of the Branch Davidians, the 1999 Columbine High School shootings in Littleton, Colorado, and John Kerry's Silver Star mission in Vietnam.

While there is a great interest these days in games that address "serious" subject matter, and also in games that take on topics of social significance, there is no currently acknowledged genre of games addressing specific historical subjects—no genre of game play that approximates the concept of documentary in film and video. But several of the designers of the games I examine have made reference to such an emerging genre, by calling their products *docu-games* or accentuating their "historical accuracy" in the product literature. These claims attempt to align the play experiences of these games with nonfiction media, a form that carries with it a set of heavily coded cultural expectations and values. It is because of this aspirational prenaming of such a genre that it becomes an

Figure 13.1. "Documentary" Games? *9-11 Survivor*, **image © Jeff Cole, Mike Caloud, and John Brennan;** *JFK: Reloaded*, **image © Traffic;** *Medal of Honor: Rising Sun*, **image © Electronic Arts.**

interesting question to try and understand how the documentary form in film and video might intersect with these game experiences, now and in the future.

Documentary itself is not a simple concept to define. Since the very moment a camera was first turned toward a scene from life—a parent feeding a baby, workers leaving a factory, a train arriving at a station— questions of objectivity, selection, omission, intent, narrative, and the nature of reality have stalked this "nonfiction" genre of filmmaking like paparazzi. Many of these issues have roots going back to the impulse towards realism in other arts. The persuasiveness of film as a medium, however, and its (seemingly) ontological connection to its subject have tended to frame these questions as a discourse surrounding problems of audio/ visual representation, such as the relationship of the filmed image to the subject, to the "real," to science, and to history.

As a basis for comparison with the games I examine, four fundamental tendencies of the documentary form—what Michael Renov calls "rhetorical/aesthetic functions attributable to documentary practice"—prove useful. As proposed by Renov in *Theorizing Documentary*, these are: (1) to record, reveal, or preserve; (2) to persuade or promote; (3) to analyze or interrogate; and (4) to express (21–25). The first tendency is the one

Figure 13.2. A range of documentary content and styles. *The Thin Blue Line*, images © 1988 Miramax Films; *The Ballad of Big Al*, image © 2001 British Broadcasting Service; *Nanook of the North*, Robert Flaherty (1922); *The Civil War*, image © 1990 PBS Home Video.

generally most associated with the documentary genre—i.e., the "replication of the historical real." It is, on the one hand, the most problematic of these four aesthetic functions when applied to the notion of games, and on the other hand the stated goal toward which the games I am interested in actively strive.

Games obviously cannot lay claim to the type of ontological relationship with their subjects in the manner of photography or film. But, as many writers have pointed out, Renov included, this relationship is not as sacrosanct as it might first seem. The issues of selection, mediation, and intervention I have already alluded to assure that no matter how sincere our efforts, "the indexical character of the photograph can guarantee nothing" (Renov 27). In his discussion of this persuasive yet untenable relationship between the "real" and the photograph, Renov quotes art historian John Tagg: "That a photograph can come to stand as evidence, for example, rests not on a natural existential fact, but on a social, semiotic process" (28). This idea that the documentary nature of a photograph or filmed image is not inherent to these media themselves, but is actually a socially negotiated sense of the image's "believability"—a phenomenological artifact of our understanding of how images are made—relates directly to the ability of simulations to stand as similar evidence.

An example of how this social negotiation of what constitutes "evidence" might impact the emergence of a documentary genre of games can be seen in the evolving status of computer simulations and animations in courtroom settings over the past fifteen years. These detailed models, created by forensic experts, have gone from being highly suspect and potentially prejudicial to being considered probative illustration of actual events. Jason Fries is the COO of Precision Simulations, a Bay Area company that makes over one hundred forensic animations every year and has a 100% courtroom admissibility record for those simulations. He says that in the early 1990s, around the time that the first simulations were being submitted as evidence, there were stringent rules that objects depicted had to be very generic. For instance, a car could not have any specific details as to make or model, and a person had to be depicted as just a biped, with no distinguishing characteristics. This was to make sure that it was clear to the jury members that their focus should be on the underlying physics and behavioral models rather than on the visual representations. According to Fries, one of the earliest trials to involve the use of computer simulations was the 1992 trial of pornographer Jim Mitchell, convicted of killing his brother.[1]

Today, however, as both judges and juries become more familiar with these simulations, the rules have changed. If foundational evidence exists for more specific details, these are allowable within the simulation. So, a collision between a yellow Corvette and a pickup truck, for example, may now be depicted using models of these particular cars, rather than generic, car-shaped blocks. Also, people may be depicted with distinguishing characteristics, including gender, age, race, and even specific colors or styles of clothes if these facts can be substantiated by other evidence. According to Fries, the representational quality of these evidentiary simulations now approaches *Toy Story* level animation.

Are these near-photorealistic simulations probative or prejudicial at this point? Both, Fries posits, and that is why they are so powerful: because they can communicate so clearly to the jury what the forensic expert *believes to have happened* based on his or her analysis of the foundational evidence. This brings us back to the idea of this socially negotiated sense of an image's—or, in this case, simulation's— "believability." The fact is that as both judges and juries have become more accustomed to the concept of computer simulations, rules of evidence and admissibility regarding simulations have changed. A perceptual shift is taking place,

Figure 13.3. *Medal of Honor: Rising Sun.* Image © 2003 Electronic Arts.

the ripple effect of which is being seen in this example of courtroom evidence rules. This shift is illustrative of how we may someday embrace the possibility of simulations that model aspects of history not only visually but structurally (and in courtroom cases, behaviorally) so that they may constitute "evidence" by that same "social, semiotic process" that gives us the concept of the documentary image.

An example of this potentially emergent genre is *Medal of Honor: Rising Sun* (2003) for the PlayStation 2. It seems useful to begin with an example from within the mainstream game industry, since most of the other games I will consider here exist, to greater or lesser extent, outside of that industry, and the question of whether some of them should even be considered games at all must be raised. In this game, the player is a witness to history. The following scenario places the player in the midst of the attack on Pearl Harbor; it is dramatic, exciting, and undeniably bears a closer resemblance to Jerry Bruckheimer's *Pearl Harbor* than anything we would call a documentary.

As the game begins, you (the player) lie half-asleep in your bunk; romantic big band music plays drearily over a scratchy radio speaker. Suddenly, something hits the ship, nearly knocking you from your bunk.

Klaxons sound an alert and an officer shouts for everyone to get moving—this is not a drill. As you stumble to your feet, you see other sailors around you tumbling out of bed, grabbing pants or boots, dressing as fast as possible. You know exactly where you are, and when—mostly from the marketing promises of the game—but soon that information is replaced by the details of this immersive experience. You are on the USS *California*, part of the doomed US fleet stationed at Pearl Harbor on the morning of December 7, 1941. It's now 8:03 a.m. and the Japanese attack has begun in force. The minutiae of Navy life circa 1940 surrounds you. Though not photorealistic, it is beautifully rich and specific: snapshots of the player and his buddies tacked to a wall, letters and papers spilling onto the floor next to a dead sailor killed in the first explosion. Everywhere you turn, there are signs of life interrupted and the sounds of battle coming from above deck.

Cued by onscreen hints, you move as quickly as possible through the ship, stopping to help put out fires or help other sailors as you go, until you reach the deck of the *California* and join the fight. This moment, where you emerge on deck into the battle proper, is elongated and dramatized in an unusual (for games) use of slow-motion. Control is stripped away from you for this moment, simulating a paralyzing fear as you leave the relative safety of the ship's interior. Another sailor is shot out of a machine gun turret; you can either use the rifle you were handed when you came on deck or climb inside the turret and take over. Either way, wave after wave of Japanese aircraft attack. The sky is so full of planes that it is a simple matter to hit one, but there is always another, another, and another.

At a certain point, an explosion on the *California* knocks you overboard and you wind up rejoining the fight from the turret of a small PT boat. As the battle intensifies, the USS *Arizona* is hit and lost. "Oh, my God!" The nonplayer characters react to this event—an historical fact that locates us in time and space once again with this specific reference to an actual event. "This can't be happening," a nonplayer character moans. The *Arizona* is obscured by waves of billowing black smoke and there is a moment of quiet as the boat moves through the smoke—there are no targets, and the magnitude of what has just happened is allowed to sink in. "God help them," another character comments.

The gunboat soon moves out of the smoke and back into battle, as the officer onboard the gunboat commands you to "get back in the game." After a successful defense of the USS *Nevada*, the level ends and the characters excitedly rejoice at this small victory amidst larger defeat. The officer reprimands them sternly, saying, "No one will ever know what it [this day] was like—except the ones that made it. Just make sure you don't forget the ones that didn't." The clear message being communicated is that you too are now a virtual veteran, having made it through the simulated day.

In this first level of *Medal of Honor*, there is a conflux of history, nostalgia, drama, and interactivity. The tone is dramatic, and the music and imagery evoke a heroic nostalgia regarding the events and a sense of honor—even pride—in this particular US defeat. By putting the player in the position of an ordinary sailor without power to make significant change to the outcome of the event, the game allows us to experience this moment from the past "first hand"—to take action but not to expect any critical difference in effect. Although we are dropped into this level without context, subsequent levels of the game use wartime footage as dramatic setup, which give the player an historical (if romanticized) perspective of the importance of their in-game actions. The levels themselves have been designed with the help of veterans and military historians with the goal of putting the player into wartime moments that are as "authentic" as possible. According to executive producer Rick Giolito, all of the objects such as weapons, vehicles, environments, and battlefields have been researched extensively by the designers—though he stresses that the primary aim of the game is to provide entertainment, not to create a realistic simulation.[2]

Part of the entertainment that *Medal of Honor* players expect, however, relates to historical accuracy. In the PC version of the game, *Medal of Honor: Pacific Assault* (2004), the game incorporates "pop-up facts" that allow players to hover over objects in the environment to find out interesting historical information. Also, the game makes a point of informing players when it is moving away from the historical timeline. The inspirations for the game, says Giolito, are the oral histories of people who were there. A great deal of the game's content is based on their recollections. "It's an homage to that generation," he says. For those who were there, the persuasiveness of the simulation can be quite powerful. Stephen Dinehart, an Interactive Media student at the University of Southern California, posted a personal note on the division weblog about the experience of playing this level of *Medal of Honor: Rising Sun* with his 83-year-old grandfather, a veteran of WWII in the Pacific. "He thought a couple of times that the in-game graphics were actual footage. He would call off the facts and numbers as we played," Dinehart writes. "It gave me this incredible sense of retouching history in a way I have never felt before."

The scenario described above, with its epic, Hollywood approach to

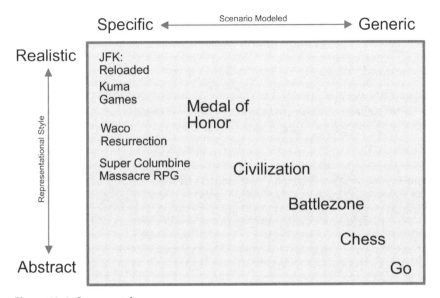

Figure 13.4. Game matrix

simulating the attack on Pearl Harbor from one sailor's perspective, is clearly more aligned with the tradition of historical narrative than that of documentary. The game uses its significant simulative powers to give players the persuasive, immersive, personal experience of being thrown into the events of December 7, 1941, and while it does make claims to historical "accuracy" in terms of the effect of simulated weaponry and battlefields in its literature,[3] it does not itself make any claim to the possibility of documentary games. *Medal of Honor* is useful, however, as a touchstone—not only for the state of the art in simulative re-creation of specific historical events in games, but also as proof of an underlying desire on the part of mainstream players to become immersed in re-created historical scenarios (though, as we will see, there are limits to that desire that create ethical and aesthetic issues for the designers of more realistic games).

Also, while *Medal of Honor* may be one of the most successful "historically accurate" game series, it is by no means atypical. On the contrary, the technological cycles that have driven the game industry to date all seem to move toward a point of convergence at which photorealistic visuals and painstakingly accurate simulations will meet. If one were to draw a matrix mapping the progress of games along a spectrum of abstract to photorealistic visual imagery on one axis and generic simulation to specific scenario model on the other, one might see a progression that looked something like Figure 13.4. *Medal of Honor*, while it models a very specific moment in time, does so from the perspective of a generic sailor—a character whose actions will make no significant difference to the larger historical events. The generality of the character's experience allows the player to easily and safely imagine himself or herself in this role—to take actions without questioning their historical value or accuracy. We are "in the moment," but we do not define the moment.

An example in a similar vein is the work of Kuma Reality Games. This company—whose games are distributed mainly through a website, rather than the larger retail channels at which one would find *Medal of Honor*—offers "accurate re-creations of real war events weeks after they occur."[4] Using reference material such as wire sources, video footage, and satellite images, Kuma has arrived at the game equivalent of the nightly news. In fact, when a player opens his or her game viewer (from which he or she can choose a specific scenario), he or she is confronted with a graphic style mimicking that of a news channel. A "text crawl" along the bottom of the screen announces new missions, which are all based on recent headlines.

Kuma CEO Keith Halper compares his company's games to an interactive version of the 1970s documentary series *The World at War*. "We step you through current events, military events that are appropriate for our tools," he says. "We try to mirror the real news, so if there is a story that is big in the news, we will try to come out that same week with a mission on that topic."[5] For example, the company's missions 1 and 2, *Uday and Qusay's Last Stand* (2004), feature a re-creation of the assault in which Saddam Hussein's sons were killed. According to Sarah Anderson, VP of Marketing at Kuma, this episode in the war was one "where the tactics and end result [i.e., killing the Hussein brother vs. taking them alive] were questioned and we feel our re-creations help people understand why it likely went down the way it did."[6]

In most of the Kuma scenarios, as with *Medal of Honor*, the player is a generic soldier, placed into the middle of a specific moment. Their actions, while they may affect that scenario, are not judged against any particular individual's historic actions within the moment that is being modeled. One particular Kuma mission stands out in contrast to this: *John Kerry's Silver Star Mission* (2004), set in Vietnam on February 28, 1969. During the 2004 presidential campaign, when much was being made of this mission in the traditional news services, Kuma released a game re-creation of the event. In the re-creation, the player maneuvers a Swift Boat up the Dong Kung River, in the role of then-Lieutenant (j.g.)

Figure 13.5. *Kuma\War: John Kerry Silver Star Mission.* **Images © Kuma Reality Games.**

John Kerry. At a certain point, the player is engaged by the enemy and must respond. How to respond to the attack is entirely up to the player, but attached to every Kuma mission is a linear video discussing the real-world events on which it is based. In the Kerry mission video, the mission objectives are given context, and the specific strategy that was used by Kerry in this scenario is explained. If players watch this video, or have a general understanding of the event, they may try to understand history here by re-enacting it. Or, they may deviate from history and find their own solution.

By comparing his company's games to well-known documentary series like *The World at War*, Halper is claiming a sense of cultural recognition for his games that is greater than that afforded to mainstream games. By aligning his re-created scenarios with the concept of documentary, he validates his work as something greater than game play, on the one hand, but more powerful than documentary on the other: "We are able to create a sense of situational awareness," he says, "that is very difficult to get in other types of media." Halper feels that with the tools available to game developers today, "we can tell sophisticated stories about real and very important events. War was a natural choice; and we felt we could really add something to the discussion."

The next example is quite controversial, to say the least, and it is worth noting that it, like the Kuma games described above, is not available through traditional retail channels. Available as a download from the

Figure 13.6. *JFK: Reloaded*: view from the sixth-floor window. Image © Traffic.

developer's website until August 2005, the game is currently unavailable. At the original download site is now a note: "Documentary history was made here 22nd November 2004. Long live the JFK Legacy."[7] *JFK: Reloaded* allows the player to reenact the assassination of John F. Kennedy. The opening screen of the game succinctly locates us with a few lines of text: "Dallas, Texas. 12:30 pm, November 22, 1963. The Texas School Book Depository, sixth floor. The weather is fine. You have a rifle." The card fades away, replaced by a view from the sixth-floor window just as the presidential motorcade pulls into sight. Because we are so familiar with this particular moment in history, we know exactly what we are supposed to do without further encouragement.

The assassination of JFK is not an easy task, however, and the fact is that in all probability even an expert game player will not successfully kill the president the first time through the simulation. Certainly, they will not make the exact series of shots that hit the correct combination of targets. Successful or not, after the motorcade has passed, the simulation takes the player to a review screen to see how they match up against the actual forensic evidence. The player's score is based on how closely their actions approximated that evidence. For example, they can score 0–200 points depending on whether or not they are able to hit the Presi-

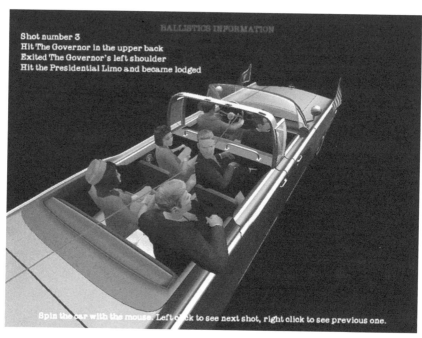

Figure 13.7. *JFK: Reloaded*: scoring based on ballistics info. Image © Traffic.

dent, where you hit him, and whether he is alive or dead at the end of the scene. The score is also dependent on the number and timing of shots (if the player shoots too many times, too early or too late, points will be deducted), and the state (injured or uninjured) of the First Lady, Texas Governor John Connally, and the governor's wife. If after seeing their score, the player feels they can do better, they can restart the scenario and try again. Or, they can use the multiple camera views to replay their assassination attempt over and over, watching from Abraham Zapruder's location, from the grassy knoll, the presidential limo, or a number of other key locations. Prior to February 22, 2005, if a player felt they had done fairly well, they could submit their score to a contest: the player who came closest to re-creating the exact timing and results of the actual events won a cash prize from the developer for their effort; the highest scoring entry was 782 points out of a possible 1000.

This game has been vocally condemned by a number of prominent people, including Senators Edward Kennedy and Joseph Lieberman. Quite honestly, everyone to whom I myself have described this game has reacted negatively to the concept. But what is it about this particular scenario that provokes such strong feelings when we are talking about an event that has been covered from every possible angle by every other

**Figure 13.8. *JFK: Reloaded*: instant replay. Image ©
Traffic.**

form of media? Do we condemn Oliver Stone's *JFK* (1991)? The History
Channel's *The Men Who Killed Kennedy* (1995)? Or any of the innumera-
ble books, websites, reports, documentaries, and other forms of discourse
surrounding this event? One has to wonder whether these reactions are
actually in response to the facts of the simulation itself, or whether the
outcry is in response to the fact that this simulation is constructed as a
game re-creation of a very specific and traumatic event.

The very notion of a "game" about the assassination of John F. Kennedy might seem at first to show a lack of respect towards the subject
matter. But, as those studying serious games and those who have read
Huizinga know, play is at the heart of the most serious pursuits of culture
such as religion, law, war, debate, and dramaturgy (Huizinga 5). And the
designers of *JFK* have a serious intent. According to them, their primary
purpose in creating the game was to finally put to rest the conspiracy
theories that continue to surround the assassination. Kirk Ewing, Manag-
ing Director of the development company Traffic, says that "we've created the game with the belief that Oswald was the only person that fired
the shots on that day, although this recreation proves how immensely
difficult his task was" (Traffic). The game took a ten-person team seven
months to research and six months to program their re-creation of the

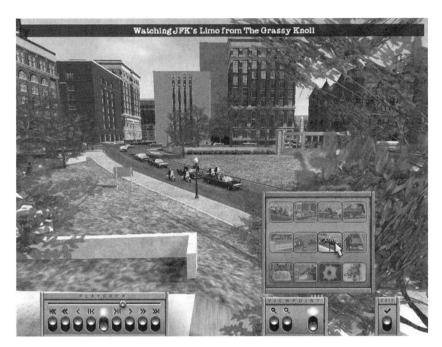

Figure 13.9. *JFK: Reloaded*: view from the grassy knoll. Image © Traffic.

events as specified in the Warren Commission report. Traffic calls their game a "unique insight into the assassination" and a way "to take people back in time and put them at the scene in Dealey Plaza to witness it for themselves" (Feldman).

As a player, however, my relationship to the event is much more complicated than just a trip back in time. I realize immediately that I must "get it right" to achieve a high score. Getting it "right" means acting on not an objective scientific knowledge of the event, or even a detailed knowledge of the findings of the Warren Commission—what it really means is negotiating my own personal memory of something I have seen hundreds of times in the past: the home movie footage shot by Abraham Zapruder. I know *when* to shoot, and *what* I should hit with each shot, primarily because I have seen the event happen so many times in clips from this footage. Unlike the *Medal of Honor* scenario, I am not only cast as a primary participant in this historical moment, with the power to make it happen "correctly" or not, but I also have a very specific set of cultural and visual "cues" which direct my actions. As I negotiate this knowledge within the scenario, I am struck by two things: first, how deeply disturbing it is to play this particular role, and second, how convinced I've become after

Figure 13.10. *JFK: Reloaded*: a disturbing view of a historical moment.
Image © Traffic.

fifteen or twenty attempts that Lee Harvey Oswald could *not* have made those shots—at least not if this simulation is in any way accurate. In fact, it is so difficult a challenge that in all of the alternate endings of the event conceived by my play of the game, only once was the president seriously injured. Every other time, the motorcade made it out of range before history could be fulfilled.

In his article "Simulation vs. Narrative: An Introduction to Ludology," Gonzalo Frasca puts forth the concept that games, as simulations, use an "alternative semiotical structure," one that offers "distinct rhetorical possibilities" and may "provide authors with essentially different tools for conveying their opinions." He emphasizes the idea that "simulation does not simply retain the—generally audiovisual—characteristics of the object but also includes a model of its behaviors." As he points out, the output of simulations may actually produce the same set of representational signs (in my example, a simulated audiovisual sequence quite similar to the Zapruder film), but he asserts—and this is clear to anyone who has played a game and then watched another person play the same game—that "simulation cannot be understood just through its output" (223–24). Which begs the question: what can we understand about these historical re-creations through their simulation? Can we understand the reasons behind an assassination? The emotions of the assassin? The nuances of the political context? Or only its basic forensic data?

More recently, another game that might be considered a part of the documentary genre has proved even more controversial. That is *Super Columbine Massacre RPG!* (2005), a game recreating the 1999 Columbine High School shootings in Littleton, Colorado. Danny Ledonne, creator of *Super Columbine Massacre RPG!*, spent six months designing the game—his first—which allows players to take on the role of killers Eric Harris and Dylan Klebold on the day of Columbine shootings. The game was released at his website for download on April 20, 2005, the sixth anniversary of the shootings. Ledonne, a documentary filmmaker by training, used videos, newspaper articles, and official documents that had been released to re-create the events of shootings in detail within the game, but this attention to documenting the details of the tragedy is rarely mentioned in general press coverage of the game. "I think there are elements of the game that are completely lost to most people," says Ledonne.

> This is in part because the subject matter doesn't flag down our most
> intellectual sensibilities and also because, of course, video games
> don't usually contain philosophers, poetry, or deeper meditations
> on society . . . In the end, SCMRPG is something of [a] chimera that
> becomes whatever the player wants it to be: a horrible exploitation,
> a thorough research project, a crappy little 16-bit game, or a point of
> fixation for someone who wants to kill people. (Crecente)

Super Columbine Massacre RPG! was pulled from the lineup of finalists in the 2007 Slamdance Guerilla Gamemaker Contest because of its controversial subject matter, though in the festival's thirteen-year history, no film finalist—no matter how controversial—had before been pulled from the screenings. In protest of this decision, which seems to promote the notion that games can but should not address provocative real world subject matter, seven of the fourteen remaining finalists and one sponsor (this author's academic institution) also withdrew from the contest (Fullerton). In a statement about his decision, game designer Jonathan Blow recognizes that the game "lacks compassion . . . but despite this, the game does have redeeming value. It does provoke important thoughts, and it does push the boundaries of what games are about." Unlike the examples of *Medal of Honor* and Kuma Games, however, *Super Columbine* explores a highly specific scenario in the relatively abstract style of a 1990s Nintendo game. Low-res, pixelated avatars and environments clash with the photographic inserts and documentary content to create an artistic expression of the killings. Echoing Frasca, *Wired*'s Clive Thompson writes that *Super Columbine* "uses the language of games as a way to think about the massacre. Ledonne, like all creators of 'serious games,' uses gameplay as a rhetorical technique." Although the game was pulled from the Slamdance festival, in an interesting move the film documentary jury tried to award it a "Special Jury Prize" for "Best Documentary" but was halted by the festival director Peter Baxtor (Flemming). This type of response by an artistic venue highlights the potential complexities surrounding the genre of documentary play, as even an "alternative" venue such as Slamdance considers a documentary game inappropriate for public screening.

Another example of this emerging genre offers an entirely different approach, one that has more in common with experimental or subjective documentary practice than the strict reconstructive simulation approach of *JFK: Reloaded* or the dramatic, almost propagandistic approach of *Medal of Honor*. This is the game *Waco Resurrection* (2003), and it is not so much a re-creation of a historic moment as an interpretation of such an event—an experiential examination of the conflicting forces surrounding it. In this game, the player dons a plastic David Koresh mask and enters a 3D re-creation of the Waco compound of the Branch Davidians. Once inside the compound, players must defend themselves against rival Koreshes (other players) and government agents while maintaining the loyalty of their followers. The soundtrack of the game, which plays eerily in the earphones of the mask, is a mix of official-sounding chatter on government radios and a hauntingly surreal song recorded by Koresh himself.

This game, it is interesting to note, is even farther removed from traditional distribution channels than even Kuma games or *JFK: Reloaded*. It is designed as an art installation and requires a custom hardware environment that includes multiplayer support and the hard-plastic David Koresh masks with embedded voice recognition technology so that players can speak the words that cause the simulation to begin: "I am David Koresh." There is no historical timeline to follow in this game, unlike in the Kerry mission or *JFK: Reloaded*. Rather, the game takes place in an imagined moment that includes within it the various ideologies at play in the historical moment it references. As the developer, C-level, states on its site, "*Waco Resurrection* re-examines the clash of worldviews inherent in the 1993 conflict by asking players to assume the role of a resurrected "cult" leader in order to do divine battle against a crusading government."[8]

Peter Brinson, one of the game's developers, contends, "*Waco Resurrection* does not attempt to accurately depict the events. It is meant to

Figure 13.11. *Super Columbine Massacre RPG!* Images © Danny Ledonne.

Figure 13.12. *Waco Resurrection*. Images © C-level.

force the player to confront their personal take on the incident." Brinson goes on to explain his take on the difference between film documentary and the potential genre of game documentary:

> In a film documentary—the filmmaker's portrayal and delivery of the events is at the foreground of the experience . . . Often a viewer will agree with the film's subjective points as well as take the portrayal of events as historical fact. Perhaps the viewer will completely disagree or form a stance somewhere in between. This negotiation of the content is a result, an after effect of the film documentary's narrative.

> In a documentary game, the player's reaction to the content—both within the game and in mind—IS the narrative. It is part of the real-time, present tense experience of the game's portrayal, rather than a personal addendum to the grand narrative. The player's perspectives aren't formed in relation or objection to the game creator's construct. The player's agency is the story. How do I feel about taking the role of David Koresh in a game? And importantly, how will I play him? Will I strive for historical accuracy or deviate from what happened? Do I know exactly what happened? Does anyone? The game's simulation of events acts as a set of supportive story threads to the player's grand narrative.[9]

Brinson's statement brings up several important issues, including one that has proven to be a critical disconnect between games and traditional forms of narrative: that of uncertainty. Later in the discussion of the rhetoric of simulations quoted above, Frasca dismisses the importance of narrative to game scenarios; by association, this includes historical narratives: "Games always carry a certain degree of indeterminacy that prevents players from knowing the final outcome beforehand" (227).

This issue of indeterminacy, or uncertainty, would then seem to be a key formal element of games that fights against the ability to create historically specific game scenarios. That conclusion assumes, however, that the purpose of a documentary genre of games would be to dramatize a single historic narrative—an accepted truth—rather than to allow players to explore and engage with a specific moment in time. The limits of the documentary genre—in both film and games—are not this clear. As we saw in *Medal of Honor,* for example, the player's role was made generic so that his or her actions, while having local effects, did not globally affect the outcome of history. In the *JFK: Reloaded* scenario, the opposite approach was taken: the player's goal is to reenact history exactly, and only by doing so can he or she "win" the game. *Waco,* by exploring the ideology surrounding an event rather than a specific timeline of events, deals with this issue by avoiding it altogether.[10]

A final example is *9-11 Survivor* (2003), a mod for *Unreal Tournament 2003* (2002) that puts the player into the towers of the World Trade Center during the September 11 terrorist attack. This game mod, which is not commercially distributed, has garnered word of mouth through conference presentations by the developers and a design document and series of screenshots on their website.[11] Its extremely limited release notwithstanding, the game has nevertheless been as highly criticized in online forums

Figure 13.13. *9-11 Survivor.* Images © Jeff Cole, Mike Caloud, and John Brennan.

as *JFK: Reloaded*. One of the game's developers, Jeff Cole, states that "the game itself is not really a game at all [. . . it] keeps not score or actual track of time. It is merely a moment caught in time."[12] Cole describes his team as "artists" using the medium they are most familiar with to "reconstruct the event." He knows that his game is controversial, and in his response touches on an important reason for this. Games, he says, echoing the earlier words of Kuma's Keith Halper, "can often provide you with a perspective that you might not otherwise have been able to experience or imagine," but, he adds insightfully, they also may fail to "capture any real sense of the emotional distress brought on by the event." This is an important point—one which is related to the pervasive notion, seen also in the cases of *JFK: Reloaded* and *Super Columbine Massacre RPG!*, that games as a medium are incapable of communicating serious emotions or ideas.

In all of these games, it is clear that there is a basic urge, similar to the first fundamental tendency of documentaries proposed by Michael Renov, to re-create a "historical real." In some cases, such as *JFK: Reloaded, Super Columbine*, or the products of Kuma Games, there is also a sense that these games are either analyzing or interrogating that history—and perhaps even attempting to persuade or promote an agenda based on that analysis. *Waco*, with its experimental, subjective approach, also explores the potential for expressive documentary within a game format. While the fact that these games simply call themselves documentaries and deal in some way with the same fundamental tendencies of documentary does not prove anything in itself, the fact is that the form of documentary is potentially quite flexible. In discussing the poetics of the documentary form, Renov makes a call for expanding the boundaries of what we recognize as documentary, pointing out "that a work undertaking some manner of historical documentation renders that representation in a challenging or innovative manner should in no way disqualify it as nonfiction, because the question of expressivity is, in all events, a matter of degree" (35). He is referring, of course, to a more experimental approach toward documentaries within the film format, but the statement holds true for this exploration of documentary games as well.

There are clearly some gating issues here. These include several problems I have only touched on, such as that of uncertainty: i.e., how can games based in fact deal with the inherent tension between the knowledge of an event's outcome and the necessity of allowing player agency to affect that outcome? There is also the problem of cultural acceptance of games as a serious medium. At odds in many ways with the perception of games as "nonserious" is the fact that all of the events I've looked at so far are moments of extreme violence that can be quite disturbing for many players. Were these issues to be solved, there remains the creative question of what we can learn from the documentaries in which we participate, and how these experiences add to our understanding of historical events and the issues surrounding them, rather than simply allowing us to be "in the moment." There may yet be an expressive mixing of the game and documentary forms that will someday carry a cultural value equal to that associated with film documentaries. We are not there today, but these games show a desire to get there, or at least to explore that potential.

Notes

1.   Personal interview, 2 March 2005. All quotations by Fries in this chapter are from this interview.
2.   Personal interview, 2 March 2005. All quotations by Giolito in this chapter are from this interview.
3.   *www.eagames.com/official/moh/pacassault/us/de_features.jsp*. Accessed 15 May 2005.
4.   *www.kumagames.com*. Accessed 15 May 2005.
5.   Personal interview, 1 March 2005. All quotations from Halper in this chapter are from this interview.
6.   Personal e-mail, 22 February 2005.
7.   *www.jfkreloaded.com*.
8.   *waco.c-level.cc*. Accessed 15 May 2007.
9.   Personal e-mail, 5 February 2005.
10. To be fair, it is unclear whether a game like *Waco* stands alone as an historical document or whether it demands extensive prior knowledge of the event in question in order to fulfill its function as an historical critique.
11. *www.selectparks.net/911survivor/index.html*.
12. Personal e-mail, 14 March 2005.

Works Cited

Blow, Jonathan. "Braid won't be at Slamdance after all." *braid-game.com* (6 January 2007).
Crecente, Brian. "Columbine RPG Creator Talks About Dawson Shooting." *kotaku.com* (20 September 2006).
Dinehart, Stephen. "MOH field test." *interactive.usc.edu/members/edinehart* (28 December 2004).
Feldman, Curt. "JFK Reloaded picks up press, none pretty." *gamespot.com* (22 November 2004).
Flemming, Brian. "Slamdance, Columbine and me." *Brian Flemming's Weblog* (*www.slumdance.com/blogs*, 13 February 2007).
Frasca, Gonzalo. "Simulation versus Narrative: Introduction to Ludology." *The Video Game Theory Reader*. Ed. Mark J. P. Wolf and Bernard Perron. New York: Routledge, 2003.
Fullerton, Tracy. "USC Interactive Media Division Withdraws Slamdance Sponsorship." *Ludicidal Tendancies* (*interactive.usc.edu/members/tfullerton*, 9 January 2007).

Huizinga, Johan. *Homo Ludens.* Boston: Beacon Press, 1955.
Renov, Michael. *Theorizing Documentary.* New York: Routledge, 1993.
Thompson, Clive. "I, Columbine Killer." *wired.com* (15 January 2007).
Traffic. "New 'Docu-Game' Recreates the Assassination of John F. Kennedy." Press release. *gamespot.com.* 22 November 2004.
Vargas, Jose Antonio. "Shock, Anger Over Columbine Video Game." *Washington Post* (*www.washingtonpost.com*, 20 May 2006).

Games Cited

JFK: Reloaded (PC). Glasgow, Scotland: Traffic, 2004.
John Kerry's Silver Star Mission (PC). New York: Kuma Reality Games, 2004.
Kuma\War (PC). New York: Kuma Reality Games, 2004.
Medal of Honor: Pacific Assault (PC). Los Angeles: Electronic Arts, 2004.
Medal of Honor: Rising Sun (PlayStation 2). Los Angeles: Electronic Arts, 2003.
9-11 Survivor (PC). Available at *www.selectparks.net/911survivor*.
Super Columbine Massacre RPG (PC). Available at *www.columbinegame.com*.
Uday and Qusay's Last Stand (PC). New York: Kuma Reality Games, 2004.
Unreal Tournament 2003 (PC). New York: Atari, 2002.
Waco Resurrection (PC). Accessed at *waco.c-level.cc*; currently listed at *c-level.org/projects.html*.

14

Of Puppets, Automatons, and Avatars

Automating the Reader-Player in Electronic Literature and Computer Games

Robert P. Fletcher

> Grace . . . appears purest in that human form which has either no
> consciousness or an infinite one, that is, in a puppet or in a god.
> —Heinrich von Kleist, "On the Marionette Theater" (1810)

> The Automaton Chess Player, built in 1769, . . . was a machine that
> seemed to think, and it caused its inventor to be called . . . a "modern
> Prometheus." The Chess Player was to elicit wonder throughout the
> world, but Kempelen, an eminent mechanician, insisted that it was
> only a toy, a trifle he had concocted for the amusement of Empress
> Maria Theresa. The machine's widespread popularity worried him; he
> dismantled it, inexplicably, soon after it was first shown.
> —Gaby Wood, *Edison's Eve: A Magical History
> of the Quest for Mechanical Life* (2002)

> [I]t is helpful to remember that by the nineteenth century puppet
> shows were widely attacked in the same way that comic books, video
> games, and action movies are today—for crudity, obscenity, violence,
> and setting an overall bad example for the young.
> —Victoria Nelson, *The Secret Life of Puppets* (2001)

Ambivalence about the human simulacrum has a long history as well as
what seems to be a very big future (in video games). Uncanny copies of
human beings have been created with strings and cogwheels as well as
through computer graphics and have gone by the names of puppet, doll,
automaton, android, and avatar. As my epigraphs show, for some time
the relationship between the human and its simulation has been fraught
with tensions between identifying with or rejecting as the other, and be-

tween experiencing a sense of wonder or of being cheated—no matter whether the simulation be created with cams, code, or even cinema, as in the example of Charlie Kaufman and Spike Jonze's 1999 film *Being John Malkovich*.[1] Looking back on the unsettling figure of the automaton allows both a work of electronic literature (eLit), William Poundstone's "3 Proposals for Bottle Imps" (2003), and a two-part adventure game, Benoît Sokal's *Syberia* (2002) and *Syberia II* (2004), to explore the automation of their own audiences, as well as to ponder the spirit-matter or mind-body dualism that has structured much of modern Western culture. As Gaby Wood points out, the Oxford English Dictionary defines an automaton as either "a figure which simulates the action of a living being" or, conversely, "a human being acting mechanically in a monotonous routine" (as cited in Wood xix). Both eLit and game provide the reader-player with the occasion to recognize in himself or herself "the puppeteer *in the service of the puppet*" (Wood 99) and to recognize in the history of mechanical life an anticipation of current contests over the significance of the simulacrum in the form of the avatar. However, "3 Proposals for Bottle Imps" foregrounds the metafictional dimension even as it engrosses its audience with its own stories of human automatism, while the *Syberia* game immerses its audience in a visually convincing world of automatons and reserves its reflexive moments for the occasional sly remark or technical shock. The difference between these cybertexts in this ratio of diegetic to extradiegetic elements suggests to me that in each the representation of precybernetic mechanical life carries a different valence: the eLit text appears to be most interested in driving home the idea of the materiality of posthuman subjectivity (what Donna Haraway means when she says, "The cyborg incarnation is outside salvation history"), while, conversely, the game seems most interested in uncovering what Victoria Nelson sees as the repressed transcendent in the human form divine. These differing commitments to be reflexive or nostalgic about the "human" have consequences for how the texts construct the history of the human-machine relationship.

Poundstone's Bottle Imps: The Automaton as Machine

Poundstone's "3 Proposals" is a Flash animation, multimedia in nature (with dynamic text, images, and sound) and consisting of three allegories and a list of frequently asked questions (FAQ) (see Figure 14.1). It takes Raymond Roussel's 1914 novel *Locus Solus* as a starting point for critical reflection on the long history of the human-machine relationship

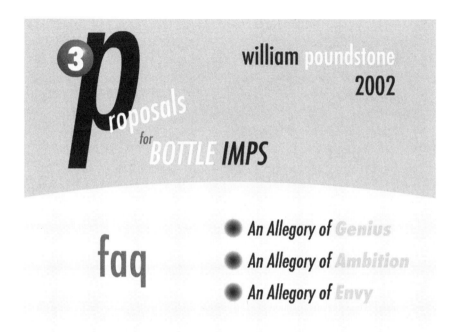

**Figure 14.1. "3 Proposals for Bottle Imps": main menu.
Image © William Poundstone.**

and its current manifestations in digital culture. The FAQ, essential to the reader's experience of the text, explain the bottle imp's function as human simulacrum, reflect on the philosophical challenge it poses to humanism, and link all this to digital textuality:

> In contrast to film, video, or conventional animation, eLit is a form of visual story-telling in which characters are mostly invisible, blurred, or glanced from a distance. Though this is sometimes put down to temporary limitations of posing and animation software, eLit is fundamentally a medium of artifice—of symbols that are perceived as symbols . . . *Locus Solus* is mainly about machines (or in one chapter, dead people who been reanimated into a mechanical, puppet-like simulation of life.) [*sic*] Roussel presents a world of avatars, virtual personages that look, move, and talk like people; beings capable of soliloquies though not conversation or introspection. This could equally describe the digital realm today.

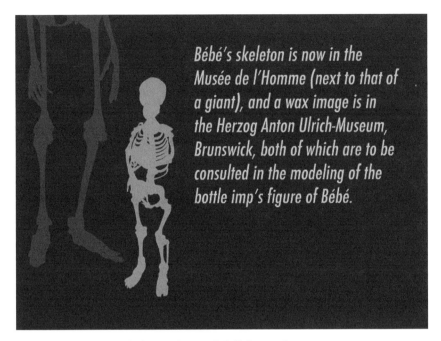

Bébé's skeleton is now in the Musée de l'Homme (next to that of a giant), and a wax image is in the Herzog Anton Ulrich-Museum, Brunswick, both of which are to be consulted in the modeling of the bottle imp's figure of Bébé.

Figure 14.2. "3 Proposals for Bottle Imps": Bébé's remains. Image © William Poundstone.

Poundstone's allegorical narratives, especially the one on envy, illustrate the mechanization of the human being, thus functioning as both proposals for "absurd automata" akin to those in Roussel's novel and "always already the stories themselves, set somewhere else in space and time (and eternally looping in 'our' time frame)." Since those narratives take the form of Flash animations, the automated stories are in some ways, as they run and then loop automatically, always already the automata themselves. In other words, they don't just tell the stories; they enact or model them with image and sound.

Poundstone's "allegory of envy" tells the story of an eighteenth-century dwarf, Nicholas Ferry, nicknamed Bébé, who is initially a marvel of nature for members of a European court but then comes to be seen as an inferior machine or a faulty toy when a second, better-behaved and better-educated dwarf arrives on the scene. Bébé proves his humanity by his revengeful rage against his competition, but when he dies his skeleton is preserved in cognac and exhibited again as an uncanny marvel in a *wunderkammer* or cabinet of curiosities.

Ultimately, as the e-text both recounts and illustrates, Bébé's remains

while preserving quality of life...

Swansea has attracted £160 million investment in **smokestack-free industries**

it was a stroke of marketing genius

Figure 14.3. "3 Proposals for Bottle Imps": "Ambition."
Image © William Poundstone.

are "retained for their scientific value" and displayed in a museum (next to a giant), as is a wax reproduction of this human being who was taken for a doll (see Figure 14.2). The story exemplifies the vexed relationship of the human and automaton in the Western world's imaginary. As Wood puts it in her examination of the lives of "The Doll Family," a German brother and three sisters by the name of Schneider who survived as living dolls in a twentieth-century America of freak shows and Hollywood munchkins, "Instead of wondering if automata were human, people now asked themselves how such purported humans could contain the requisite 'machinery'" (217). For Poundstone, Roussel's bottle imp simulates this ready potential for the human to be construed as the mechanical.[2] In its staging of the fight between the temperamental Bébé and his beatific counterpart Joujou, the allegory of envy also represents the battle between the two versions of the automaton haunting Western culture, as either wickedly nonempathic or benignly prelapsarian.

The metaphor of person as machine has become central in Western culture since the advent of industrialization, and Poundstone engages this history obliquely in "An Allegory of Ambition," a proposal/bottle imp that satirizes the industrialized world's attempts to erase its uglier aspects through things like civic pride and technological progress. The proposal begins with a silhouette of Dylan Thomas and his oft-cited words of contempt for his hometown, "Swansea is the graveyard of ambition." The second largest city in Wales, Swansea has been a casualty of de-industrialization (memorably depicted in the 1997 film *Twin Town*) and the proposal/bottle imp tells the story of its civic leaders' attempts to counter such a reputation by trumping the poet's observation with a slogan, "Ambition is critical," which they engraved "in brass letters on a granite pavement in Swansea City Centre" (the artwork actually turns up in the film). Poundstone explains that the engraving has become detached from its original context and inspired a marketing campaign by recent city leaders, who have designated Swansea "the City of Ambition." At this point, the proposal/bottle imp animates Swansea's ambitions by combining an energetic melody, an urban skyline that covers over the green Welsh countryside, and dynamic text phrases such as "component assembly," "website design," and "biotechnology," and then informing the reader-player that the city has indeed attracted a lot of investment in "smokestack-free industries" (see Figure 14.3). However, as the melody continues to pulse along ambitiously, the morphing text points out one more irony—that working-class youth have been left behind by this techno-economic progress and hang out at the City Centre, where they leave liquor bottles and rewrite the city slogan in graffiti as "Ambition is Crap." Poundstone's imp captures these ironic transformations and the contest over the meaning of post-industrial society they represent by reproducing the letters of the slogan in magnets that are mechanically, reflexively rearranged at regular intervals into anagrams like "claims it's a bit ironic" and "I am a strict iambic lion." Thus, this allegory and its bottle-imp automaton moralize on the lingering effects of an industrial disease that Thomas implicitly criticized and Western societies are eager to transform through carefully controlled public relations and new technologies.

Sokal's *Syberia* Games: The Automaton as Human Divine

> The Voralberg reputation crossed the oceans, dispatching its fine precision mechanisms across the globe to delighted buyers who began to believe that Voralberg automatons had a life of their own.
> —"Welcome to Valadilene" brochure in *Syberia* (2002)

Figure 14.4. *Syberia*: automaton mourners. Image © Microïds.

When we turn to the adventure game *Syberia* and its sequel (or completion, actually), we find a cybertext that tries through impressive graphics and interactive storytelling to reenvision the wonder of the automaton, even as it gestures at its dark side. The game begins with a cutscene of the funeral of Anna Voralberg, the owner of an automaton factory, whose hearse is attended by creepy mechanical mourners. The combination of near-cinematic realism in the sequence, mournful strings in the background, and the presence on the scene of the player's avatar, the relatively fleshlier American lawyer Kate Walker, creates an uncanny moment, as both Kate and the player apprehend an illusion of life in this return of the dead (see Figure 14.4). Victoria Nelson has argued that the human simulacrum has traditionally been one way to access the holy, but that,

> [i]n our officially postreligious intellectual culture, we miss the idols . . . Just as the mad scientist figure carries the negative but still highly charged projection of the holy man who would otherwise have no place in our living culture, the repressed religious is also visible in representations of puppets, robots, cyborgs, and other artificial humans in literature and film. It endures as a fascination

Figure 14.5. *Syberia*: the Voralberg crypt. Image © Microïds.

with the spiritualizing of matter and the demiurgic infusion of soul into human simulacra—a fascination that manifested itself, in the twentieth century, both in avant-garde theater and in popular entertainments (comics, films, and cybergames). (20)

Syberia takes the New York lawyer's growing acceptance of that spirit-matter relationship and its implications for her life as its very subject. Originally sent to the depressed town of Valadilene in the French Alps to acquire the factory for "the Universal Toy Company [. . .] a multinational which has a monopoly on the toy market," Kate must abort her mission, descend into the crypt (or in Nelson's terms the grotto, source of the grotesque) (see Figure 14.5), and retrieve the clues that will help her pursue a quest to find the long-lost inventor of the automatons, Anna's brother Hans Voralberg, who as a boy fell from a height when reaching for a toy mammoth he found in a Lascaux-like cave with his sister and emerged from the resulting coma as an idiot savant whose innocence mimics that of his creations (or vice versa). Along the way, Kate must reject the calls (via cell phone) of boss, fiancé, friend, and even mother, who all insist that she return to the artificial, affect-less relationships she has

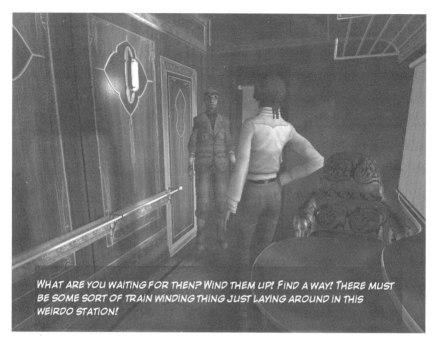

Figure 14.6. *Syberia*: Oscar and Kate. Image © Microïds.

been maintaining in the "real world" of corporate America; in promising instead to help Hans reach a mystical island of mammoths called Syberia, she reclaims her own repressed sense of the transcendent. She is aided and hindered in her quest to find Hans and take him to Syberia by various good and bad automaton-like characters, such as the "simple" child Momo; assorted unhelpful, robot-like clerks, storekeepers, and bartenders; and, most importantly, an actual automaton—the latest model, with an "additional soul auxiliary"—a mechanical railway engineer named Oscar (see Figure 14.6) who drives the marvelous wind-up train that takes Kate on her journey into Eastern Europe and Russia. Oscar plays something like the subaltern role of C3PO to Kate's Luke Skywalker, manifesting a charmingly naive (or stubborn) literal-mindedness at times and at one point becoming the victim of a scavenger of automaton parts who resides in an old Soviet mine.

That particular stop on the journey reveals that Hans has worked for the Soviet government following WWII, and this part of his history allows the game to engage, as it does occasionally, that other meaning of the automaton, the human who is taken for a machine. But whereas Poundstone's eLit examines the long shadow cast on Western cities by industrial

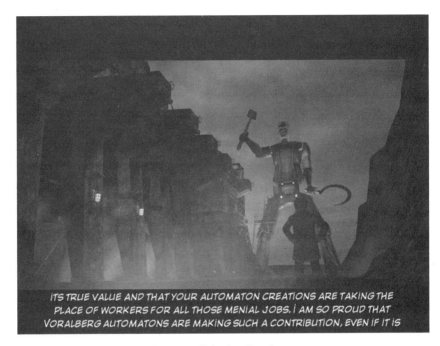

Figure 14.7. *Syberia*: Soviet imagery, linked to Hans's automatons. Image © Microïds.

history, Sokal's game exports that history to Eastern Europe and Russia. In interviews, Sokal has spoken of his fascination with the former Soviet Union (see Figure 14.7):

> When I started to think of "Syberia" I though[t] that there were no places for explorers anymore, except in the former USSR. All these countries were hidden behind the "iron curtain" and we knew very little. I was also amazed by places such as the Sea of Aral and the way some people thought that they could just change the nature [*sic*]. (Wajer)

In the game, the West is represented primarily by the silhouette of Kate's obstreperous boss, law partner Edward Marson, who presides in a fuzzy, soft-lit boardroom that looks out onto an iconic Manhattan skyline. Although Kate originally goes to a fictional town in the French Alps to buy the closed factory, the signs of post-industrial depression and alienation are reserved by-and-large for the East. The "journey from West to East" advertised in the teaser for the game is also a journey back in time, from

Figure 14.8. *Syberia*: bureaucratic automatism. Image © Microïds.

a transformed, powerful West of acquisitive multinationals to a languishing, inefficient Russia of rusted machinery. A recovered voice cylinder from Anna to her brother reveals that the marvelous Voralberg automatons played a role in the post-war modernization of Soviet industry:

> But it's so good to hear that your talent is being recognized for its true value and that your automaton creations are taking the place of workers for all those menial jobs. I am so proud that Voralberg automatons are making such a contribution, even if it is small, to the improvement of people's lives.

Not surprisingly, this tale of an infusion of fantastic technology from the West and the subsequent salvation of the dehumanized worker doesn't explain the consequences of such sudden unemployment for a Soviet society wherein a guaranteed job and the relative prosperity of the 1950s and 1960s were among the few bright spots of economic history (Hanson 48–70). Now, however, these wonders have been abandoned, with the implication that not only innovative technology but its maintenance must come from the West. The human characters and automatons that Kate, Oscar, and later Hans encounter along the way are likewise dysfunctional and barely surviving in a world of junk and refuse, and the puzzles in the game often involve getting the machinery up and running.

The meaning of automaton as mechanized subject is also at play in a more humorous context when Kate's train is stuck in Barrockstadt, site of a university whose rectors, in a satire of bureaucratic automatism, do what they can to block the heroine's attempt to get on her way again because she is not following the rules, while at the same time insisting that she must move her train. "Out of the question!" one shouts when Kate explains that her train must sit while she finds the clues to get it moving again, "Trains should first stop, then subsequently leave. That is the rule!" (see Figure 14.8). This is one of several spots in the game where the clunky adventure-game convention of clicking down a list of dialogue topics and getting canned responses repeated to you over and over actually reinforces the narrative and thematic context. The rectors (as well as those obstructive storekeepers) are supposed to sound like automatons, and indeed they do.

This soulless life in corporate America and post-Soviet, post-industrial Russia is countered in the game by the spirituality of the Youkals, the indigenous people whom Kate encounters in Part Two. Seemingly modeled on a myth belonging to the Nenets, one of the "small peoples" of the Yamal Peninsula in Northern Siberia, the mysterious Youkals live apart from Russians in underground villages and maintain a culture built around domesticated mammoths, the bones and hides of which constitute the raw materials of Youkal technology.[3] Youkal legend centers on a magical "ice ark" that periodically traveled to the north and brought back frozen mammoths with which the modern Youkals fed and clothed themselves. Kate finds the ark in dry dock and must reinitiate its journeys to the lost island. In fact, the game ends when, upon reaching Syberia, Kate reunites Hans with the marvelous in the form of real, live mammoths like those that he had found on the island when he had left home as a young man decades before, and she thereby enables him to cross over into a spiritual realm. This end to the quest links the game's use of the automaton to represent the repressed spirituality of the West with what Nelson terms the "'colonized transcendent'—that is, the twentieth-century Western fascination with the religions of pretechnological cultures around the world, which amounted to an allowable means by which to experience vicariously one's inclinations toward the holy" (12).

Indeed, the *Syberia* games take full, if not always conscious, advantage

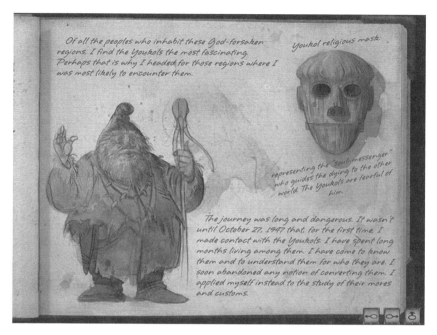

Figure 14.9. *Syberia II*: Youkol ceremonial mask resembling an automaton. **Image © Microïds.**

of the Romantic myth of the noble savage. Cultural anthropologists and historians of Siberian colonization write of the contradictory values attached to the small peoples of the North in Russian culture. Much like Native Americans in the United States, the indigenous peoples of Siberia have been seen as exotics that are alternately ridiculous and sublime, monstrous and angelic, backward and pure (Diment and Slezkine 3–5; Slezkine 33–35; Mandelstam Balzer 6 and 51–52). Sokal invests the Youkals with an authenticity missing from the corrupt and decrepit Russian towns through which the heroine and her train pass, linking them (like the automatons) to a timeless world immune from political economy. The game even provides an ethnological study of the Youkals in the form of a priest's journal, and the native mask therein resembles an automaton face (see Figure 14.9). However, Mandelstam Balzer and others have demonstrated the complexity of the history of the Siberian peoples since Russian expansion to the east and north began in earnest in the eighteenth century. Russians came to dominate southern Siberia, "uneasy interdependence" characterized northern towns and villages, and only in the northern "backwoods" did the cultural practices of the indigenous

Figure 14.10. *Syberia II*: Youkol train station built of mammoth tusks.
Image © Microïds.

peoples remain dominant (Mandelstam Balzer 29–53). In the Soviet
Union, "Siberian peoples were considered to be less advanced along the
Marxist scale of historical progress," but the government saw itself as he-
roically bringing "the indigenous population out from timelessness and
[. . .] into history" at an accelerated pace (Grant 227). There is a hint of
such social divisions in a minor episode of the game, where the hierarchy
of Romansbourg is reflected in the town's layout, with the train station
and depressed commercial interests of the ex-communists sitting on platforms high above a poor, vaguely "ethnic" population represented by the
orphan girl Malka. Colonel Emeliov, left in charge of this "last bastion of
civilization," explains that "low down is low down, and high up is high
up. People who are low down got different points of view from those who
are high up. Different kettle, different fish, if you get my meaning, Miss
Walker." When Kate suggests that she may explore the sub-station, he
warns her that "all the undesirables of the plateau wash up in our little
town sometime," and he responds to her objection to this line of thinking
with the defense that he is merely "carrying out a soldier's orders."

By and large, though, the reality of the Siberian peoples in the twentieth and twenty-first centuries is lost to a vision of a remote, untouched society of shamanic rituals and technological marvels constructed from native materials (à la TV's *Gilligan's Island*), such as a train station of wood and mammoth tusks (see Figure 14.10). The Youkals' monopoly on religious ritual in the game (despite the train's stop at an Orthodox monastery) represents, I believe, an example of what Renato Rosaldo has called "imperialist nostalgia," in which the "agents of colonialism long for the very form of life they intentionally altered or destroyed" (69). Eggert has extended this concept to include texts that reproduce the indigenous culture "as tribute or museum display" (75). This nostalgia links the Siberian peoples intimately with the other agent of transcendence and innocence in the game, the human divine in the form of the automaton. Indeed, I would contend that the game purifies its mechanical technology through association with the indigenous peoples. Soviet and Russian "exploration and exploitation of gas and oil fields on Yamal has gained in importance at both the national (Soviet/Russian) and international levels" since the 1960s and has led to the

> loss of pastureland owing to allotment for oil and gas development and related transport; damage to additional areas from industrial activity; contamination of rivers and sea-coast areas by oil, oil products, and other chemical agents; damage to bird, mammal, and fish breeding grounds, habitat, and migratory routes; and destabilization of the permafrost. (Golovnev and Osherenko 11–13)

In Sokal's vision, the marvelous wind-up train, carrying its inventor, mechanical operator, and American passenger, brings no exploitation or pollution and little damage to the environment, with the exception of some comic relief in the form of two bumbling villains who want to capitalize on Hans's genius. Once past the Russian towns, Hans's train takes Kate through pristine, gorgeously rendered landscapes and eventually comes to rest before the hidden Youkal village itself, where it is dragged inside by the natives to its final resting place. Kate and Hans transfer to the magical ice ark for the final leg of their journey to the island and the mammoths, but only after the automaton Oscar sacrifices himself to restore the dying Hans to health in a scene that brings together the wonders of technology and shamanism. Oscar's demise takes place under the auspices of the Youkal shaman, who nonetheless shows surprise when the automaton self-destructs. She then pulls a lever that lowers Hans, suspended from

Figure 14.11. *Syberia II*: Hans's transformation echoes Frankenstein. Image © Microïds.

Figure 14.12. *Syberia II*. Image © Microïds.

her hut roof in a shot reminiscent of cinematic versions of both *Frankenstein* (1931) and *A Man Called Horse* (1970), into the waiting remains of Oscar, which are assimilated to Hans's frail body, transforming the innocent creator into a cyborg god capable of making the trip to Syberia (see Figures 14.11 and 14.12). Thus, the repressed transcendent is accessed through a unique combination of romanticized images of technological invention and "primitive" culture.

Reflexivity in Game and Electronic Literature

In its combination of satire and quest, *Syberia* sets up a structural contrast between the mechanical and soulful characters and, unlike Poundstone's "Bottle Imps," it seems at times unaware of the artifice of its nostalgic narrative. At some points, it does play self-consciously with the ambiguities of the automaton by exploiting the pervasive irony of a human simulacrum (our avatar) watching various other human simulacra (the automatons) and reacting with wonder at the sublime sight (see Figure 14.13). Moreover, one subplot offers a self-reflexive parody that suggests an awareness of the issues in gaming such as gender and power, and fetish and desire. If Kate Walker is not exactly Lara Croft (reaction to her appearance from contributors to the "Syberia Blows" forum thread at *idlethumbs.net* was mixed, ranging from "she's hot!" to "bloody non-descript euro-chick"), she is nevertheless a female avatar created by a male artist. In the promotional short *The Making of Syberia* as well as in an online interview, Sokal expresses something like paternal pride in Kate's ingenuity and ability to solve her problems with intellect rather than violence: "I simply like to show women who are not just 'like man' (i.e., using weapons, fighting)" (Wajer). However, the game also includes a parody of the Pygmalionism at work both here and in the long history of male artists and their female muses. A phantom haunting the derelict Soviet mine steals Oscar's hands and will return them only if Kate retrieves an opera singer he has worshipped for years so she can perform for him one more time. He shows Kate his shrine filled with simulacra of Madame Helena Romanski, but once Kate fulfills her part of the bargain he traps the diva, whom Kate must free (see Figure 14.14). Thus, the game has fun with a *Phantom of the Opera* parody while slyly raising the issue of the author's and possibly the reader-player's fantasy of manipulating the female figure.[4] It is also during this episode near the end of the game's first part that one of its more explicitly self-referential moments occurs. As Kate prepares to take Helena back to the mine for her performance, she receives a cell-phone call from her friend Olivia, who gushes with affected guilt over an indiscretion with Kate's fiancé Dan. When Kate responds that this doesn't seem "real, right now" and that she needs to "process this new bit of data," Olivia warns her (and us) that she is (and we are) becoming an automaton in her (and our) abandonment of conventional commitments for this single-minded quest to find the inventor of a set of marvelous automatons. The quest is invested with genuine affect in the game, though represented here by Olivia as an obsessive, mechanical

Figure 14.13. *Syberia*: **Kate's reaction. Image © Microïds.**

compulsion, while the melodramatic confession, we find, is "soulless," as Olivia quite quickly recovers her good spirits when she finds Kate doesn't care about the cheating. In the meantime, with a nudge and a wink, the reader-player has been reminded of his/her own compulsion to succeed in the game's quest and of the possibility that in identifying with Kate he/she may indeed be becoming an automaton of sorts.

For the most part, however, *Syberia* seeks to immerse its player in its surreal Eastern Europe and Russia—this world of decaying industry, wondrous automatons, and ancient magic—despite surprises such as this episode, when the player is prodded to reflect on the relationship between him/herself and the simulated identities through which he/she is living at the moment. In the eLit text "3 Proposals for Bottle Imps," this metafictional critique is the primary focus. Poundstone links cybertextual literature to Roussel's modernist experiments in narrative form, claiming that both marginalize the human and are instead "mainly about machines." Like the modernist novel, eLit calls attention to its own mediation of reality:

Figure 14.14. *Syberia*: a madman's shrine to an opera singer. Image © Microïds.

In contrast to film, video, or conventional animation, eLit is [a] form of visual story-telling in which characters are mostly invisible, blurred, or glanced from a distance. Though this is sometimes put down to temporary limitations of posing and animation software, eLit is fundamentally a medium of artifice—of symbols that are perceived as symbols.

For Poundstone's reader, a main lesson of the encounter with the automaton should be an awareness of story as machine; like the modernist text, the eLit machine is estranging. He effects that estrangement in part by manipulating the Flash animations with virtuoso skill. In each allegory, music, dynamic words, and images pulse along together—images and text morphing, music looping—the machine in control of the reader's experience of the text, and thus in control of the reader. The reader's time must be the machine's time. In a 3D graphic environment, that dimension of 'real time' action may add to the effect of immersion, but with the textual automation of eLit, I think the feeling of a less than 'human' expe-

Figure 14.15. *Syberia*: **a display bug reveals Kate to be another kind of puppet. Image © Microïds.**

rience more probable. I find this hypothesis confirmed by my students' experience of the work of other eLit artists besides Poundstone who have exploited this mechanization of the textual experience. For example, a pair of web artists calling themselves Young-Hae Chang Heavy Industries has published Flash narratives and monologues told in a spare, synchronized combination of mostly instrumental music and plain black text on a white background.[5] In their "Orient," the thoughts of young singles in a bar speed along at an almost unreadable pace to keep up with the jazz soundtrack. As the *Iowa Review Web* has put it, "Writing in three different languages, Young Hae Chang and Marc Voge strip away interactivity, graphics, photos, illustrations, and colors to leave viewers with language and sound." My students expressed both fascination with and a feeling of alienation from their cybertexts.[6]

While immersion, a transparent virtual reality, and the hiding of the "story-telling illusions" may be the goals of many game designers, several theorists of games have pointed out that there always resides in the experience of any given game the potential for the medium to reveal itself—for the puppet's strings to be exposed. Fencott categorizes various kinds of "perceptual opportunities" in games as "sureties, shocks, and surprises," with shocks being those moments of poor design when some element jars a user out of his/her sense of "presence." A rather grotesque example of such a shock comes in the first part of *Syberia* should the player decide voluntarily to leave Kate Walker for even a moment by hitting Alt-Tab on the keyboard. When one tries to reimmerse in the pleasure of the game, one is confronted with a mutilated avatar, the lower face of which has been effaced and whose status as the most human character in the world—evidenced importantly by a mouth that is both handsomely simulated and the source of Kate's affect-laden speeches—has been thereby thrown into doubt (see Figure 14.15). Kate Walker is revealed to be one more automaton. But I would argue that more than such accidental shocks, the very interface and gameplay of this adventure game, and of adventure games in general, work to undermine the illusion of presence, to reveal the automaton in the reader-player, and thereby to link it in another way to the self-imposed marginalization Poundstone claims for electronic literature.

Conclusion: Requiem for a Game

> Simulation is not a new tool . . . However, the potential of simulation
> has been somehow limited because of a technological problem: it is
> extremely difficult to model complex systems through cogwheels.
> Naturally, the invention of the computer changed this situation.
> —Gonzalo Frasca, "Simulation versus Narrative: Introduction to
> Ludology" (2003)

In the past it may have indeed been difficult to create a persuasive model through mechanical means, but both Poundstone's "3 Proposals for Bottle Imps" and Sokal's *Syberia* demonstrate how long-standing is the fantasy of succeeding, and the game in particular acknowledges the pleasure of the fantastic to be found in the mechanical wonder, even if it does so self-consciously. But this game and others of its kind have also been criticized for disallowing the kinds of pleasures other games provide—for not simulating some kinds of affective experience well enough, for breaking the illusion. I want to conclude this essay with some speculations, inspired by the juxtaposition of electronic literature and adventure game, about why adventure games get under some people's skin. What gets talked of in terms of superior and inferior designs may also have something to do with the paradoxes of time and eternity that the automaton once again teases out in our thought.

In a review of the sequel to *Syberia* in *Computer Gaming World*, Charles Ardai praises the "breathtaking visuals" of the follow-up (though, he notes, "the periodic injections of wonder and delight don't come as often as they did" in the predecessor), but he also complains of the gameplay in a way that makes the *Syberia* games stand in for the entire adventure-game genre:

> We've come a long way since the days of the first *King's Quest* games in terms of graphics, sound, animation, and interface design, but you're still moving a little figure around, picking up objects here and delivering them there, scouring each screen for just the right spot to click on, and mechanically plowing through dialogue trees. (90)

He concludes that this limitation—the mechanical nature of the gameplay—will keep this adventure game and by implication most others from converting "naysayers." What interests me about such a complaint—and Ardai's is a perspective representative (I think) of a lot of game reviewers—is that it inverts the value of what some theorists say is the peculiar pleasure of computer games: that they exploit their audience's taste for rehearsing procedural behaviors, or what Grodal has termed the video game's focus on "coping strategies" (147). Grodal argues that video games allow one not just to hear about people or events (as in a narrative), but to manipulate them: "Video games are . . . the full, basic story that the retelling has to omit, including its perceptual and muscular realization." The exigencies of our day-to-day lives often center around such a need to manipulate the world around us (e.g., floss our teeth, back the car out of the driveway, incorporate the butter into the sauce), but, in first-person stories, claims Grodal, "such 'procedural' experiences are often not very interesting for other people, they do not like to hear about all those 'low-level' procedures and learning processes, but only to get to the bottom line, whereas video games communicate such procedural knowledge" (148). They "provide an *aesthetic of repetition*, similar to that of everyday life," and the end result of "the learning process [involved in playing a game] is what the Russian Formalists called *automation*." In some cases, we seem to like behaving like automatons.

So it may not be so much what happens in adventure games that turns off some players—my hunch is that it is more about how long it takes to do things and what that element of duration forces upon the player.

Grodal points out that the emotional experiences most taken advantage of by the first-person shooter and similarly intense games are of the "fight and flight" variety (151). But, he continues, an adventure game like *Myst* or *Syberia* exploits "associative and contemplative situations and feelings." Grodal genders these affective experiences and the gaming styles that support them rather predictably, but what strikes me is the emphasis on contemplation that the adventure game shares with the literary text (whether electronic or not). Even more important than the "aesthetic of repetition" to the adventure game (which it can indeed exploit beyond the endurance of many) may be the "convention of notice" at its center, a term I borrow from Peter Rabinowitz's discussion of the literary reading process (47). Here's David Richter's explanation of the idea:

> In some stories, an author might describe the street on which the narrator lives and mean nothing more by it than the dateline to a newspaper story, but in the style system in which "Araby" is written (modernist realism), any elaborate description can almost be counted on to have thematic significance going beyond face value. (236)

In an adventure game or a modernist short story or a dynamic eLit text, the user is pressed to notice everything, and that takes time—whether that is the mechanical beat of machine time ("it's going too fast, I can't keep up!"), or the slow-motion of the second reading of the short story, or the "tedious backtracking" of the adventure game. In demanding that the user take time to notice everything, especially the artifice, the adventure game may have condemned itself to museum status, making itself one more marvel of automation to be appreciated by the few willing to take time to reflect on the mechanism.

Notes

1. For a brief discussion of the "exchange of souls between the puppeteer and his cohorts" in *Being John Malkovich*, see Nelson 215–16. Both she and other cultural historians trace the links extending from puppetry through mechanical automata to present-day computer simulations. For example, see the delightful description of the nineteenth-century acrobat puppet or "false automaton" named "Antonio Diavolo," who "operated not by clockwork but by pistons and pullcords," in Stafford and Terpak 273. Their individual discussions of the history of puppets, automata, and other "devices of wonder" demonstrate how complex and yet consistent the imaginary functions of human simulacra have been from the times of Hero of Alexandria until now. See for instance 35–47 and 266–74. Another espe-

cially good example of the wonder associated with both the automaton and the human simulacra in cinema (specifically, the early films of Georges Méliès) exists in Brian Selznick's graphic novel for children *The Invention of Hugo Cabret*.

2. The bottle imp, he explains in the FAQ, "is a toy consisting of a gas-filled figurine sealed in a container of water. By changing the fluid pressure of the container, the figure may be made to rise and descend." Thus, both Roussel and Poundstone in their separate media (novel and Flash animation) focus on the reality effects of pointedly crude simulacra.

3. I have not been able to identify definitively the specific people on whom Sokal modeled his Youkals—he may have had in mind the Khanty, the Nenets, or some other group. For a good introduction to the complex indigenous societies of Siberia and their history with the Russians, see Slezkine. To me, the mythic dimensions of the Youkals most closely resemble the Sihirtia of Nenets legend:

> Sihirtia, the legendary small people once gone and still living underground, are considered to be the Nenets' predecessors on the tundra, sometimes hostile but more often friendly. They can appear on the earth only at night or in a mist. Underground they pastured earthen reindeer (mammoths), whose "horns" are used for the door handles of their pit houses. They seem to be skillful blacksmiths and magicians, presenting iron or bronze objects to people. (Golovnev and Osherenko 28)

4. See Rehak for a discussion of the complex negotiations of identification and rejection between player and avatar in computer games.

5. For a list of links to their various works, see their homepage, *www.yhchang.com*.

6. About "Orient," one student, Elizabeth Sammonds, wrote,

> That poem confused me because there was obviously something the poet was trying to say but it was so fast you I [*sic*] couldn't get a full grip on anything and when I would finally get something I would try to remember it but that then became a problem because I would forget it trying to keep up with the rest of the poem. I think that poem would have been more effective had it been shorter[;]

while another, Daniel D'Aprile, responded,

> I enjoyed the rushed pace of the poem, and I forgave the accompanying presence of jazz because it helped with the frenzied pace—I saw this as what Kerouac might have attempted had he access to html. A writing so rushed, constant and cacaphonous that it could only compare to the wild, uncontrollable music of Jazz.

(Online discussion at *blackboard.wcupa.edu*, 15 November 2004, for LIT 400: Reading Cyberliterature, West Chester University.)

Works Cited

Ardai, Charles. Review of *Syberia II*. *Computer Gaming World* (May 2004). 90–1.

Diment, Galya, and Yuri Slezkine, eds. *Between Heaven and Hell: The Myth of Siberia in Russian Culture*. New York: St. Martin's, 1993.

Eggert, Katherine. "Sure Can Sing and Dance: Minstrelsy, the Star System, and the Post-postcoloniality of Kenneth Branagh's *Love's Labour's Lost* and Trevor Nunn's *Twelfth Night*." In *Shakespeare, the Movie II: Popularizing the Plays on Film, TV, Video and DVD*. Eds. Richard Burt and Lynda E. Boose. London: Routledge, 2003. 72–88.

Fencott, P. C(live). "Presence and the Content of Virtual Environments" (1999). Accessed 28 July 2005 at *web.onyxnet.co.uk/Fencott-onyxnet.co.uk/pres99/pres99. htm*.

Frasca, Gonzalo. "Simulation versus Narrative: Introduction to Ludology." In Wolf and Perron. 221–36.

Grant, Bruce. "Siberia Hot and Cold: Reconstructing the Image of Siberian Indigenous Peoples." In Diment and Slezkine. 227–54.

Golovnev, Andrei V., and Gail Osherenko. *Siberian Survival: The Nenets and Their Story*. Ithaca: Cornell University Press, 1999.

Grodal, Torben. "Stories for Eye, Ear, and Muscles: Video Games, Media, and Embodied Experiences." In Wolf and Perron. 129–56.

Hanson, Philip. *The Rise and Fall of the Soviet Economy: An Economic History of the USSR from 1945*. London: Longman, 2003.

Haraway, Donna. "A Cyborg Manifesto: Science, Technology, and Socialist-Feminism in the Late Twentieth Century." In *Simians, Cyborgs and Women: The Reinvention of Nature*. New York: Routledge, 1991. 149–81. Also available at *www.stanford. edu/dept/HPS/Haraway/CyborgManifesto.html*. Accessed 27 July 2005.

Iowa Review Web. Editorial introduction to Young-Hae Chang Heavy Industries. *www.uiowa.edu/~iareview* 4 (1 February 2002). Accessed 28 July 2005.

Kleist, Heinrich von. "On the Marionette Theater." Trans. Christian-Albrecht Gollub. In *German Romantic Criticism*, ed. A. Leslie Willson. New York: Continuum, 1982. 244. Quoted in Nelson 30.

Making of Syberia. CD-ROM. Montreal: Microïds, 2003.

Mandelstam Balzer, Marjorie. *The Tenacity of Ethnicity: A Siberian Saga in Global Perspective*. Princeton: Princeton University Press, 1999.

Nelson, Victoria. *The Secret Life of Puppets*. Cambridge: Harvard University Press, 2001.

Poundstone, William. "3 Proposals for Bottle Imps." *The Iowa Review Web* (*www. uiowa.edu/~iareview*) 5 (1 February 2003). Accessed 28 July 2005.

Rabinowitz, Peter. *Before Reading: Narrative Conventions and the Politics of Interpretation*. Ithaca: Cornell University Press, 1987.

Richter, David. *Falling into Theory: Conflicting Views on Reading Literature*. 2nd ed. Boston: Bedford/St. Martin's, 1999.

Rosaldo, Renato. *Culture and Truth: The Remaking of Social Analysis*. Boston: Beacon, 1989.

Selznick, Brian. *The Invention of Hugo Cabret*. New York: Scholastic, 2007.

Slezkine, Yuri. *Arctic Mirrors: Russia and the Small Peoples of the North*. Ithaca: Cornell University Press, 1994.

Stafford, Barbara Maria, and Frances Terpak. *Devices of Wonder: From the World in a Box to Images on a Screen*. Los Angeles: Getty Research Institute, 2001.

"Syberia Blows." *forums.idlethumbs.net* (15 May 2004). Accessed 28 July 2005.

Wajer, Adrian. "Benoît Sokal interview." *przygodoskop.gry-online.pl* (February 2005). Accessed 28 July 2005.

Wolf, Mark J. P. and Bernard Perron, eds.. *The Video Game Theory Reader*. New York: Routledge, 2003.

Wood, Gaby. *Edison's Eve: A Magical History of the Quest for Mechanical Life*. New York: Knopf, 2002.

Young-Hae Chang Heavy Industries (Young Hae Chang and Marc Voge). "Orient." *www.yhchang.com* (2002). Accessed 28 July 2005.

Games Cited

Syberia (PC). Montreal: Microïds, 2002.

Syberia II (PC). Montreal: Microïds, 2004.

Contributors

Wm. Ruffin Bailey is a graduate student in Communication, Rhetoric, and Digital Media at North Carolina State University. His past research has dealt with Henry David Thoreau's expressions of non-modern sexuality through the use of unconventional reproductive imagery. Before attending the University of South Carolina, he spent several months studying comparative primate ecology in the rain forests of the former Zaire, followed by six years working as a database administrator and customizations programmer specializing in Internet mapping, Visual Basic, T-SQL, and dynamic HTML. He was a contributor to the eighth edition of *The Macintosh Bible* and has written a number of demos for the Atari 2600. Current projects include studying the influence of discoveries in the Americas on the rhetoric of comparative anatomy and interrogating operating systems through the application of ecological metaphors.

James Campbell is an associate professor of English at the University of Central Florida, where he teaches in the Texts and Technology doctoral program. He has published work on twentieth-century war and literature in *LIT: Literature Interpretation Theory, ELH,* and *NLH,* and the recent *Cambridge Companion to the Literature of the First World War.* He is currently working on a book on computer games and political ideology. In his other academic life as a literary scholar, he continues work on the connections between Oscar Wilde and the First World War poets; to that end, he recently received an NEH grant to participate in a summer seminar focused on the Wilde collection at the William Andrews Clark Library in Los Angeles.

Sean Fenty began his research on video games as a graduate student at the University of Florida. While there, he developed and taught several courses in the Networked Writing Environment, and helped maintain the Department of English's website. He is currently an instructor at the University of Louisville, where he continues to pursue his research interests in video game narratives, genre studies, and popular culture. He has published articles in

Currents in Electronic Literacy, ImageTexT: Interdisciplinary Comics Studies, and *Blesok: Literature and Other Arts.*

Robert P. Fletcher is professor of English at West Chester University of Pennsylvania, where he teaches courses in Victorian literature and culture and, increasingly, cyberliterature and culture. He has published articles in *PMLA, ELH, Studies in the Novel, Clio, JEGP,* and *Victorian Literature and Culture.* He is currently revising a study of the post-cyberpunk fiction of Canadian SF writer and blogger Cory Doctorow. This is his first foray into video game criticism, though he came to understand the unique power of simulations over their users long ago when, as a young man playing the WWII strategy game *Squad Leader,* he found board, cardboard chits, and dice sufficient to generate belief in the reality of the game.

Tracy Fullerton is a game designer, educator, and writer. She is currently an assistant professor in the Interactive Media Division of the University of Southern California School of Cinematic Arts, and co-director of the Electronic Arts Game Innovation Lab where she does research in new genres of gameplay. She is also the author of *Game Design Workshop: Designing, Prototyping and Playtesting Games,* a design textbook in use at game programs worldwide. Her design credits include faculty advisor for the award-winning student games *Cloud* and *flOw* and game designer for *The Night Journey,* a unique game/art project with media artist Bill Viola.

Thomas E. Gersic lives north of Chicago with his wife Sharol, and his son Tyler. He works professionally with interactive multimedia as a composer, sound designer, and audio programmer for Teleologic Learning Company. He completed his graduate studies in music technology and sound design in 2005 at Northwestern University, where he worked with interactive/adaptive music and multimedia technologies. Tom continues to be particularly interested in the ability of music and sound to influence the perception and cognition of visuals, especially with adaptive and generative scores for games. He has taught sound design at Northwestern University and is an adjunct professor in the College of Computing and Digital Media at DePaul University. He has also written a number of unique audio applications, available for download from his personal website.

Terry Harpold is an associate professor of English, Film and Media Studies at the University of Florida. His essays and reviews have appeared in journals such as *Bulletin de la Société Jules Verne, Game Studies, ImageTexT, IRIS, Postmodern Culture, Revue Jules Verne,* and *Science Fiction Studies*; and in edited collections such as *The Routledge Encyclopedia of Narrative Theory* and *Glossalalia*. His book *Ex-Foliations: Reading Machines and the Upgrade Path* will be published by the University of Minnesota Press in 2008.

Colin Harvey is a writer and part-time academic with a long-standing interest in the interrelationship of storytelling and play, reflected in his PhD study entitled "Play the Story: An Affective Perspective on the Video Game." He has worked as a freelance video game story designer for Sony and contributed journalism to the British magazines *Edge, RetroGamer, Develop*, and *ScriptWriter*. For two years, he wrote the regular *Trivial Pursuit* column for the Chicago-based webzine *PopMatters*. In 2004, Colin originated and ran the BA (Hons) Game Cultures degree at London South Bank University. His book, entitled *Grand Theft Auto: Motion-Emotion*, was published in 2005 by Ludologica. His short story "The Stinker" won the prestigious *SFX Pulp Idol* award in 2006, and most recently he contributed two BBC-licensed *Doctor Who* short stories to the *Short Trips* collections *Snapshots* and *Ghosts of Christmas*. Colin is currently establishing The Writing Lab at London South Bank University.

Andrew E. Jankowich is the founder of Metaboston Media, a new media publisher and consultant. He has been a lecturer at Simmons Graduate School of Library and Information Science and Brandeis University. He has been awarded fellowships at the Center for Internet and Society at Stanford Law School and Brandeis University. He concentrates his research on intellectual property law and digital art and culture. His articles have been published in the *Boston University Journal of Science and Technology Law* and the *Tulane Journal of Technology and Intellectual Property*. His audio work *Horror of Place* was exhibited at ProvFlux 2007 in Providence, Rhode Island. He graduated from the University of Pennsylvania Law School cum laude, received an MA with Distinction in English from King's College, University of London, and graduated cum laude from Dartmouth College.

Scott Magelssen teaches theatre history at Bowling Green State University in Ohio. He received his PhD in theatre history, theory, and dramatic literature at the University of Minnesota. His articles appear in *Theatre Journal, Theatre Topics, TDR (The Drama Review), Theatre Survey, Theatre History Studies, Theatre Annual, New Theatre Quarterly, Visual Communication, National Identities, The Journal of Religion and Theatre, Journal of Dramatic Theory and Criticism*, and *Performance Research*. He is the author of *Living History Museums: Undoing History Through Performance* and co-editor, with Ann Haugo, of *Querying Difference in Theatre History*, published by Cambridge

268 Playing the Past

Scholars Publishing in 2007. Scott won the 2005 Gerald Kahan Award for the Best Essay in Theatre Studies by a Younger Scholar for his article, "Performance Practices of Living Open Air Museums."

Sheila C. Murphy is an assistant professor in the Department of Screen Arts and Cultures at the University of Michigan and is the program's digital media scholar. Murphy received her BA in Art History from the University of Rochester and her MA and PhD in Visual Studies from the University of California at Irvine. She has worked as the assistant director of the UC Irvine Film and Video Center and served on the Society for Cinema and Media Studies' information technology committee. She is currently revising her dissertation, "Lurking and Looking: Media Technologies and Cultural Convergences of Spectatorship, Voyeurism, and Surveillance," into a book-length study of the emergence of lurking as a mode of passively yet actively engaging with contemporary audiovisual media ranging from television and personal computers to the Internet and video games.

Matthew Thomas Payne is a doctoral student in the Department of Radio-TV-Film at the University of Texas at Austin. His research focuses on the social impacts of communication technologies and new media, video games, alternative media practices, and teaching film/video production. He holds a master's degree in media studies from the University of Texas and a Master of Fine Arts in Film Production from Boston University. Matthew has previously served as the coordinating editor for *FlowTV* (*www.flowtv.org*), an online journal and forum dedicated to television and new media culture.

Anna Reading gained her PhD from the University of Westminster, London, in 1996. She is Director of Research in Arts and Media at London South Bank University. She is the author of a number of books and articles on memory and the media, including *The Social Inheritance of the Holocaust: Gender, Culture and Memory*. She is an editor of the international journal *Media, Culture and Society* and is on the editorial board of *Memory Studies*. Her current work concerns mobile phones and the development of mobile digital memories, or "memobilia." She is the author of a number of plays for the stage performed in the UK and overseas and is a member of the Women's National Commission (Cabinet Office). She is editing a book, *Save As . . . Digital Memory*, and writing one on mobile memories.

Laurie N. Taylor researches digital media and creates digital projects as an assistant university librarian in the University of Florida's George A. Smathers Libraries. Her articles have appeared in various journals and edited collections, including *Game Studies, Media/Culture, Computers and Composition*

Online, Works and Days, Videogames and Art: Intersections and Interactions, and The Player's Realm: Studies on the Culture of Video Games and Gaming. She also writes about games and digital media in popular venues. Her current research studies methods to digitally represent and contextualize archival materials.

Zach Whalen is an assistant professor of English at the University of Mary Washington, specializing in New Media studies. His dissertation at the University of Florida is on the textuality of videogame typography. He has published articles on video games and media studies in the journals *Game Studies, Media/Culure,* and *Works and Days,* and the edited collections *The Meaning and Culture of Grand Theft Auto* (edited by Nathan Garrelts) and *Music, Sound, and Multimedia* (edited by Jamie Sexton). He also edits and contributes to the game studies blog *Gameology.org* and is Production Editor for *ImageTexT: Interdisciplinary Comics Studies.*

Natasha Whiteman is a lecturer at the Institute of Education, University of London. Her doctoral thesis, which was funded by the Economic and Social Research Council, examined pedagogic activity in two online fan communities and explored a range of issues pertaining to Internet research methodology. She is the coauthor of "(Dis)possessing Literacy and Literature: Gourmandising in Gibsonbarlowville" in *The World Yearbook of Education 2004* (with Soh-Young Chung and Paul Dowling).

Index

Page numbers in bold indicate illustrations.